Supervision in Transition

**1992 Yearbook of the Association for
Supervision and Curriculum Development**

Supervision
in Transition

1992 Yearbook of the Association for Supervision and Curriculum Development

Carl D. Glickman, Editor

Developing Leadership for Quality in Education for All Students

Printed in the United States of America. Typeset on Xerox™ Ventura Publisher 2.0.

Ronald S. Brandt, *Executive Editor*
Nancy Modrak, *Managing Editor, Books*
Carolyn R. Pool, *Associate Editor*
Cole Tucker, *Editorial Assistant*
Gary Bloom, *Manager, Design and Production Services*
Karen Monaco, *Designer*
Stephanie Kenworthy, *Assistant Manager, Production Services*
Valerie Sprague, *Desktop Specialist*

Price: $19.95
ASCD Stock No. 610-92000
ISBN: 0-87120-188-7
ISSN: 1042-9018

Library of Congress Catalogue Card No. 44-6213

Supervision in Transition

III. The Preparation

IV. The Reflection

Foreword

The question of "supervision," with the national cry for a retooling of supervisory skills, is of great interest to me. My own district, Salt Lake City School District, has embraced "shared governance" for many years. And my tenure as director of the Utah Principals Academy has further confirmed my view that current and future educational administrators must have skills that transcend the old supervisory norms. No longer can we accept a "top-down" approach to supervision.

I applaud Carl Glickman's view that leadership, to be effective, must be shared. Those working together at a local school site must participate in goal setting and decision making. The entire school community needs to be involved—teachers, support staff, parents, and administration. "People support what they help create" is a motto that has guided me during my administrative career.

For example, as principal, I can observe, make notes, confer, and advise—but the stigma of "boss" is always there. Teachers view the administrator as the "snoopervisor" rather than as an advocate and colleague. I have learned to trust the teachers, involve them in all decisions regarding the school—and cope with the cry that our meetings are *too* long. Shared decision making does take longer, but it is the one way that professionals can have a collective voice in planning goals and guiding practice in a school. The combined effort of our school community is one reason we were selected by the U.S. Department of Education as a National Blue Ribbon School.

As the educational system struggles with "restructuring" and organizational shifts, the old bureaucratic style of supervision is in flux. Teachers, who are the ultimate experts in curriculum and instruction, must be involved in the planning and delivery of instruction. They are the best judge of effective instructional strategies and should be given the latitude of working together to enhance each other's skills. The yearbook gives many explicit examples of teachers becoming involved in making decisions at their schools.

Glickman has organized the yearbook in a way that should be most useful to practitioners. The introductory section, a splendid historical overview of the supervision process, leads into the next section, on promising practices. The third section of the yearbook explores the preparation of teachers—in ways that encourage professional inquiry and true collegiality. And the final section reflects on the great transformation—one might say, revolution—in supervision today.

Especially significant to me is Chapter 4, by Andrew Gitlin, a professor at the University of Utah, and Karen Price, a teacher involved in his study of "horizontal evaluation." Five teachers in my school were also a part of this research as students in the master's program. They were hesitant initially, but quickly moved into a mode of mutual trust and support. These teachers valued the observation and feedback sessions and saw them as a way to help one another grow professionally.

Several chapters address a "peer coaching" approach to supervision; others speak of peer assistance, teacher mentors, and collegial support. By whatever name, *teachers helping teachers* is the best method of improving the practice of teaching. Supervisors—at whatever level—must involve those with whom they work and those affected by the system. *Supervision in Transition* provides educators with a fascinating combination of sound research and practices that will serve as a guide for such a transition.

CORRINE HILL
ASCD President, 1991–92

Introduction: Postmodernism and Supervision

Carl D. Glickman

> *All of us, writing now, are post modernists, whether voluntarily or in—you can't escape your era, can't pretend to not know what is known, what is in the very air.*
>
> *Joyce Carol Oates, "Excerpts from a Journal: July 1989," 1990, p. 122*

It is perhaps time for those of us who have toiled, practiced, and written about supervision to no longer "pretend to not know" that events in education are shaking our deep-rooted conceptions of instructional supervision. Might I even suggest that the term *instructional supervision* itself may be outliving its usefulness? The reordering and redefining of societies, governments, and economies have been in "the very air." People are rethinking old ways of doing business, dismantling hierarchies, and formulating new expressions of "life, liberty, and the pursuit of happiness." It is no historical accident that the democratization and decentralization of governments across the world are happening at the same time similar activities are being asked of public schools. Providing administrators, teachers, students, and parents a real voice in educational decisions at the time of perceived educational crisis is a bold attempt to rethink our schools, the ways that we teach, and the ways students learn. We know what we will have if we operate as we have in the past—and the prospects are not promising. However, we don't know what we will achieve by operating differently; those prospects are both frightening and exhilarating. But, at last, citizens and school people are willing to do what we have not easily done before: take risks.

Where does this leave educational supervision as a concept and set of activities? When I was asked to edit the 1992 ASCD Yearbook, I grappled with this question. As the director of the Program for School Improvement (which operates the League of Professional Schools) and as a professor and author of past textbooks in supervision, I found myself caught between my "old" viewpoints and the realities of how public schools are actually moving ahead to improve teaching and learning. When schools become decentralized, engage in shared governance, and see themselves as the center of action research, the term *supervisor* or *supervision* has little meaning to staff members. Instead, they think of enhancing education through shared leadership and collegiality; through their own plans for staff development and curriculum development; and through their own goal setting, actions, and research. A "supervisor" with hierarchical control of these activities—whether a principal or central office member—is antithetical to them. "Supervision," as a term derived from its industrial roots of closely inspecting the work of employees, is also antithetical (and a bit disgusting) to them. Instead, educators, students, and parents see themselves in control of their own actions and their own concepts. They see themselves as committed, intelligent, resourceful, and dignified people who can discuss, debate, and make informed decisions to reform and sustain meaningful education.

Most activities or programs that I, and others, have clearly articulated in the past as "supervisory" or "supervision" are not called by that name by today's risk-taking practitioners. Instead they use terms such as *coaching, collegiality, reflective practitioners, professional development, critical inquiry*, and *study or research groups*. Practitioners shun the word "supervision" to describe the what and why of their actions. Given Joyce Carol Oates' quandary that I "can't pretend to not know what is known," the idea of an ASCD yearbook called *Supervision in Transition* dawned on me. I thought how interesting it would be to ask young and experienced women and men from public schools and universities, who work in varying settings and who speak from different perspectives, to tell us how supervision is being construed in places struggling to reshape education. The challenge that I invited the authors to write about was this:

> Over the past decade, school supervision has been in the midst of swirling, transitional views. One view of supervision—as a district-based, inspector-type function carried out by line supervisors who understand generic processes of effective teaching—has gained ascendancy. A shifting view of supervision as a school-based collegial process, based on reflection, uncertainty, and problem solving, has been

finding acceptance in schools that are recasting the roles and responsibilities of teachers. A further area of shifting views has been from an emphasis on pedagogy to a focus on the interaction of content (subject knowledge) and instruction. These transitions in supervision have created volatile issues, tugging at the security of people's professional lives, and changing previous organizational structures. The 1992 yearbook intends to bring fresh insights from the varying perspectives of theorists, researchers, and practitioners to inform those who will decide and implement programs of supervision for the 21st century.

The authors' responses to my challenge were remarkably candid and thought provoking. It was a joy for me to read their contributions and uncover more of what we already know, as well as what else we need to know. Some writers take us into their schools and provide immediate and vivid portrayals of the actual and changing experiences of supervision. Other writers teach us from a distance to rethink the related philosophical and psychological issues of a changing school and supervision world.

There is a logical order to this book; it moves from perspectives on context, to practice, to preparation, and concludes with reflection. But, to me, the book is really a collection of voices pushing our thinking and actions about supervision. The authors went beyond my challenge; they reshaped it. Their words echo the words of Joyce Carol Oates: "Don't pretend to not know what you know." Supervision is in such throes of change that not only is the historical understanding of the word becoming obsolete, but I've come to believe that if "instructional leadership" were substituted each time the word "supervision" appears in the text, and "instructional leader" substituted for "supervisor," little meaning would be lost and much might be gained. To be blunt: as a field, we may no longer need the old words and connotations. Instead, we might be seeing every talented educator (regardless of role) as an instructional leader and supervisor of instruction. If so, indeed, the old order will have crumbled.

Reference

Oates, J.C. (1990). "Excerpts from a Journal: July 1989." *Georgia Review* 44, 1 & 2: 121–134.

I

The Context

1

Policy and Supervision

Linda Darling-Hammond with Eileen Sclan

State and local policies have exerted a growing influence on the supervision and evaluation of teachers. The increased role of policy is intimately related to recent attempts to improve and "professionalize" teaching. On one hand, policymakers recognize that teacher competence is a critical component of educational quality—and they press for policies aimed at enhancing teacher knowledge and skill. On the other hand, states and districts mandate specific supervision and evaluation strategies that reinforce nonprofessional conceptions of teaching and modes of assessment. This apparent paradox can be resolved only by reshaping the governance of the teaching occupation so that evaluation functions are designed and carried out according to professional standards of practice.

Professionalism and the Press for Teacher Policy

During the 1980s, a number of reform proposals discussed the professionalization of teaching (see, e.g., Carnegie Forum 1986, Holmes Group 1986, National Governors' Association 1986). The proposals focused attention on the nature of teacher preparation, evaluation, support, and involvement in decision making as key to effective schooling and teaching. These proposals were based on a different theory of educational improvement than were reforms launched in earlier decades, which focused more on "teacher-proof" curriculums and management techniques than on investments in teacher knowledge:

> One theory, which may be called bureaucratic in orientation, assumes that specialized knowledge for teaching is unnecessary because techniques, tools, and methods can be prescribed from above; they need not be crafted by teachers themselves. The other theory, which may be called professional in orientation, assumes that pedagogical preparation is essential, because teachers must be capable of making complex

educational decisions on behalf of diverse students (Darling-Hammond and Berry 1988, p. xi).

The bureaucratic management of teaching has involved a quest for instructional tools and systems that can be prescribed for teacher use. "Standardized" and "routine" are the key words here: the bureaucratic model assumes that students are standardized enough in their responses that they will respond in routine and predictable ways to a common stimulus, and that teaching tasks are routine enough to be converted to procedures. The professional conception starts from a different assumption: because students learn in different ways and at different rates, teaching must be responsive to their needs if it is to be effective. As a consequence, teachers must make decisions in nonroutine situations using a complex knowledge base augmented by highly developed judgment and skill.

The professional conception of teaching places more emphasis on the following:

• Teacher preparation and ongoing opportunities for learning.

• Evaluation of teaching, as well as a different kind of evaluation.

• The *appropriateness* of teaching decisions to the goals and contexts of instruction and the needs of students, not just prescribed routines.

• Evaluation as a constant feature of organizational and classroom life, not as a discrete annual event. In such ongoing evaluations, teachers continually inquire about the usefulness of their plans and actions and continually revise them in light of these inquiries (Darling-Hammond 1986, Glickman 1985). (See also Chapter 8 for further comparisons of bureaucratic and "emerging" practice.)

The professional conception of evaluation is not based on an inspection system featuring supervisors bearing checklists on brief visits to classrooms. Rather, evaluation is an ongoing set of experiences in which teachers examine their own and each others' work, determine its effectiveness, and explore alternative strategies. In fact, a professional structure for teaching may not include traditional, bureaucratic supervision, defined as the one-to-one relationship between a worker and a presumably more expert superordinate who is charged with overseeing and correcting the work (Gitlin and Smyth 1990). Instead, organizational strategies for team planning, sharing, evaluating, and learning may create methods for peer review of practice. These strategies—like those used in other professional organizations and restructured businesses—may better fill the needs previously addressed by traditional supervisory functions (Darling-Hammond 1986).

The emphasis of recent reforms on "professionalizing" teaching has engendered a great deal of policy activity aimed at teachers and teaching. During the 1980s, states developed more than 1,000 legislated acts regarding teachers and implemented a substantial number of them in schools (Darling-Hammond and Berry 1988). Many of these enactments introduced new requirements for teacher preparation, certification, the induction and evaluation of beginning teachers, and the evaluation or recertification of veteran teachers. Other legislation introduced funding for mentors for beginning teachers, or for "lead" teachers assuming a variety of supervisory or other roles in schools. Still other legislation sought to institute performance-based compensation systems for teachers, accompanied by changes in evaluation methods and supervision strategies.

This legislative activity and its resultant policies have been launched under the banner of professionalism, reflecting the view that teachers are an important part of the educational equation. The reforms, however, have often adopted a bureaucratic view of teaching. And because many of the changes are lodged in law and regulation, they have greatly influenced supervision and evaluation practices—and consequently teaching and learning. These policy changes are not only more far reaching, but also more resistant to revision than would be true if formal policy tools were not the vehicles for change. Competing visions of teaching and learning, as well as supervision and evaluation, are embodied in this raft of new teacher policies.

Policies Influencing Teacher Supervision

Many kinds of policies influence teacher supervision. Obviously, formal evaluation policies for beginning and veteran teachers are frequently accompanied by supervisory structures and requirements. For beginning teachers, these policies may be part of a state licensing system, as well as a local district evaluation system. Increasingly, legal requirements for assisting and assessing beginning teachers are part of changes in states' licensing standards.

The standards soon to be established by the National Board for Professional Teaching Standards may have important effects on teacher supervision. Alongside performance-based assessments that are part of certification examinations, the board is considering the use of portfolios whose contents will engage teachers in critiquing and coaching their peers as part of the certification process. Moreover, the sorts of references, recommendations, and other evidences of performance that teachers may be required to produce when they sit for board examinations would require departures from traditional teacher supervision and evaluation practices.

In addition to these obvious influences on supervision practices, other federal, state, and local district policies can affect how teachers are supervised, by whom, and by what criteria.[1]

State Policy Trends

The school reform movement has expanded state roles in educational policy-making generally. This has been especially true in the area of teacher supervision and evaluation, given the states' concerns about teacher quality and school accountability. By 1990, 44 of the 50 states and the District of Columbia had legislative or regulatory requirements for the evaluation of veteran teachers (Valentine 1990; AACTE 1988; Flakus and Mosqueda 1986). In addition, 47 states and the District of Columbia are implementing, piloting, or considering induction programs for beginning teachers (Valentine 1990; AACTE 1988; NASDTEC 1988; Bray et al. 1985; Defino and Hoffman 1984; Hawk and Robards 1987; Darling-Hammond and Berry 1988; Goertz 1988). All told, 31 states require or suggest specific procedures or instruments for evaluation (Valentine 1990). Nearly all of the remainder require that evaluation occur, though they are less prescriptive about the methods used.

Veteran Teacher Supervision and Evaluation

For tenured teachers, more than half of the states (27) require scheduled classroom observations by a supervisor, varying from twice a year to once every three years. Summative evaluation reports are required by 29 states, varying from once every year to once every three years (Valentine 1990). The supervisory process is often stipulated to include such activities as note-taking by the supervisor (sometimes on a specified form), post-observation conferences, uses of (or constraints against using) particular types of nonobservational or artifact data, and

---

[1]Federal, state, and local policies may include (1) highly prescriptive curriculum guidelines that specify teaching practices in great detail—and thus point supervision toward the inspection and monitoring of these practices; (2) teaching "models" that envision standard teaching routines to be followed for each lesson; and (3) test-driven instructional strategies that trigger teacher reviews based on student outcomes. New efforts to aim both teaching and testing at higher order cognitive skills and performance activities will also affect teacher supervision. For example, Vermont's efforts to institute portfolios for examining student progress will also provide indicators of teaching activities; these indicators will likely influence supervision of teaching.

written plans for professional development or remediation under specified circumstances (Valentine 1990).

Of the 44 states that require evaluation of veteran teachers, 12 mandate the use of state-developed instruments or procedures, while 22 require that local districts develop their own, sometimes according to state guidelines (e.g., New Mexico and Indiana) or subject to state approval (e.g., Pennsylvania). Others require only that evaluation occur, without specifying how it must be performed.

Among the 12 states that mandate the use of state-developed instruments or procedures, most have drawn their criteria and indicators from a particular subset of what is known as the "teaching effectiveness research." This aspect of the research establishes behaviors associated with generic skills in a small number of domains as the basis for observation, supervision, and evaluation (Valentine 1990; French, Holdzkom, and Kuligowski 1990). These criteria are even more widely used in beginning teacher evaluation programs, which are generally more highly specified by states because the criteria are often directly linked to licensing as well as tenure decisions.

State and local forays into merit pay and career ladder programs have created another arena in which policies are influencing teacher supervision practices. During the 1980s, more than 40 states considered or experimented with programs intended to reward teachers based on their performance. Though most merit pay initiatives have already folded, career ladder efforts continue in many places (Darling-Hammond and Berry 1988). Career ladder approaches have wide-ranging influences on teacher supervision, including various forms of self-evaluation, peer review, and portfolio development.

Career ladder programs also often include new roles for senior teachers as supervisors, coaches, or mentors of beginning teachers and as consultants to other veteran teachers, thus changing traditional bureaucratic arrangements governing supervisory relationships.

Beginning Teacher Supervision and Evaluation

There has been a substantial increase in state involvement in the supervision of beginning teachers throughout this past decade. Though requirements for some local evaluation of beginning teachers have existed for many years (29 states require some evaluation beyond that received by tenured teachers), new state programs tend to mandate (and occasionally fund) particular kinds of assistance and assessment for beginners.

The first of these recent state initiatives for beginning teacher induction was in 1980 (Ishler 1988). By 1984, 8 states had enacted policies; and by 1988, 12 states required some specified supervision or evaluation procedures for beginning teachers (NASDTEC 1988). At the beginning of 1990, the number of states implementing beginning teacher supervision/evaluation programs was 18, including the District of Columbia (Valentine 1990; AACTE 1988; NASDTEC 1988; Hawk and Robards 1987), while another 30 had proposals on the drawing board or under consideration.

Most of the 18 state-implemented programs mandate both assistance and assessment of new teachers. (Illinois requires assistance only; states like California and Maryland provide funding for some mentors but do not yet require that beginning teachers receive their assistance) (Wagner 1985). Fourteen of the states have developed state performance observation instruments and supervisory procedures, with varying degrees of prescriptiveness. For example, Connecticut, Georgia, and Kentucky require the use of a state-developed instrument for evaluating beginning teachers. Districts in Florida may choose whether to use the state's instrument or develop their own; all but one use the Florida Performance Measurement System (FPMS). New Mexico districts may choose among four state models or design their own. Oklahoma's state-developed instrument, though required, uses a narrative format less constraining than many other checklist approaches.

Four of the 18 states allow local districts to choose their instruments and procedures. Pennsylvania and Maine require districts to attend to state guidelines when developing their plans; California and Oregon allow districts wide discretion in developing their own plans.

Thirteen of these states require completion of the programs for certification (Goertz 1988). The structure of most of these programs is similar: assistance and assessment teams of two or three people (usually an administrator, "mentor" teacher, and state department or university education department representative) observe new teachers two or three times during the first year. Observers are usually trained to use state-developed performance observation instruments that list criteria deduced from a portion of the teaching effectiveness literature. In some cases, new teachers are given a development plan to follow. In addition to a varying number of formative evaluations, at least one summative evaluation is required during the first year.

If new teachers fail to demonstrate the behaviors designated as indicators for the required list of competencies, then they are to receive assistance from the team or attend staff development (Goertz 1988).

Those who still fail to master the competencies cannot receive a teaching license. Thus, supervision is focused on the specific behaviors required by the form rather than on actual problems of practice (Borko 1986). As Fox and Singletary (1986) point out: "Few [programs] focus on the goals of developing a reflective orientation and the skills essential to self-evaluation."

Prototypes of the more prescriptive programs are found in states such as Florida, Georgia, Mississippi, South Carolina, North Carolina, Tennessee, Virginia, Kentucky, and Connecticut. Louisiana and Arizona are piloting similar types of programs. By contrast, California's mentor program emphasizes developmental supervision. Although the type of teacher support offered to California teachers varies from district to district, assistance may take any form that supports the teacher's growth; it is not limited to a prescribed set of behaviors (Wagner 1985), and completion of the program is not tied directly to certification.

Other states, such as Illinois and Ohio, emphasize support for beginning teachers rather than focusing on a prescribed form of evaluation. Their assistance, too, is not limited to behavioral indicators of generic skills. States such as Minnesota and New York are developing full-fledged internship programs like those used in other professions. They will provide clinical supervision and training to beginning teachers aimed at the translation of a complex knowledge base into judgmentally sound practice.

Local Policy Trends

In many cases, the reform movement has been led by local school districts intent not only on improving teaching, but also on changing the relationships governing the management of schools and teaching. In some places, local teachers' unions have taken leadership roles; in others, enlightened superintendents or school board members have led the way. Wherever significant reforms have occurred, both "management" and "labor" have joined together to redefine their roles and relationships regarding professional standards for teaching (McDonnell and Pascal 1988; Wise, Darling-Hammond, McLaughlin, and Bernstein 1984).

One important example of this trend was the creation of an intern/intervention program in Toledo, Ohio, in the early 1980s (see Chapter 9). This program has become the model for similar initiatives in Cincinnati, Ohio; Rochester, New York; Washington, D.C.; and elsewhere (Darling-Hammond 1984). The teachers association in Toledo bargained for a new model of professional accountability in which expert "consulting" teachers provide intensive supervision to both new entrants and to veterans having difficulty. The consulting teachers' efforts are overseen by a committee of teachers and administrators, who consider evidence from the school principal and the consulting teacher in the course of making evaluation decisions concerning continued employment of interns and intervention candidates. Shared norms of professional practice are both defined and enforced in this clinical problem-solving model. Shared responsibility for teaching is also created.

The importance of these kinds of initiatives has been underscored by more recent reforms aimed at shared decision making and joint accountability in schools, but these programs have not always been greeted with open arms. When the teachers' union and school board in Rochester, New York, negotiated a similar mentoring program, the district was sued by its Council of Supervisors and Administrators, the chief principals' union, on the grounds that only certified administrative staff should be allowed to supervise teachers. The case was thrown out of court because the judge could not see how such an effort to coach beginning teachers could be anything but helpful; however, the sense of threat manifested in the administrators' complaint is still present in many school systems experimenting with forms of peer assistance and review for teachers.

Many local efforts to revamp supervision and evaluation practices include opportunities for teachers to observe and consult with their peers in a variety of formal and informal ways. These may range from peer-mediated self-appraisal strategies (Barber 1984) to released time for mutual classroom observation and the provision of time for joint planning and consultation (see Chapter 4). These strategies are one way to introduce expertise related to a teacher's subject area or grade level into the dialogue about teaching. They also provide a means for helping teachers to encounter and develop richer understandings of teaching in various contexts and to develop the shared norms of practice so critical to a profession (Darling-Hammond 1986; Darling-Hammond, Gendler, and Wise 1990).

Local initiatives to rethink and restructure teachers' opportunities to learn, however, must contend with state policies that may or may not support the conceptions of teaching and teacher learning that undergird their own reforms. As the field takes shape, it is increasingly clear that reformers have differing ideas about how to improve teaching and, in fact, very different ideas about what good teaching is and what knowledge and skills it demands. These ideas, in turn, bode very different futures for teaching as a profession and for the nature of education that students are likely to receive (See Section II for examples of local initiatives). In what follows, we seek to illuminate these futures by examining the content, methods, and assumptions embodied in two policy approaches to teacher supervision.

Policy Effects on Teaching and Teacher Learning

As noted earlier, different conceptions of the work of teaching have important implications for the ways in which teaching and learning are structured. These conceptions vary primarily in the extent to which they view learning as either predictable and standardized or differentiated and complex—and teaching as the mastery of simple routines or as the exercise of informed judgment.

Several analysts have recently described the different views of teaching that undergird two identifiably different supervision strategies and policies. The first kind of supervision model focuses on the development of a reflective teaching orientation stimulated by attention to teachers' individual contexts and felt needs (e.g., Garman 1982, Glickman 1985). The second emphasizes the production of specific teacher behaviors thought to represent "effective teaching" (e.g., Minton 1979, Hunter 1984).

Tracy and MacNaughton (1989) characterize the proponents of these two approaches to supervision as "neo-progressive" in the first instance and "neo-traditionalist" in the latter. Their analysis—and that of the proponents themselves (see, e.g., Garman, Glickman, Hunter, and Haggerson 1987)—locates neo-progressives in the intellectual tradition of cognitive developmentalists such as Dewey, Piaget, and Bruner. Neo-traditionalists derive much of their intellectual heritage from behavioral psychologists such as E.L. Thorndike. Neo-progressives are concerned with developing deliberative classrooms that support both teachers and students in constructing meaning from their interactions with each other and with the world they study. Neo-traditionalists are concerned with specifying and producing teacher behaviors thought to increase those student behaviors thought to be associated with learning.

Although both approaches claim the mantle of "clinical supervision" (Cogan 1973, Goldhammer 1969), neo-traditionalists bypass several fundamental tenets of clinical supervision models by deriving observation criteria and desired outcomes from correlational research on teaching behaviors rather than from the concerns and intentions of teachers working in different contexts (Garman et al. 1987, Pavan 1986, Costa 1984). The goal is to coach teachers to display these behaviors rather than to identify and solve actual problems of practice. As such, this kind of strategy has been criticized for failing to encourage or assess teacher reflectiveness (Macmillan and Pendlebury 1985; Peterson, P.L., and Comeaux 1989a; Gitlin and Smyth 1990). The neo-traditionalist approach has even been dubbed "unrelated to the cultivation of conscious thought" (Gibboney 1987).

The behavioral approach has been adopted by many of the states that were among the first to mandate beginning teacher induction programs in the early 1980s (French et al. 1990). These states also tended to adopt low-inference evaluation instruments requiring only the observation and tallying of specific behaviors. Because use of these observations for making a licensure decision demands reliability and "objectivity," the challenge is ostensibly met by allowing the evaluator only to note the presence or absence of behaviors, not their appropriateness or effectiveness. When evaluation is made "evaluator-proof" in this way, the supervisor's job is simplified, as supervision can focus only on the search for and production of these behaviors. This approach typifies the reductionism attacked by Sergiovanni (1984) as symptomatic of the "web of primitive scientism" in which teacher supervision seems trapped:

> Examples of reductionism in the supervision and evaluation of teaching would be the reducing of complex patterns of human interaction to tallies on a data collection schedule and reducing the phenomenon of student response to teaching to the timing of specific student task behaviors (p. 355).

Sergiovanni continues:

> The consequence of this stance is a preoccupation with "looking" at classrooms, teachers, and teaching at the expense of "seeing." To look is to attend and describe; to see is to discover and understand. . . .

> The scientific-technical view argues that looking must be emphasized to avoid perceptual problems and evaluation bias. . . . [However], the choice of such a framework (for reliably recording events) corresponds to some preconception of the issue. This preconception guides the inquiry and helps to determine the findings, and thus the evaluation is biased from the beginning (p. 361).

Because bias is unavoidable, even when "objective" methods are used, the real question is, What is the framework that guides the behaviorally oriented teacher induction and evaluation programs? The research cited as the basis for most of these behaviorist supervision models is generally a subset of process-product research on teaching (Valentine 1990, French et al. 1990) indicating that "direct instruction" techniques[2] correlate with elementary school students' performance on multiple-choice basic skills tests. Many researchers have criticized the use of this research base to derive standardized rules for practice—because of its correlational nature (Griffin 1985) and its contextual limitations (Darling-Hammond 1986; Macmillan and Pendlebury 1985; Peterson, P.L., and Comeaux 1989a). This subset of process-product research, however, is still widely used in "research-based" teacher evaluation and supervision models adopted by many states and districts.

The "effective teaching" research supporting direct instruction strategies has unearthed many of its own limitations. For example, teaching behaviors found effective in some situations are ineffective or even counterproductive when used too much or under the wrong circumstances (Peterson, K., and Kauchak 1982; Medley 1977; Soar 1972). Meanwhile, other research has found that students' performance on tasks requiring higher order skills, creativity, and problem-solving abilities benefits from very different instructional approaches (see e.g., Peterson, P.L., 1979). Other researchers have found that effective teaching behaviors vary depending on student characteristics, subject matter demands, and instructional goals (Brophy and Evertson 1974; Cronbach and Snow 1977; Peterson, P.L., 1976; Gage 1978; McDonald and Elias 1976).

A major problem with inferring generalized rules for practice from correlational studies is that cause-effect relationships are unproved.[3] Moreover, the use of such a practice frequently reduces rather than enhances a teacher's effectiveness. These problems occur because important context variables change the relationship between a given behavior and its outcome. Thus, the fact that teachers vary their behaviors across teaching situations can produce more effective teaching, even though these behaviors may not contribute to evaluation results, as measured by low-inference behavioral instruments (Shavelson and Dempsey-Atwood 1976, Stodolsky 1984). These same context

---

[2] These are defined as teacher-directed activities using materials congruent with achievement test tasks monitored by frequent use of low-cognitive-level questions and drill (Rosenshine 1979)
[3] That is, a correlation may occur for many noncausal reasons. For instance, another independent factor may be associated with both of the variables under study. Also, a small correlation across many cases, though statistically significant, means that one variable generally accounts for very little of the variance in the other, and it may mask dramatic differences in the relationship between the same two variables under varying conditions..

factors produce the inconsistencies among findings in process-product studies that have undermined confidence in simple applications of their results (Doyle 1978, Peterson, P.L., 1979).

Sometimes, the limitations of such simple applications are pointed out by additional process-product research. For example, in one study seeking to validate Georgia's Teacher Performance Assessment Instrument, two of the instrument's behaviors[4] actually produced significant negative correlations with teachers' effectiveness, as measured by student achievement gains (Ellett, Capie, and Johnson 1981).

Unfortunately, as we describe in the next sections, even where studies have noted contextual nuances and limitations, these findings are ignored when the research is translated into supervision and evaluation schemes. Other bodies of research—such as research on cognition, child development, motivation and behavior, subject-specific pedagogy, and effective schooling—are typically not included at all in these schemes (French et al. 1990; Darling-Hammond 1986; Darling-Hammond, Wise, and Pease 1983).

This might be an academic issue if policy were not currently the major vehicle for models of teacher supervision. State-level induction and evaluation policies not only affect beginning teachers, but they also affect the state's teacher education institutions, which are often evaluated by the number of their graduates prepared to "pass" the standards (Darling-Hammond and Berry 1988). Griffin (1985) expresses a concern that such simplistic applications of limited research findings produce a lowest-common-denominator standard for certification. A related concern is the following: When teacher supervision and evaluation are guided by these lights, what kind of teacher learning occurs? What are the results for teaching and, ultimately, for student learning?

In the following sections, we examine these concerns with reference to two distinctive models of beginning teacher supervision: Florida's Performance Measurement System (FPMS) and Minnesota's newly endorsed teacher internship program standards.

---

[4]One behavior—the way in which the teacher "attends to routine tasks"—was significantly and negatively related to students' progress in both reading and mathematics. Another—the way in which the teacher "specifies and selects learner objectives for lessons"—was significantly and negatively related to students' progress in mathematics. Interestingly, related planning behaviors concerning the selection of procedures, materials, and assessments were also negatively related to students' mathematics progress, though not significantly. This latter result leads one to question whether the behavioral indicators selected were rigid or inappropriate.

The Florida Performance Measurement System

The Florida Beginning Teacher Program had its origins in an omnibus school reform package enacted in 1979. Beginning in 1982, new teachers in Florida were to receive a year of supervision and were to be evaluated on a number of "generic" competencies through a "performance measurement system." The FPMS is an extreme form of an observation-based behavioral tally: the observers record the frequencies of specific behaviors in two columns, one for "effective" behaviors, the other for "ineffective." The observer does not record any other behaviors, any information about contextual factors, or any information about the behaviors of students or other individuals in the classroom, nor does any interpretive narrative accompany the tally.

The system was also adopted for use with veteran teachers in many Florida districts and became a requirement for the state's ill-fated "Master Teacher Program," later accounting in part for the program's demise. The system has since been used in Kentucky; and many of its principles have been used in teacher evaluation instruments in South Carolina, North Carolina, and Texas (Hazi 1989). Similar systems of behavioral tallies are also in use in Mississippi, Tennessee, and Virginia (French et al. 1990).

In an important sense, then, the FPMS approach represents a prototype of an evaluation model that has had widespread policy consequences. Within Florida, the instrument has been used to drive many different types of decisions about teacher certification, tenure, retention, and compensation. Outside the state, the instrument has had an impact as others looking for reform guidance have found it a readily available tool for their own goals.

In addition, the greater the number of uses found for such instruments, the more far reaching their influences on teacher preparation and continuing supervision. Where important decisions are to be made based on a measure, the "high stakes" associated with its use tend to cause behaviors required by the measure to increase; and performances not emphasized by the measure will frequently decrease (Haney and Madaus 1986). Thus, one might expect that high-stakes policy uses of a teacher evaluation tool would increase the importance of the evaluation model as a basis for supervision while decreasing attention to other educational concerns. One study suggests that such uses of the Florida instrument have also strengthened the normally weak effects that supervision practices generally have on teacher learning and teacher performance (Peterson, P.L., and Comeaux 1989b).

What do teachers who learn to teach to the FPMS actually learn? First, evidence suggests that the range of teaching concerns they are likely to encounter and consider will be much narrower than would otherwise be true. For example, Hoover and O'Shea (1987) compared the post-observation conferences of supervisors who used the FPMS with those who used a more open-ended "analytical recording form." They found that the FPMS users discussed a much narrower range of relevant behaviors, and these focused almost exclusively on the behaviors listed on the FPMS checklist.

Among the concerns that would likely be missing from such discussions are those ignored by the instrument: the teacher's content knowledge and treatment of subject matter; the relationship between teacher practices and student responses or outcomes; practices related to emerging bodies of research, such as the use of collaborative learning strategies or inductive methods for stimulating higher order thought processes; and the teacher's performance outside of the observation context (French et al. 1990).

Nonobservable aspects of teaching using the FPMS approach include the following important dimensions of good teaching:

- Curriculum planning.
- The types of assignments and feedback given to students.
- The quality and variety of materials used.
- Diagnostic efforts on behalf of pupils having difficulty.
- The depth and breadth of content covered.
- The coherence among lessons or units over time.
- Interactions with parents and colleagues.

Teachers trained to teach to the FPMS indicators would not learn to vary their behaviors according to the needs of students and the demands of the teaching situation. In fact, as the following example shows, teachers would explicitly learn not to do so, even where research and experience would suggest they should. In the process they would likely learn to disdain complexity in both research and teaching, as the FPMS itself does. Ironically, the instrument frequently ignores or contravenes the findings presented in the substantial research summary prepared for the Florida initiative (Florida Coalition 1983). Though the massive summary document excluded some bodies of research entirely from its purview, it did provide an honest, thoughtful, and thorough examination of the "effective teaching" research it sought to review.

For example, in a dense, nine-page discussion of the research on praise, the research document notes the differential effects of generalized and specific praise on children at different ages, of different genders, and under different circumstances. It goes on to note that "even identical teacher statements made under the same circumstances and with the same intent (to provide encouragement or reinforcement) may be experienced very differently and may have very different effects in different individuals" (Florida Coalition 1983, p. 32).

Nonetheless, the FPMS instrument provides only two behavioral indicators regarding praise to guide its tallies: "gives specific academic praise" (to be tallied as effective), and "uses general non-specific praise" (to be tallied as ineffective). The coding manual includes the following note: "The use of general praise is pedagogically acceptable in the kindergarten and primary grades, for students have not yet learned to discount it. Even so, tally it on the right side [as an ineffective behavior]" (Florida Department of Education 1989, p. 7). The system thus consciously conveys to teachers that their use of pedagogically acceptable practices is not acceptable, and that they should ignore research which suggests that they should adjust their behaviors to different student responses or circumstances.

Similarly, despite research that suggests the importance of linking classroom work to students' personal experiences, the FPMS codes as "ineffective" any teacher questions that "call for personal opinion or that are answered from personal experience." Here again, the coding manual notes that "these questions may sometimes serve useful or even necessary purposes; however, they should be tallied here [in the "ineffective" column] since they do not move the class work along academically" (Florida Department of Education 1989, p. 5b).

The FPMS instrument is littered with such statements, suggesting that beginning teachers should be trained to be insensitive to the students they teach and ignorant of a broader knowledge base on teaching. Floden and Klinzing's (1990) conclusion is to the point:

> Training teachers to follow a fixed set of prescriptions discourages teachers from adapting their instruction to the particular subjects and students they are teaching. Hence, the instructional effectiveness of teachers given such training is unlikely to be at a high level (pp. 16–17).

Similarly, expert veteran teachers must ignore their knowledge to pass such assessments. In fact, the most dramatic evidence of the results of these distortions is the fact that Michael Reynolds, Florida's 1986 Teacher of the Year (and a runner-up in NASA's Teacher in Space program), did not pass the FPMS assessment when he was being evaluated for a merit pay award. His principal and vice-principal could not find enough of the required behaviors during the laboratory lesson they observed to qualify him for merit pay. Furthermore, they had to mark him down for answering a question with a question, a practice forbidden by the FPMS, though popular with Socrates and many other effective teachers. This particular example is symptomatic of an especially egregious flaw of the instrument: it favors an approach to teaching that is distinctly ill suited to the development of students' critical thinking abilities and apparently not cognizant of most recent research on student cognition.

If the ultimate test of the validity of this type of evaluation instrument is whether it correctly differentiates between "effective" and "ineffective" teachers, the FPMS ought to fail. If a test of its utility is whether it encourages the use of knowledge and more informed judgment in teaching, it should doubly fail. Although Florida's merit pay plan was ultimately rescinded because of widespread evaluation problems (Hazi 1989, Darling-Hammond and Berry 1988), the FPMS is still being used as the basis for supervising and evaluating both beginning and veteran teachers, as are its relatives in many other states.[5]

Recent critiques of similar systems in Texas (Tyson-Bernstein 1987) and South Carolina (Berry and Ginsberg 1988) point out the limitations of attempts to establish context-free behavioral indicators as the basis for evaluation and the primary goal for teacher learning. These researchers echo Shulman's (1987) concern that such initiatives are evidence of the "currently incomplete and trivial definitions of good education held by the policy community" (p. 20).

Other states, including California, Minnesota, New York, and a growing number of others, especially in the Midwest, Northwest, and Northeast, are creating internship programs that seek to incorporate a very different conception of teaching and teacher learning. These initiatives recognize the importance of relying on a broader base of knowledge to provide a foundation for teachers' judgments and reflections on their teaching. They envision a full internship year of heavily supervised practice and graduated responsibility as an extension of teacher preparation before teachers are ready to be licensed. They aim to develop teachers who

> possess broad and deep understandings of children, the subjects they
> teach, the nature of learning and schooling, and the world around

---

[5]However, Georgia has recently eliminated use of its Teacher Performance Assessment Instrument as the basis for beginning teacher certification decisions. A raft of difficulties with the evaluation contributed to this decision, including at least one lawsuit in which the court could not find a legitimate basis for the instrument's criteria, claiming they appeared "arbitrary and capricious" (*Kitchens v. State Dept. of Education*, Fulton County Superior Court, Civil Action File #D–54773, July 29, 1988).

them . . . [and who] exemplify the critical thinking they strive to develop in students (Holmes Group 1986, p. 28).

Recently published, proposed standards for Minnesota's internship program provide an outline of how such an alternative policy model might function.

Minnesota's Internship Program for Beginning Teachers

Minnesota's newly proposed internship model emanates from both a different conceptual basis and a radically different governance structure than many of the existing state prescriptions for teacher supervision and evaluation. Minnesota is one of only a handful of states that accord teaching the same kind of professionally governed standards board as states generally accord all their other professions.

The Minnesota Board of Teaching (MBOT) is creating a structure for teacher education and licensure similar to that followed in other professions:

• Teacher education managed by reference to desired learning outcomes rather than counts of required course titles.

• A supervised internship as a prerequisite to sitting for board examinations.

• Licensure examinations based on a broad view of knowledge as a foundation for teaching.

• Performance-based assessments of abilities to apply knowledge in complex teaching situations (Wise and Darling-Hammond 1987)

Minnesota's conception of teaching knowledge is grounded in a view of teachers as "thoughtful, creative persons who use a set of principles and strategies derived from an informed personal philosophy of education and the multiple demands of learning contexts" (MBOT 1986). The dispositions, skills, and knowledge required for teaching include, among others, dispositions to "reflect on [one's] own teaching and its effects on learners," to "respect and value individual and cultural differences," and to "engage in critical and divergent thinking and problem-solving with students." A knowledge base for such practice includes knowledge of scientific inquiry and epistemology, as well as knowledge about behavior and cognition, cultures, human growth and development, social organizations, ethics, communication and language, learning contexts, and subject matter (MBOT 1986).

The proposed internship experience differs from the beginning teacher programs in most other states in that it is not merely a set of evaluations to which beginners are subject during their first year of employment as a teacher. Like internships in other professions, it is to be a carefully planned clinical experience for beginners who are *not* full-fledged teachers allowed to practice unsupervised. Interns will teach partial loads under supervision and will assume greater responsibility over time.

Internship programs will be conducted by schools in conjunction with university teacher education faculty[6] and will ultimately be accredited by the Board of Teaching. This process is intended to ensure that beginning teachers will be exposed to state-of-the-art practices in the areas in which they are likely to need assistance, rather than experiencing a haphazard introduction to teaching under circumstances that more closely resemble hazing than guidance and support. The optimal structure for such programs will likely be professional development schools explicitly authorized to support the clinical preparation of beginning teachers (Darling-Hammond, Gendler, and Wise 1990).

The proposed standards for internship programs consciously embrace a conception of teaching as complex and context-dependent and a conception of teacher learning as deliberative. The standards require that interns experience—through a combination of study, observation, and direct practice—a variety of teaching situations, including variety in student age or grade levels, subject areas, student learning characteristics, students' cultural backgrounds, and types of communities. The proposed standards require that interns gain experience in applying their knowledge to major tasks of teaching as well as difficult problems of practice, analyzing and using research, and reflecting on their own and others' teaching experiences.

The standards also require that interns participate in teaching observations, conferences, and seminars, as well as meeting with individual supervisors at least two hours weekly. These deliberations are to include discussions of professional ethics; general and specific concerns relating to planning, instruction, and assessment; and the diagnosis and understanding of student needs and progress. In short, rather than learning to ignore differences among students and teaching contexts while unquestioningly displaying a set of uniform behaviors, beginning teachers in Minnesota will learn to examine different needs and contexts, to question their teaching strategies, and to apply wide-ranging sources of knowledge to the complex problems of practice they face. They will be evaluated not by fixed lists of behaviors that have been

---

[6]Several alternative methods of developing such collaborative programs are currently being piloted in Minnesota.

"evaluator-proofed," but by their ability to exhibit professional modes of thinking and judgment as assessed by master teachers and teacher educators whose judgment in turn can be trusted because they were chosen for their professional expertise.

Minnesota's internship aims to develop teachers who are "reflective professionals":

> The reflective professional is engaged continuously in the process of learning. Not only is the reflective professional engaged in "learning to learn" and in "higher-order learning," but she also inspires and facilitates this kind of higher-order learning in her students. . . . The image of the reflective professional defines the teacher in terms of the kind and quality of the decision making, thinking, and judgment in which the teacher engages, not just in terms of her behavioral competencies (P.L. Peterson and Comeaux 1989a, p. 133).

The Minnesota plan demonstrates that it is possible for policy to enlarge horizons for teacher learning, rather than narrowing them. Minnesota, like a growing number of other states, is betting that policy can support a professional conception of teaching rather than a bureaucratic one. (See Chapter 7 for a discussion of school renewal in a Minnesota district.)

The likelihood that this type of policy will become more prevalent depends on several factors:

• The enlightenment of researchers about the nature of interactions between research and policy.

• The involvement of teachers and teacher educators in shaping state requirements for teacher supervision and evaluation.

• The creation of a policy community that can legitimately define and enforce professional standards.

In the first instance, researchers and others who advise policymakers must become more aware of many policymakers' natural inclination to want to reduce research findings into regulations, that is, into rules permitting little or no variation in practice. In offering research as a tool for improving teaching, researchers must educate "consumers" in its proper use. At the same time, teachers and teacher educators must become proactive in developing—and enforcing—the standards by which they would like teaching to be judged.

Both of these conditions are more likely to be achieved when policies concerning teacher supervision and evaluation are placed in the hands of professional standards boards, where—as in other professions facing complex problems of practice—expert members of the profession determine the best means by which practitioners can be taught to responsibly evaluate and address such problems. Ultimately, the nature of the standards will be greatly influenced by the knowledge and commitments of those charged with creating them. If they are to be professional standards, the profession will need a place at the center of the policy structure, not just a voice at the periphery.

References

American Association of Colleges for Teacher Education (AACTE). (1988). *Teacher Education Policy in the States. A 50-state Survey of Legislative and Administrative Actions.* Washington, D.C.: AACTE.

Barber, L.W. (1984). *Teacher Evaluation and Merit Pay: Background Papers for the Task Form on Education for Economic Growth* (Working Paper No. TF-83-5). Denver: Education Commission of the States.

Berry, B., and R. Ginsberg. (1988). "Legitimizing Subjectivity: Meritorious Performance and the Professionalization of Teacher and Principal Evaluation." *Journal of Personnel Evaluation in Education* 2: 123–140.

Borko, H. (1986). "Clinical Teacher Education: The Induction Years." In *Reality and Reform in Teacher Education*, edited by J.V. Hoffman and J. Edwards. New York: Random House.

Bray, J.L., P. Flakus-Mosqueda, R.M. Palaich, and J.S. Wilkins. (1985). *New Direction for State Policies.* Denver: Education Commission of the States. (No. TR-85-1).

Brophy, J.E., and C. Evertson. (1974). *Process-Product Correlations in the Texas Teacher Effectiveness Study: Final Report.* Austin: Research and Development Center for Teacher Education, University of Texas.

Carnegie Forum on Education and the Economy. (1986). *A Nation Prepared: Teachers for the 21st Century.* New York: Carnegie Forum.

Cogan, M.L. (1973). *Clinical Supervision.* Boston: Houghton Mifflin.

Costa, A.L. (1984). "Reaction to Hunter's 'Knowing, Teaching, and Supervising.'" In *Using What We Know About Teaching,* (pp. 196–202), edited by P.L. Hosford. Alexandria, Va.: ASCD.

Cronbach, L.J., and R.E. Snow. (1977). *Attitudes and Instructional Methods: A Handbook for Research on Interactions.* New York: Irvington.

Darling-Hammond, L. (1986). "A Proposal for Evaluation in the Teaching Profession." *Elementary School Journal* 86, 4: 531–551.

Darling-Hammond, L. (1984). "Toledo's Intern-Intervention Program." In *Case Studies for Teacher Evaluation: A Study of Effective Practices* (pp. 119–166), edited by A.E. Wise, L. Darling-Hammond, M.W. McLaughlin, and H.T. Bernstein. Santa Monica, Calif.: RAND Corporation.

Darling-Hammond, L., and B. Berry. (1988). *The Evolution of Teacher Policy.* Santa Monica, Calif.: RAND Corporation.

Darling-Hammond, L., T. Gendler, and A.E. Wise. (1990). *The Teaching Internship: Practical Preparation for a Licensed Profession.* Santa Monica, Calif.: RAND Corporation.

Darling-Hammond, L., A.E. Wise, and S. Pease. (1983). "Teacher Evaluation in the Organizational Context: A Review of the Literature." *Review of Educational Research* 53, 3: 285–328.

Defino, M.E., and J.V. Hoffman. (1984). *A Status Report and Content Analysis of State Mandated Teacher Induction Programs.* (Report No. 9057) Austin: University of Texas, Research and Development Center for Teacher Education.

Doyle, W. (1978). "Paradigms for Research on Teacher Effectiveness." In *Review of Research in Education,* Vol. 5, edited by L.S. Shulman. Itasca, Ill.: F.E. Peacock.

Ellett, C.D., W. Capie, and C.E. Johnson. (1981). *Teacher Performance and Elementary Pupil Achievement on the Georgia Criterion Referenced Tests.* Athens, Ga: Teacher Assessment Project, University of Georgia.

Flakus-Mosqueda, P. (1986). "Teacher Testing and Performance Standards: A Survey of Selected State Policies." *Teacher Education Quarterly* 13: 8–27.

Floden, R.E., and H.G. Klinzing. (1990). "What Can Research on Teacher Thinking Contribute to Teacher Preparation? A Second Opinion." *Educational Researcher* 19, 4: 15–20.

Florida Coalition for the Development of a Performance Evaluation System. (1983). *Domains of the Florida Performance Measurement System.* Tallahassee: Florida Department of Education.

Florida Department of Education. (1989). *Manual for Coding Teacher Performance on the Screening/Summative Observation Instrument: Florida Performance Measurement System.* Tallahassee: Florida Department of Education.

Fox, S.M., and T.J. Singletary. (1986). "Deductions About Supportive Induction." *Journal of Teacher Education* 37, 1: 12–15.

French, R.L., D. Holdzkom, and B. Kuligowski. (April 1990). "Teacher Evaluation in SREB States. Stage I: Analysis and Comparison of Evaluation Systems." Paper presented at the annual conference of the American Educational Research Association, Boston.

Friske, J.S., and M. Combs. (1986). "Teacher Induction Program: An Oklahoma Perspective." *Action in Teacher Education* 8: 67–74.

Gage, N.L. (1978). *The Scientific Basis of the Art of Teaching.* New York: Teachers College Press.

Garman, N.B. (1982). *Supervision of Teaching. ASCD 1982 Yearbook.* Alexandria, Va.: ASCD.

Garman, N.B., C.D. Glickman, M. Hunter, and N.L. Haggerson. (1987). "Conflicting Conceptions of Clinical Supervision and the Enhancement of Professional Growth and Renewal: Point and Counterpoint." *Journal of Curriculum and Supervision* 2, 2: 152–177.

Gibboney, R.A. (February 1987). "A Critique of Madeline Hunter's Teaching Model from Dewey's Perspective." *Educational Leadership* 44: 46–50.

Gitlin, A., and J. Smyth. (1990). "Toward Educative Forms of Teacher Evaluation." *Educational Theory* 40, 1: 83–94.

Glickman, C.D. (1985). *Supervision and Instruction: A Developmental Approach.* Boston, Mass.: Allyn and Bacon.

Goertz, M.E. (1988). *State Educational Standards in the 50 States: An Update.* Princeton: Educational Testing Service.

Goldhammer, R. (1969). *Clinical Supervision: Special Methods for the Supervision of Teachers.* New York: Holt, Rinehart and Winston.

Griffin, G.A. (January–February 1985). "Teacher Induction: Research Issues." *Journal of Teacher Education.* 36, 1: 42–46.

Hawk, P.P., and S. Robards. (1987). "Statewide Teacher Induction Programs." In *Teacher Induction: A New Beginning* (pp. 33–43), edited by D.M. Brooks. Reston, Va.: Association of Teacher Educators.

Haney, W., and G. Madaus. (1986). "Effects of Standardized Testing and the Future of the National Assessment of Educational Progress," Working Paper for the NAEP Study Group. Chestnut Hill, Mass.: Center for the Study of Testing, Evaluation, and Education Policy.

Hazi, H.M. (1989). "Measurement Versus Supervisory Judgment: The Case of *Sweeney v. Turlington.*" *Journal of Curriculum and Supervision* 4: 211–229.

Holmes Group. (1986). *Tomorrow's Teachers: A Report of the Holmes Group.* East Lansing, Mich.: Holmes Group.

Hoover, N.L., and L.J. O'Shea. (1987). "The Influence of a Criterion Checklist on Supervisors' and Interns' Conceptions of Teaching." Paper presented at the Annual Meeting of the American Educational Research Association, Washington, D.C.

Hunter, M. (1984). "Knowing, Teaching, and Supervising." In *Using What We Know About Teaching*, edited by P.L. Hosford. Alexandria, Va.: ASCD.

Ishler, P. (1988). "A Report on Successful Teacher Induction Programs: The Whys, Whats, and Wherefores for Texas." Paper presented at the Annual Texas Conference on Teacher Education. (ED 301 562), Dallas, Texas.

Macmillan, J.B., and S. Pendlebury. (1985). "The Florida Performance Measurement System: A Consideration." *Teachers College Record* 87: 67–78.

McDonald, F.J., and P. Elias. (1976). *Executive Summary Report: Beginning Teacher Evaluation Study, Part II.* Princeton: Educational Testing Service.

McDonnell, L.M., and A. Pascal. (1988). *Teacher Unions and Educational Reform.* Santa Monica, Calif.: RAND Corporation.

Medley, D.M., E.P. Rosenblum, and N.C. Vance. (1989). "Assessing the Functional Knowledge of Participants in the Virginia Beginning Teacher Assistance Program." *The Elementary School Journal* 89: 495–510.

Minnesota Board of Teaching (MBOT). (1986). *Minnesota's Vision for Teacher Education: Stronger Standards, New Partnerships.* St. Paul: Task Force on Teacher Education, Minnesota Higher Education Coordinating Board and MBOT.

Minton, E. (1979). *Clinical Supervision: Developing Evaluation Skills for Dynamic Leadership* (cassette recording). Englewood, Colo.: Educational Consulting Associates.

National Association of State Directors for Teacher Education and Certification (NASDTEC). (1988). "Support Systems for Beginning Teachers". In *Manual on Certification and Preparation of Educational Personnel in the United States.* (pp. 1–18), edited by D. Mastain. Sacramento: NASDTEC.

National Governors' Association (NGA). (1986). *Time for Results: The Governors' 1991 Report on Education.* Washington, D.C.: NGA.

Pavan, B. (March 1986). "A Thank You and Some Questions for Madeline Hunter." *Educational Leadership* 43: 67–68.

Peterson, K., and D. Kauchak. (1982). *Teacher Evaluation: Perspectives, Practices, and Promises.* Salt Like City: University of Utah.

Peterson, P.L. (1976). "Interactive Effects of Student Anxiety, Achievement Orientation, and Teacher Behavior on Student Achievement and Attitude." Unpublished doctoral dissertation, Stanford University.

Peterson, P.L. (1979). "Direct Instruction Reconsidered." In *Research on Teaching*, edited by P.L. Peterson and H.J. Walberg. Berkeley, Calif.: McCutchan.

Peterson, P.L., and M.A. Comeaux. (1989a). "Assessing the Teacher as a Reflective Professional: New Perspectives on Teacher Evaluation." In *The Graduate Preparation of Teachers* (pp. 132–152), edited by A.E. Woolfolk. Englewood Cliffs, N.J.: Prentice-Hall.

Peterson, P.L., and M.A. Comeaux. (1989b). "Evaluating the Systems: Teachers' Perspectives on Teacher Evaluation." Paper presented at the Annual Meeting of the American Educational Research Association, San Francisco, Calif.

Rosenshine, B.V. (1979). "Content, Time, and Direct Instruction." In *Research on Teaching* (pp. 28–56), edited by P.L. Peterson and H.J. Walberg. Berkeley, Calif.: McCutchan.

Sergiovanni, T.J. (1984). "Expanding Conceptions of Inquiry and Practice in Supervision and Evaluation." *Educational Evaluation and Policy Analysis* 6, 4: 355–365.

Shavelson, R.J., and N. Dempsey-Atwood. (1976). "Generalizability of Measures of Teacher Behavior." *Review of Educational Research* 46: 553–612.

Shulman, L.S. (1987). "Knowledge and Teaching: Foundations of the New Reform." *Harvard Educational Review* 57: 1–22.

Soar, R.S. (1972). *Follow-Through Classroom Process Measurement and Pupil Growth*. Gainesville: University of Florida.

Stodolsky, S. (1984). "Teacher Evaluation: The Limits of Looking." *Educational Researcher* 13: 13–22.

Tracy, S.J., and R.H. MacNaughton. (1989). "Clinical Supervision and the Emerging Conflict Between the Neo-traditionalists and the Neo-progressives." *Journal of Curriculum and Supervision* 4, 3: 246–256.

Tyson-Bernstein, H. (1987). "The Texas Teacher Appraisal System: What Does It Really Appraise?" *American Educator* 11: 26–31.

Valentine, J. (April 1990). "A National Survey of State Teacher Evaluation Policies." Unpublished research paper, University of Missouri, Columbia.

Wagner, L.A. (November 1985). "Ambiguities and Possibilities in California's Mentor Teacher Program." *Educational Leadership* 43: 23–29.

Wise, A.E., and L. Darling-Hammond. (1987). *Licensing Teachers: Design for a Teaching Profession*. Santa Monica, Calif.: RAND Corporation.

Wise, A.E., L. Darling-Hammond, M.W. McLaughlin, and H. Bernstein. (1984). *Case Studies for Teacher Evaluation: A Study of Effective Practices*. Santa Monica, Calif.: RAND Corporation.

2

Searching for a Common Purpose: A Perspective on the History of Supervision

Frances S. Bolin and Philip Panaritis

> **The past is never dead. It's not even past.**
>
> *William Faulkner,* Requiem for a Nun, *Act 1, Scene 3, p. 80, 1975*

Supervisors have always held sharp differences of opinion about schooling, teaching, and curriculum. It stands to reason that they would also differ in their ideas about the role of the supervisor. The history of supervision is characterized by these differences, surfacing both as internal struggles over mission and a more external struggle for identity as a distinct field of practice. These struggles cannot be understood apart from broader social trends that changed both the role of the school and that of the teacher during the 20th century.

Supervision emerged as a field of practice around the turn of the century in response to increased levels of bureaucracy in schools and the public demand for more control over the curriculum (Karier 1982, Bolin 1987). Conflicting conceptions of the supervisor's role are closely related to differences of opinion about the purposes of school in a democratic society and how to achieve these purposes. It was in response to changing public expectations of the schools that the fields of curriculum and supervision grew hand in hand.

There have always been educators who raised questions about definition and theory in supervision, but literature in the field is dominated by a concern for the practical. Rhetorical questions about definition and theory, scattered through the literature from the turn of the century, have been the work of a handful of academics who have had their own concerns about identity, definition, and purpose in relation to schools of education (Bolin 1988).

Questions about what supervision is and what it is supposed to do—for whom and by whom—have never been insignificant questions. Supervisory training and standards of professional practice depend on some consensus about these issues. But there are essentially only two areas around which a loose consensus has been built over the years:

1. The function of supervision is an important one whether it is carried out by a superintendent (as in the early history of the field), a supervisor, curriculum worker, or peer.

2. Supervision is primarily concerned with the improvement of classroom practice for the benefit of students, regardless of what else may be entailed (e.g., curriculum development or staff development).

This consensus has not been easily won, nor is it inconsequential. Furthermore, agreement on the importance of improving classroom practice was never more than a surface agreement that obscured conflicting ideas about what ought to be practiced in the classroom and what appropriate practice would look like if it were to be found.

The term *classroom practice* has had different, often contradictory meanings. It stood for teaching, broadly conceived as creating environments for learning and development of curriculum and instructional practices. This was central to the early textbook definition of supervision employed by W.H. Burton in 1922. It was also consistent with Jessie Newlon's supervisory leadership in the Denver schools in the late 1920s and 1930s. Classroom practice was used in a much more narrow sense to mean efficiency and effectiveness of classroom instruction in the Detroit schools under the leadership of A.S. Barr in the early 1920s and in his initial textbook definition of supervision.

One can argue that definitions of supervision have had little significant impact on education. Study of definition is instructive, however. Discussions about the function of supervision and the role of the supervisor have mirrored a public attitude about the means and ends of education that has disenfranchised the teacher as curriculum decision maker.

Supervision as Inspection

As social forces acted to shift the responsibility for education from parent to church and society, the fields of supervision and curriculum emerged (Karier 1982, Kliebard 1987). The teacher represented family in the vital role of instruction. Respected but poorly paid, the teacher was trusted to inculcate the values of family and church in much the way that the master craftsperson of days gone by instructed apprentices in the skills and values of practicing a trade. The social role of schools— and teachers—in the United States shifted from one of developing community ideals to mediation between families and diverse, complex communities. Individuals who were available to teach did not necessarily embody community ideals because community ideals were no longer homogeneous. Therefore, what was taught—the curriculum—took on new importance.

Early supervisors were inspectors, assigned the task of ascertaining "the tone and spirit of the school, the conduct and application of the pupils, the management and methods of the teacher, and the fitness and conduction of the premises" (Philbrick 1876, pp. 3–4). Supervisors commended excellence and suggested improvement. The teacher guided students in development of rudimentary skills of reading, mathematics, and writing; and most teachers followed a traditional curriculum rooted in the classics. Teacher imagination, skill, and whatever materials could be found determined the details of curriculum development. For most students, schooling ended with primary school. Those who wished to pursue a profession apart from family apprenticed themselves to someone who could guide them, were self-taught, or attended one of the few secondary schools that prepared a handful of students for college.

By the end of the Civil War, all of this was dramatically changing. Martin Trow (1977) describes the Civil War as "the great watershed of American history," separating agrarian society with small farmers and businesses from an urbanized, industrial society (p. 106). When the war broke out, the U.S. population was less than 30 million. Within fifty years it had grown to almost 100 million (Risjord 1986). No longer just shopkeepers, farmers, or self-employed artisans, this population had diversified. The 1890 census revealed that two-thirds of all workers had become wage-labor employees (Bowles and Gintis 1976). Problems of urban crowding, a large and uneducated immigrant population, and unemployment were already beginning to have their effect. "We girdle the land with iron roads and lace the air with telegraph wires," wrote economist Henry George in 1879, "yet it becomes no easier for the masses of our people to make a living. On the contrary it is becoming harder" (cited in Madgic, Seaberg, Stopsky, and Winks 1979, p. 267).

Education seemed the obvious answer to the needs of an industrial and increasingly multicultural society, and the public began to favor secondary education for all. This, as Trow points out, was "in large part a response to the pull of the economy for a mass of white collar employees with more than an elementary school education" (1977, p. 107). The high school curriculum that had been designed for an elite, homogeneous population of students who were bound for college no longer served.

Teachers, in short supply, were not prepared for the demands of public schooling increasingly thrust on them. New recruits were often "immature" and "unevenly prepared" (Lowry 1908, p. 4) and ill equipped to handle the unruly young people, many of whom were taken off the streets and put in their charge as a result of newly enacted compulsory education laws (Cremin 1964). William Torrey Harris attempted to solve the problems created by unqualified teachers in the St. Louis schools: he placed textbooks in classrooms, a practice that was duplicated across the country. This ushered in what Harold Rugg described as the "era of curriculum making by textbook writers" (1926, p. 7), a shift from curriculum making by the teacher.

By the turn of the century, the problem of the schools was clearly before the public. Joseph Rice, pediatrician turned school reformer, attacked schools from the pages of *Forum*. Articles appeared in *Harper's Weekly* and *Atlantic Monthly* highlighting the need for school reform and the deplorable salaries and working conditions of teachers. Kliebard points out that "Rice's genuine dismay and disgust of what was going on in American schools in the 1890s had evolved into grim determination that teachers and administrators must be *made* to do the right thing" (1987, p. 23).

But how were schools to be improved? Teachers (mostly female and disenfranchised) were seen as a bedraggled troop—incompetent and backward in outlook.

Supervision as Social Efficiency

In the early 1900s, efficiency in organization of supervision and increased control over the curriculum were seen as ways to deal with teacher deficits. The role of the supervisor expanded to include that of on-the-job teacher training. Writers of the *Seventh Yearbook of the Society for the Scientific Study of Education* urged that the supervisor, in most cases a school superintendent, take on the role of "teacher of teachers" because of the complexity of teaching and "the profound injury that results when the work is badly done" (Lowry, 1908, p. 64.)

The school superintendent was to "be first of all a teacher of teachers, an expert critic teacher" (Edison 1893, p. 301).

A new understanding of child growth and development, coupled with the new psychology of learning, challenged the assumptions of traditional education. These new concepts brought about "constant change in methods and curriculum" (Lowry, 1908, p. 64). The curriculum was no longer to be left to the teacher's inventiveness. Even equipped with the textbook, the teacher was unlikely to be able to keep up with developments in education. "Lacking a half-million dynamic teachers, are we not forced to put into our schools a dynamic curriculum?" asked Harold Rugg (1926, p. 7). Supervisors became responsible for curriculum development, preparing courses of study for teachers to follow.

Still, with teachers most often alone in their classrooms, there was little guarantee of uniformity in the way they implemented the course of study. One promising solution was to apply the "neutral" tools of science to curriculum development and supervision. By objectively determining "standard specifications for the educational product" (Bobbitt 1913, p. 18), educators had at their disposal a powerful criterion for developing what they believed to be a socially useful curriculum and determining the extent to which it had been efficiently and effectively implemented. Franklin Bobbitt (1913) called for standardization in the curriculum, based on analysis of the real-life needs of adult citizens. The supervisor, a curriculum specialist, was to develop curriculums based on activity analysis and direct the teacher in its proper execution.

By applying principles of "scientific management" taken from the "activity analysis" that Frank Winslow Taylor had perfected in industry, W.W. Charters developed a framework for thinking about teaching that inspired supervisors and administrators across the United States. It directly addressed the issue of wasted time in schools, the issue Rice had dramatically brought to public attention. Spurred on by the work of Bobbitt, Charters, and the Committee on Economy of Time in Education, supervisors began devising rating scales for measuring teacher efficiency and effectiveness in ways that they believed to be more objective than had previously been possible. The scientific management movement became "a kind of crusade" that swept the nation (Tyack and Hansot 1982).

The underlying premise of the crusade was the Hegelian notion that society was basically just and was evolving toward an even more just and progressive order. Social Darwinism seemed a confirmation of this idea; schooling was the vehicle through which society could control its own evolution.

Not everyone was caught up in the crusade. Boyd H. Bode (1931) challenged the premises of the scientific management movement. Many administrators, supervisors, and teachers went on about their work as usual. In fact, despite the rhetoric about standardization and control of outcomes, teachers were actually allowed "considerable latitude" in practice (Courtis 1926).

In some instances, teacher freedom and involvement in curriculum making was seen as a crucial part of teachers' supervision. For example, Jesse Newlon, school superintendent in Denver, urged that teachers work with supervisors to develop courses of study. Reporting to the Board of Education in 1925, Newlon defended this practice as superior to attempts "by more arbitrary methods to obtain rigid uniformity of practice at the expense of the teacher's initiative and resourcefulness" (p. 22).

But freedom under the law was not satisfactory to those who distrusted the teacher with curriculum decisions. There was considerable tension between those who held Newlon's perspective and those more taken with the ideas of Bobbitt, a tension that found its way into the literature of the professional organizations that were concerned with supervision. Improvement of the teacher's classroom practice seemed to be an area upon which all could agree, however. The Commission on Supervision, appointed in 1927 to develop the *Eighth Yearbook* of the National Education Association's (NEA) Department of Superintendence, defined supervision in terms of the teacher's role in the classroom: "Supervision has for its object the development of a group of professional workers who attack their problems scientifically, free from the control of tradition and actuated in the spirit of inquiry" (Commission on Supervision 1930, p. 4). This definition seemed to be sufficiently ambiguous to encompass a wide array of contradictory viewpoints. Yearbook writers George E. Strayer and Zenos E. Scott (1930) spoke of teachers as the focal point of the supervisor's creative work. Scott, with I. Jewell Simpson, devoted a chapter of the yearbook to a discussion of "creative supervision," which they believed would unite democratic and scientific supervisory practices. "Supervision is creative when objective standards, built upon the findings of research and the best in educational theory and practice, are applied subjectively with the human element in mind" (Scott and Simpson 1930, p. 346).

Enthusiasm for bringing ideas together into a united perspective belied the fact that supervisors could not have it both ways. Some educators envisioned the creative work of supervision as involving the teacher in the intellectual work of curriculum development. In contrast, others saw creativity in curriculum development as the supervisor's province and creativity in teaching as creative implementation of instructional strategies.

Another professional society (still part of the NEA) emerged during this period. It would eventually replace the Department of Superintendence. Drawing its membership from the Department of Superintendence, the National Conference on Educational Method was organized in 1921. Members of the Conference were more directly concerned with classroom practice than were members of the Department of Superintendence—a result of significant changes in the role of the superintendent. School systems were increasingly organized along the lines of corporate business, with boards of education drawn from "men of affairs" in the community (Urban 1982).

By 1929 the National Conference had changed its name to the Department of Supervisors and Directors of Instruction. This organization reflected the fact that supervisors now represented a new level of school personnel between teacher and school superintendent. In 1910, nearly all of the fifty big-city superintendents had increased powers. By 1920, the urban school administrator held power to hire and fire, design curriculum and prescribe instruction, and supervise teachers (Cuban 1976). Bureau of Census figures confirm the story. Between 1910 and 1920, nationwide public school expenditures for instruction increased by nearly two and a half times, while during the same decade spending on administration rose over five times (Tyack 1967, p. 474). Educational method, which had been a broad area uniting these professionals, did not sufficiently describe their interests. Some administrators and supervisors were becoming more interested in curriculum development and what was referred to as "installation," whereas others were interested in support and improvement of the teacher. In 1943 the group that had begun in 1921 as the National Conference on Educational Method became known as the Association for Supervision and Curriculum Development (ASCD). The separation between supervision (concerned with instruction) and curriculum (concerned with curriculum development and implementation) was well underway.

Supervision as Democratic Leadership

Preparation of the school supervisor was a concern of those who were interested in advancing the profession. As superintendents increasingly delegated the work of classroom inspection, teaching, and evaluation of teachers, those who were left with the task needed a specialized training that was distinct from that of the teacher and the school administrator. Determining what it is that supervisors are actually supposed to do continued to be problematic. Clifford Woody chided the committee who developed the *Seventh Yearbook of the Department of Supervisors and Directors of Instruction* for their failure to reach a satisfactory definition of supervision. The committee had adopted a statement of purpose—"pupil growth through teacher growth"—that did little to clarify what supervision should do. It was a problem similar to the one faced by the fourth yearbook committee, which Woody had chaired. "This previous committee proceeded on this assumption, 'Supervision is like electricity; we don't know what it is, but we've got it and can measure its amounts and effects'" (1934, p. 396).

Several textbooks had been written to guide training of superintendents. In 1926 a new textbook, *The Supervision of Instruction*, by A.S. Barr and William H. Burton, addressed the unique problems of the supervisor. This text brought together conflicting perspectives by defining supervision as *the improvement of classroom practice*, and the book became the predominant textbook in supervision for the next several decades. Barr and Burton defined supervision in consensus terms:

> Supervision is . . . coexistensive with the range of things physical and spiritual which are primarily concerned with bettering the conditions which surround learning. A direct attack may be made upon improving learning through the improvement of instruction (1926, p. 21).

When Barr and Burton began to collaborate on their 1926 textbook, both had written on the subject. Barr was author of a work on school standards published in 1924. The book had been developed in the Detroit schools and went into tedious detail about the activities and objectives in teaching various subjects. In a 1925 textbook with Fred Ayer, Barr wrote of supervision as oversight for the purpose of improving the work of the teacher.

Burton was the author of a basic textbook on supervision published in 1922. He was interested in supervision based on principles of human growth and development and had defined supervision in terms of improving the conditions of learning. Burton was interested in the potential of new work that applied objective standards of measurement to supervision and recognized in Barr someone with skill in development of "scientific" strategies for the improvement of teaching.

Barr continued to work on scientific supervision. Left to himself, Barr (1931) defined supervision as educational leadership for the improvement of teaching, to be accomplished through research, training, and guidance.

Through each revision of the influential Barr and Burton textbook, there is a subtle tension, obscured by consensus language. Both authors agreed that supervision was about "bettering the conditions which surround learning," which can be done directly through "improvement of instruction"; but it is doubtful that the authors really agreed to the same concept of supervision.

A great depression and second world war focused the attention of society on education as preparation for democratic citizenship. As Karier (1982) points out, many professional educators were engaged in a philosophical discussion about the meaning of democracy and the democratic school. By the 1940s, it was widely recognized that curriculum programs would be stronger if teachers were involved in their development. Prudence Cutright (1945) urged that teachers be provided release time from teaching to develop and write these materials. Teacher involvement in development of courses of study in Denver had evolved to teacher-pupil planning for the curriculum. The Denver schools had been selected to be one of the progressive schools in the Eight-Year Study in 1933. "Where previously the course of study had been prepared by a committee of teachers for use by all, now teachers and pupils, planning in terms of their own situation and needs, developed units of study with a minimum of prescription by others" (Caswell 1950, p. 153). Many concurred with this approach. Notably, Alice Miel (1946) saw supervision as a function that involved teachers in the process of democratic, cooperative curriculum development.

By 1947 Barr and Burton's textbook reflected these social trends. The two were joined in authorship by L.J. Brueckner, who brought an interest in democratic leadership to their work. Brueckner had come to their attention much earlier as a result of his work in development of a *self-diagnostic* tool for teachers to use in thinking about their own practices. It combined activity analysis with time spent on various activities. The definition of supervision offered by the three showed a shift in the consensus language used to describe supervision. Supervision was still described as "an expert technical service," albeit one "primarily concerned with studying and improving the conditions that surround learning and pupil growth" (Barr, Burton, and Brueckner 1947, pp. 11–12).

Brueckner's self-supervision tool, in itself, illustrates how supervisors ascribed different meanings to the same events. Many supervisors who read Brueckner's report, published in *The Elementary School Jour-*

nal in 1925, immediately saw the potential for improving "efficiency and effectiveness" by combining activity and time analysis in teacher assessment and evaluation. Brueckner, whose professional contribution reflects high regard for the teacher as a professional, capable of curriculum decision making, self-evaluation, and political action for improvement of society, must have been appalled at the uses found for his rating scale.

Differences of opinion about the purpose and practice of supervision continued to exist despite consensus language of professional organizations and the mainstream textbooks. Fred Wilhelms called for a broader definition of supervision in 1946, arguing that neither the role of expert technician nor that of inspiring leader was useful in itself. "The supervisor is an organizer of opportunity, and . . . good supervision is the facilitation of opportunities," he wrote (Wilhelms 1946, p. 222). Wilhelms urged that teachers be given opportunity "to learn what they need and want to learn" and "to play their full part in policy-making" (p. 119). Even so, Wilhelms did not reconcile the conflicting views about what these opportunities should entail.

The consensus textbook by Barr, Burton, and Brueckner (1947) underwent another revision in 1955. By this time, Barr had dropped out, intent on pursuing his work on teacher effectiveness. Burton and Brueckner's textbook reflects interest in the cooperative group work in the schools, heralding supervision of the 1950s and 1960s with its emphasis on curriculum development. Supervision, still defined as an expert technical service, was now "primarily aimed at studying and improving co-operatively all factors which affect growth and development" (Burton and Brueckner 1955, p. 11).

The wide appeal of the Barr, Burton, and Brueckner textbook was undoubtedly due to its consensus definition of supervision. Refinements in definition reflected wider social forces affecting education. At the same time, there was always sufficient ambiguity and latitude in the definition to satisfy a wide array of interests and inclusion of a broad range of material that appealed to both "technicians" and "inspiring leaders" described by Wilhelms (1946). The strong link between improving conditions of learning and improvement of teaching was supportive of those who chose to focus on supervision as improvement of instruction, but it did not preclude a broader definition of teaching.

In the long run, the technicians won out. The trend involving the teacher as curriculum developer was never a dominant one in the field. As efforts to bring new curriculums to classrooms continued to be problematic, curriculum implementation became a study in itself.

Caswell (1946, 1950) and others drew on new work being done in social psychology, particularly Lewin's notion of factors constraining and contributing to organizational change. As a result, curriculum specialists began to consider the psychological factors, such as security and recognition, that teachers needed in order to risk curriculum change (Snyder, Bolin, and Zumwalt in press). Many who were interested in the democratic, cooperative group process became taken with new theories related to group dynamics and human relations. Karier (1982) identifies the role of the National Training Laboratories in developing "a highly effective apparatus," which was effective in bringing "individual thought, identity, and freedom" into line with "the bureaucratic 'group' in thought and action" (p. 13). Group dynamics and human relations techniques were often highly manipulative of teachers and were used by supervisors to make a curriculum that was increasingly efficiency oriented more palatable.

Attacks on schooling in the 1960s and efforts to produce teacher-proof curriculums further diminished the role of the teacher. At about the same time that Dwayne Huebner (1976) was describing the field of curriculum as moribund, supervision was suffering from its own identity crisis. Between 1944 and 1981, ASCD had published more than forty yearbooks; but only four of these were devoted to supervision.

It is significant that the form of supervisory practice that evolved during the late 1960s was clinical supervision, developed by Morris Cogan and colleagues in their work with student teachers. Whatever else it was intended to be, the clinical cycle was rooted in an educational process Cogan defined in behavioral terms. The clinical approach was easily co-opted by those who were interested in a technological approach to teaching. Yet its emphasis on "collegiality," a term coined by Cogan (1973), broadly appealed to many educators. The past decade has been dominated by articles about what does and does not constitute clinical practice, further removing supervision as a field from coming to terms with its identity.

The Illusion of Consensus

We began with Faulkner: "The past is never dead. It's not even past." The problems facing our society have taken on new forms since the turn of the century. New words and concepts, such as nuclear fusion and AIDS—unimaginable in the 19th century—now populate our vocabulary. Both new problems and our approaches to solving them, however, are rooted in facets of the human condition and human perspectives on life that are as old as history.

Nor is the past gone from schools. Schools in our society were created in response to changing social conditions and have always been expected to respond. As social forces have compelled schools to take on more and more of the work of family and community in educating children, the public has demanded that schools be more and more accountable for outcomes. The acceptable means of evaluating school outcomes has been primarily limited to standardized tests of student performance. These in turn have driven the curriculum of schools. Supervision as an expert technical service aimed at the improvement of classroom practice—seen as instruction—is compatible with this point of view. Though individual supervisors and alternative schools of supervisory practice might have it otherwise, their views were largely beside the point. As Karier (1982) pointed out: "Unexamined, unchecked, and uncontrolled, the criteria of efficiency cut deeply into our traditional views of the dignity of life, knowledge, the meaning of words, and the overall political process by which we govern ourselves" (p. 15).

The illusion of consensus may have made it possible for scholars in supervision to work together to produce yearbooks and textbooks in the field. In agreeing to a definition of supervision that supposedly contained everyone's interests without sufficiently considering what this definition left out, supervisors mirrored and perhaps unconsciously facilitated a narrowing of the teacher's role and their own.

References

Barr, A.S. (1931). *An Introduction to the Scientific Study of Classroom Supervision*. New York: Appleton.

Barr, A.S., and W.H. Burton. (1926). *The Supervision of Instruction*. New York: Appleton.

Barr, A.S., W.H. Burton, and L.J. Brueckner. (1947). *Supervision: Democratic Leadership for the Improvement of Learning*. 2nd. ed. New York: Appleton-Century.

Bobbitt, F.W. (1913). "Some General Principles of Management Applied to the Problems of City School Systems." In *The Supervision of City Schools, 12th Yearbook of the National Society for the Scientific Study of Education*, Part I, edited by F.W. Bobbitt et al. Chicago: University of Chicago Press.

Bode, B.H. (1931). "Education at the Crossroads." *Progressive Education* 8: 543–549.

Bolin, F.S. (Summer 1988). "Does a Community of Scholars in Supervision Exist?" *Journal of Curriculum and Supervision* 3: 296–307.

Bolin, F.S. (Summer 1987). "On Defining Supervision." *Journal of Curriculum and Supervision* 2: 368–380.

Bowles, S., and H. Gintis. (1976). *Schooling in Capitalist America: Educational Reform and the Contradictions of Economic Life*. New York: Basic Books.

Brueckner, L.J. (1925). "The Value of a Time Analysis of Classroom Activity as a Supervisory Technique." *Elementary School Journal* 25: 518–21.

Burton, W.H. (1922). *Supervision and the Improvement of Teaching*. New York: Appleton.

Burton, W.H., and L.J. Brueckner. (1955). *Supervision: A Social Process*. 3rd ed. New York: Appleton-Century-Crofts.

Caswell, H.I. (1946). *The American High School: Its Responsibility and Opportunity*. Eighth Yearbook of the John Dewey Society. New York: Harper and Brothers.

Caswell, H.I. (1950). *Curriculum Improvement in the Public Schools*. New York: Teachers College Press.

Cogan, M.L. (1973). *Clinical Supervision*. Boston: Houghton Mifflin.

Commission on Supervision, Department of Superintendence, NEA. (1930). *The Superintendent Surveys Supervision. Eighth Yearbook of the Department of Superintendence*. Washington, D.C.: National Education Association.

Courtis, S.A. (1926). "Reading Between the Lines." In *Curriculum- making: Past and Present. 26th Yearbook of the National Society for the Study of Education*, Part I, edited by G.M. Whipple. Bloomington, Ill.: Public School Publishing Co.

Cremin, L.A. (1964). *The Transformation of the School*. New York: Random House.

Cuban, L. (1976). *The Urban School Superintendency: A Century and a Half of Change*. Bloomington, Ind.: The Phi Delta Kappa Educational Foundation.

Cutright, P. (1945). "Curriculum Development in the Postwar Period." In *American Education in the Postwar Period: Curriculum Reconstruction. 44th Yearbook of the National Society for the Study of Education*, Part I, edited by R.W. Tyler. Chicago: University of Chicago Press.

Edison, A.W. (1893). "School Supervision." *Education* 13: 391.

Faulkner, W. (1975). "Intruder in the Dust." In *Requiem for a Nun* (Act 1, Scene 3, p. 80). New York: Vintage.

Huebner, D.E. (1976). "The Moribund Curriculum Field: Its Wake and Our Work," *Curriculum Inquiry* 6: 156.

Karier, C. (1982). "Supervision in Historic Perspective." In *Supervision of Teaching* (pp. 2–15), edited by T.J. Sergiovanni. Washington, D.C.: ASCD.

Kliebard, H.M. (1987). *The Struggle for the American Curriculum: 1893–1958*. New York: Routledge and Kegan Paul.

Lowry, C.A., ed. (1908). *The Relation of Superintendents to the Training and Professional Improvement of Their Teachers. Seventh Yearbook of the Society for the Scientific Study of Education*, Part I. Chicago: University of Chicago Press.

Madgic, R.F., S.S. Seaberg, F.H. Stopsky, and R.W. Winks. (1979). *The American Experience: A Study of Themes and Issues in American History*. Reading, Mass.: Addison-Wesley.

Miel, A. (1946). *Changing the Curriculum: A Social Process*. New York: Appleton-Century-Crofts.

Newlon, J.H. (1925). *20th Annual Report of School District Number One in the City and County of Denver and State of Colorado*. Denver, Col.: Denver School Press.

Philbrick, J.D. (1876). "The Examination of Graded Schools." In *Educational Addresses and Pamphlets in Teachers College Library*. New York: Teachers College, Columbia University.

Risjord, N.J. (1986). *History of the American People*. New York: Holt, Rinehart and Winston.

Rugg, H.O. (1926). "Curriculum-Making: Points of Emphasis." In *Curriculum-Making: Past and Present. 26th Yearbook of the National Society for the Study of Education*, Part I, edited by G.M. Whipple. Bloomington, Ill.: Public School Publishing Co.

Scott, Z.E., and I.J. Simpson. (1930). "Creative Supervision." In *The Superintendent Surveys Supervision. Eighth Yearbook of the Department of Superintendence.* Washington, D.C.: National Education Association.

Snyder, J., F.S. Bolin, and K.K. Zumwalt. (in press). "Curriculum Implementation." In *AERA Handbook of Research on Curriculum,* edited by P.W. Jackson.

Strayer, G.E., and Z.E. Scott. (1930). "The Meaning and Necessity of Supervision." In *The Superintendent Surveys Supervision. Eighth Yearbook of the Department of Superintendence.* Washington, D.C.: National Education Association.

Trow, M. (1977). "The Second Transformation of the American Secondary Education." In *Power and Ideology in Education,* edited by J. Karabel and A.H. Halsey. New York: Oxford University Press.

Tyack, D.B., ed. (1967). *Turning Points in American Educational History.* Waltham, Mass.: Blaisdell.

Tyack, D.B., and E. Hansot. (1982). *Managers of Virtue: Public School Leadership in America, 1800–1980.* New York: Basic Books.

Urban, W.J. (1982). *Why Teachers Organized.* Detroit: Wayne State University.

Wilhelms, F. (1946). "Tomorrow's Assignment." In *Leadership Through Supervision,* edited by T.J. Sergiovanni. Washington, D.C.: ASCD.

Woody, C. (1934). "Evaluation of the 7th Yearbook." *Educational Methods* 13: 396.

3

Changing Perspectives in Curriculum and Instruction

James Nolan and Pam Francis

Come writers and critics, prophesy with your pen
And keep your eyes wide, the chance won't come again
But don't speak too soon for the wheel's still in spin
And there's no tellin' now where she's aimin'
And the losers now will be later to win
For the times they are a-changin'

Bob Dylan, "The Times They Are A'Changin," 1964

This chapter* considers the potential impact of contemporary theories of learning and teaching on supervisory practice. Although
theorists usually conceive of curriculum and instruction as separate
entities, we have chosen not to consider the two separately in this
chapter. Curriculum and instruction are frequently separated for purposes of discussion and analysis of the educational process; but in the
learning-teaching act, decisions about what to teach (i.e., curriculum)
and how to teach it (i.e., instruction) must be reconciled and unified. It
is in the learning-teaching act that supervision finds its focus and
direction.

Educational practices—and indeed all of human behavior—are
guided largely by what Sergiovanni (1985) has termed *mindscapes*.
Mindscapes are mental frameworks or paradigms through which we
envision reality and our place in reality. They are usually more implicit
and unexamined than explicit. As such, mindscapes are taken for
granted and provide a set of beliefs or assumptions that exert a tremendous influence on behavior. Sergiovanni states:

---

*We are grateful to Bernard Badiali, J. Robert Coldiron, and Lee Goldsberry for comments
on earlier versions of this chapter.

Mindscapes provide us with intellectual and psychological images of the real world and the boundaries and parameters of rationality that help us to make sense of the world. In a very special way, mindscapes are intellectual security blankets on the one hand, and road maps through an uncertain world on the other (Sergiovanni 1985, p. 5).

The major thesis of this chapter is that the mindscapes that currently drive both supervision theory and practice will undergo significant alteration as a result of important changes in educators' conceptions of learning and teaching that have evolved during the 1980s. We have developed this thesis through a three-part structure: (1) an examination of traditional views of the learning-teaching process, (2) an examination of changing perspectives on the learning-teaching process, and (3) an examination of the implications of these changing perspectives for the practice of supervision.

Traditional Views of Learning and Teaching

The traditional view of the learning-teaching process, which has dominated instruction in most schools, can be captured in five fundamental beliefs about learning. The power of these beliefs rests not in any particular one, but rather in the fact that they constitute a mutually reinforcing system of beliefs. Even though these beliefs are very powerful in driving much of what we currently do in the name of educational practice, for most educators they have remained largely implicit and unexamined. In fact, we derived our descriptions of these beliefs from an analysis of what schools and educators actually do as they attempt to educate learners, rather than from an analysis of what schools and educators espouse. These five fundamental beliefs are:

1. *Learning is the process of accumulating bits of information and isolated skills.*

2. *The teacher's primary responsibility is to transfer his knowledge directly to students.*

3. *Changing student behavior is the teacher's primary goal.*

4. *The process of learning and teaching focuses primarily on the interactions between the teacher and individual students.*

5. *Thinking and learning skills are viewed as transferable across all content areas.*

These five beliefs have important implications for teaching. Given these beliefs, the most important teaching tasks are the following:

- Organizing and structuring the learning material in the most appropriate sequence.
- Explaining concepts clearly and unambiguously.
- Using examples and illustrations that can be understood by students.
- Modeling appropriate application of desired skills.
- Checking student comprehension of the material that has been presented.
- Structuring and organizing practice sessions with instructional material so that it will be retained more effectively in long-term memory and transferred appropriately to other contexts.
- Assessing student learning by requiring students to reproduce the desired knowledge and skills on paper-and-pencil tests or through other observable means.

These beliefs have resulted in a teacher-centered conception of teaching and supervision in which the teacher's observable behavior during instruction, occupies the center stage of the educational drama. The supervisor works one-to-one with each teacher in a two-step process: (1) the supervisor uses paper-and-pencil observation instruments to carefully capture and document the teacher's observable behavior during instruction; and (2) the supervisor and teacher come together in a conference designed primarily to relate the teacher's observable behavior to both individual student behavior and to research findings on generalizable teaching behaviors that seem to be effective in promoting student learning.

Changing Perspectives on Learning and Teaching

During the 1980s, the shape of educational practice slowly began to change, creating a new mindscape about human learning. This new framework has the potential not only to change teaching behavior on a large-scale basis, but also to cause us to fundamentally alter our beliefs about supervision. This new mindscape, or view of learning and teaching, can also be encapsulated in several interrelated beliefs about the nature of learning and teaching. Some of these beliefs are based on theories of learning that are relatively new; others are based on theories of learning that have existed for many years but have exerted little influence on practice.

1. *All learning, except for simple rote memorization, requires the learner to actively construct meaning.* Learners construct meaning by taking new information, relating it to their prior knowledge, and then putting their new understandings to use in reasoning and problem solving. "In this process, each person is continuously checking new information against old rules, revising the old rules when discrepancies appear and reaching new understandings or constructions of reality" (Brooks 1990, p. 68). For learning to occur, the learner must actively engage in the mental processes necessary to construct the new meanings and understandings. Although learning theorists have held this belief for many years (see Dewey 1902), only recently have concerted efforts been made to help practitioners put this notion into practice (see Lampert 1990).

2. *Students' prior understandings of and thoughts about a topic or concept before instruction exert a tremendous influence on what they learn during instruction.*

> What people learn is never a direct replica of what they have read or been told or even of what they have been drilled on. We know that to understand something is to interpret it and further that an interpretation is based partly on what we've been told or have read but also on what we already know and on general reasoning and logical abilities (Brandt 1988–89, p. 15).

One of the teacher's most important tasks must be to explore the conceptions that learners bring with them to the classroom and help them achieve a new, more refined understanding of those concepts. When learners' preexisting conceptions are inaccurate, the teacher must provide experiences that assist the learners to recognize the inaccuracies. Otherwise, their misconceptions are not likely to change as a result of instruction. "It is not sufficient to simply present students with the correct facts. One has to change the concepts or schemas that generated the inaccurate beliefs" (Bransford and Vye 1989, p. 188).

3. *The teacher's primary goal is to generate a change in the learner's cognitive structure or way of viewing and organizing the world.* The most important factor in any learning-teaching situation is not the observable behavior of either the teacher or the learner. The single most important factor in determining how much a student learns during instruction is the learner's cognitive processing of information during instruction (Anderson 1989). Changes in observable behavior are important because they can be used to infer that the learner's cognitive structure has changed, but changes in behavior are an indicator of learning and a result of learning, not the learning itself.

4. *Because learning is a process of active construction by the learner, the teacher cannot do the work of learning.* Students must do the work of learning (Schlechty 1990). The teacher's task is to help learners acquire the skills and dispositions needed to carry out the work of learning. This means: (a) helping learners acquire learning and thinking strategies; (b) helping learners acquire the metacognitive understanding needed to choose the appropriate learning strategy for a given instructional task and to self-monitor the use of the strategy; and (c) motivating learners to engage in appropriate thinking during instruction. The teacher moves from the role of protagonist to that of director or drama coach, and the student becomes the main character in the educational drama.

5. *Learning in cooperation with others is an important source of motivation, support, modeling, and coaching.* In contrast to the traditional view of learning as a solitary process, the new mindscape recognizes the important role that peers can play in the learning process by sharing responsibility for the learning of all group members. Most successful instructional programs designed to teach higher order cognitive skills prescribe the use of cooperative learning groups focused on meaning-construction activities. Such activities provide a type of cognitive apprenticeship in which students have multiple opportunities to observe others do the work that they are expected to do (Resnick and Klopfer 1989). There is ample evidence that when students are engaged in cooperative learning activities that are structured to include both group interdependence and individual accountability, they learn more (Slavin 1989–90).

6. *Content-specific learning and thinking strategies play a much more important role in learning than was previously recognized.* Until the past decade, much of the research on learning focused on learning strategies and skills that were general in nature and applied across subject matter. "One of the great luxuries of the old style research on learning was that you could look for principles that had general validity. Now we believe that we must first immerse ourselves in the study of how people learn particular things in particular environments" (Brandt 1988–89, p. 14). In the past few years, the pendulum has swung from an exclusive emphasis on general thinking and learning skills to an increasing emphasis on content-specific learning and thinking skills. Perkins and Salomon (1989) agree with the contention that content-specific learning skills were neglected by educational researchers for a long period of time and suggest that learning and thinking skills are most likely a

synthesis of general cognitive strategies and context or content-specific techniques.

As was true for research on learning, process-product research on teaching (which provides the basis for much of our current work in supervision and staff development) has focused almost exclusively on teaching techniques that are applicable across grade levels and subject matter. This heavy emphasis on general principles and methods of teaching to the exclusion of content-specific principles and methods has come under fire from a number of educational researchers in recent years.

One content specialist, Henry (1986), argues that the field of instructional supervision and its emphasis on general notions of teaching has violated the field of English education through the institutionalization of behaviorist views of learning and teaching. Henry paints a picture of thousands of English teachers scurrying to write behavioral objectives, create improved feedback and management loops, and use mastery learning strategies. He sees these activities as antithetical to the very nature of English.

> What is neglected or generally omitted is the fundamental probing of instruction which lies not solely in overt, externally observable behavior but also in the internalized arrangement of ideas most of which are predetermined by the discipline. Time is different in history, in physics, in biology, in mathematics, and in English (Henry 1986, p. 20).

Henry's views concerning the importance of content-specific conceptions of learning and teaching have been well supported in recent years by the work of several teacher educators, such as Buchman (1984).

> Curriculum practices and development in many schools and colleges of education can be interpreted as a flight away from content. Teachers without content are like actors without scripts. Teaching is conditional on the presence of educational content and essential activities of teaching are conditional upon the content knowledge of teachers (pp. 29–30).

The importance of content knowledge in the teaching process has also been the primary focus of study of Shulman and his associates. They have identified general pedagogical knowledge, subject matter knowledge, and pedagogical content knowledge as critical components of the professional knowledge base in teaching (Wilson, Shulman, and Richert 1987). Pedagogical content knowledge is a relatively new and illuminating construct that refers to the "capacity of a teacher to transform the content knowledge he or she possesses into forms that are pedagogically powerful and yet adaptive to the variations in ability and background presented by the students" (Shulman 1987, p. 15). Included among the various aspects of pedagogical content knowledge are: (1) the teacher's view of how the discipline should be represented to students, (2) the teacher's understanding of how easy or difficult particular concepts will be for specific groups of students to learn, and (3) the teacher's possession of a variety of examples, metaphors, analogies, and narratives that can be used to make the concepts in the discipline more understandable for students. Wilson, Shulman, and Richert (1987) see the teacher's pedagogical content knowledge as a critical attribute in the process of preparing for, delivering, and reflecting on instruction.

In short, to paraphrase Shulman (1990), when the content to be taught becomes a starting point for the process of inquiry and researchers begin to ask what is good teaching of mathematics or what is good teaching of *Romeo and Juliet*, the answers and related questions seem to be quite different from the answers received when one begins by asking what is good teaching in general.

These six beliefs, which characterize the changing mindscape on learning and teaching, call into serious question the portrait that we painted earlier of the supervisor who works one on one with each teacher to document observable behavior and move that behavior into greater alignment with the research on general teaching effectiveness. Indeed, the new mindscape on learning and teaching demands a significantly altered mindscape on supervision.

Implications for Supervision

The changing perspectives on learning and teaching have five important implications:

1. Teachers should be viewed as active constructors of their own knowledge about learning and teaching.

2. Supervisors should be viewed as collaborators in creating knowledge about learning and teaching.

3. The emphasis on data collection during supervision should change from almost total reliance on paper-and-pencil observation instruments to capture the events of a single period of instruction to the use of a variety of data sources to capture a lesson as it unfolds over several periods of instruction.

4. Both general principles and methods of teaching as well as content-specific principles and methods of teaching should be attended to during the supervisory process.

5. Supervision should become more group oriented rather than individually oriented.

Teachers as Active Knowledge Constructors

Just as students must actively construct new knowledge, teachers must be active participants in constructing their own knowledge. The mindscape that has been dominant in supervision has viewed supervision and staff development as vehicles for training teachers to adopt practices and to use knowledge that has been produced by others, principally by researchers on teaching. Just as it is impossible for teachers to pour their knowledge into the heads of students, it is equally impossible for supervisors and staff developers to pour the knowledge and practices recommended by researchers into the heads of teachers. Teachers who choose to adopt new practices are not empty vessels to be filled with someone else's ideas. They are learners who are re-educating themselves to become experts in another mode of teaching (Putnam 1990). Much of our knowledge about learning remains unused in classrooms not because teachers are unwilling to use it, but because they have not been given the opportunity and the time to work with the concepts and practices in order to relate them to their own knowledge, experience, and contexts—to truly make them their own. Before teachers can use a new model of teaching effectively, they must acquire a deep, personalized understanding of the model. Support for this statement can be derived from the work of Joyce and Showers (1988), which demonstrates that at least thirty to forty hours of study, practice, and feedback are required before teachers gain executive control over complex teaching models. Executive control means that the trainer can use the model well technically, can distinguish between appropriate and inappropriate opportunities for applying the model, and can adapt the model to particular students and contexts.

Perhaps most important, teachers must be looked on as generators of knowledge on learning and teaching, not merely as consumers of research. "What is missing from the knowledge base for teaching, therefore, are the voices of teachers themselves, the questions teachers ask, the way teachers use writing and intentional talk in their work lives, and the interpretive frames teachers use to understand and improve their own classroom practice" (Cochran-Smith and Lytle 1990, p. 2).

When driven by the new mindscapes on learning and teaching, supervision becomes a vehicle for inquiry and experimentation—aimed at knowledge generation, not simply knowledge adoption. The primary purpose of supervision becomes *the improvement of teaching and learning by helping teachers acquire a deeper understanding of the learning-teaching process.* Knowledge generation can be achieved when supervision becomes a process of action research in which the supervisor and the teacher use classroom learning and teaching activities as a vehicle for testing their own ideas, ideas and practices of colleagues, and findings derived from more formal research studies in terms of their application to the unique educational context in which the teacher and supervisor function.

This view of supervision has been advocated quite powerfully by Schön (1989) and Garman (1986). Garman has taken the view of clinical supervision espoused by Cogan (1973), one of the originators of clinical supervision, and expanded it to be more compatible with current perspectives on learning and teaching. Cogan's model of supervision was grounded in the traditional views of learning, which saw the teacher as the adopter of practices that had been shown as effective through the work of researchers and developers. He did not envision teachers as researchers (Garman 1986). Garman, on the other hand, points out the necessity for clinical supervisors to engage teachers in the process of self-supervision through reflection and knowledge generation. "At some point in a teacher's career, he/she must become a clinical supervisor of sorts because only the actors themselves can render the hermeneutic knowledge needed to understand teaching" (Garman 1990, p. 212). When teachers engage in the process of generating knowledge about their own teaching, they realize important benefits. "Their teaching is transformed in important ways: they become theorists articulating their intentions, testing their assumptions, and finding connections with practice" (Cochran-Smith and Lytle 1990, p. 8).

Supervisors as Collaborators in Creating Knowledge

Just as the teacher's role will change when students are seen as active partners in constructing knowledge, so too the supervisor's role will change when teachers are viewed as constructors of their own knowledge about learning and teaching. From its traditional perspective, supervision is viewed as a process intended to help teachers improve instruction. The supervisor often, intentionally or unintentionally, takes on the role of critic whose task is to judge the degree of congruence between the teacher's classroom behavior and the model of teaching that the teacher is trying to implement or the generic research on teaching.

When the supervisor is viewed as a critic who judges the teacher's performance, supervision tends to concentrate on surface-level issues because the supervisor is denied access by the teacher to the dilemmas, issues, and problems that every teacher experiences and struggles with on an ongoing basis (Blumberg and Jonas 1987). These dilemmas and problems reach to the very heart of the teaching enterprise and cannot be resolved by simply adding new models to our repertoires of teaching behaviors. They must be confronted head on and resolved through action and reflection in the classroom (Schön 1983). Supervision should play a central role in understanding and resolving complex, perennial problems such as:

• how to reconcile individual student needs and interests with group needs and interests;

• how to balance the need to preserve student self-esteem with the need to provide students with honest feedback on their performance;

• how to balance student motivation against the need to teach prescribed content that may not match students' current needs or interests; and

• how to maintain a reasonable amount of order while still allowing sufficient flexibility for the intellectual freedom needed to pursue complex topics and issues.

When the supervisor relinquishes the role of critic to assume the role of co-creator of knowledge about learning and teaching, the teacher is more willing to grant the supervisor access to these core issues and dilemmas of teaching because the teacher does not have to fear a critique from the supervisor. Relinquishing the role of critic also benefits the supervisor by removing the awesome burden of serving as judge, jury, and director of the supervisory process.

When supervision is viewed as a process for generating knowledge about learning and teaching, data collection is transformed from a mechanism for documenting behavior to a mechanism for collecting information. This information can be used to deepen both teacher's and supervisor's understanding of the consequences of resolving problems, dilemmas, and issues in alternative ways. Conferences are also transformed. In the traditional conference scenario, the supervisor provides a neat, well-documented list of praiseworthy behaviors, as well as some suggestion for future improvement. When the supervisor relinquishes the role of critic, conferences become collaborative work sessions in which both teacher and supervisor try to make sense of the almost always messy data that are gathered in the process of relating teacher action to its consequences for learners. Finally, the outcomes of conferences are transformed. In most current practice, both partners sign written narrative critiques, which are filed away to collect dust until next year's observation. When teacher and supervisor become co-creators of knowledge, they produce jointly developed, tentative understandings of the learning-teaching process. These insights can then be tested against the reality of the classroom in future cycles of supervision.

To engage effectively in inquiry-oriented supervision, supervisors need a different type of expertise. They will need a passion for inquiry; commitment to developing an understanding of the process of learning and teaching; respect for teachers as equal partners in the process of trying to understand learning and teaching in the context of the teacher's particular classroom setting; and recognition that both partners contribute essential expertise to the process. They will also need to feel comfortable with the ambiguity and vulnerability of not having prefabricated answers to the problems that are encountered in the process. Supervisors will need to trust themselves, the teacher, and the process enough to believe that they can find reasonable and workable answers to complex questions and problems.

Greater Variety in Data Collection

The emphasis in traditional conceptions of learning on observable behavior, coupled with the emphasis on the teacher as the central actor, has resulted in the use of paper-and-pencil observation instruments as the primary and often sole vehicle for data gathering in supervision. When the supervisor's task is viewed as capturing the observable behavior of one actor (the teacher), paper-and-pencil instruments seem to work reasonably well. However, when learning is viewed as an active process of knowledge construction by the learner, student cognition becomes the critical element in the learning process. Learning is then seen as a collaborative process between teacher and learner, and the task of gathering useful data changes dramatically. Now, the data-gathering task becomes one of simultaneously capturing information about multiple actors which can be used to make inferences about the thinking processes that are occurring in the minds of the actors. This type of data collection requires supplementing paper-and-pencil instruments with a wide range of data-gathering techniques including audiotapes, videotapes, student products (essays, projects, tests), student interviews, and written student feedback regarding classroom events.

The use of multiple sources of data will bring about another important change in the expertise required of those who function as supervisors. The supervisor will need to become an expert in helping the teacher match various types of data collection strategies to the questions that are being addressed in the supervisory process and in helping the teacher interpret and reflect on the data that have been gathered. This change in the focus of data collection techniques will parallel closely the changes that have taken place in educational research techniques over the past decade. Just as the paper-and-pencil instruments used in the process-product research on teaching have been augmented by qualitative data collection strategies, so too observation and data collection in supervision can be expanded to include many more data sources. Data alone, however, are never sufficient. They never tell the full story. Only human judgment, in this case the collaborative judgment of teacher and supervisor, can give meaning to the richness of the learning-teaching process. Human judgment functions much more effectively in capturing that richness when it is augmented by a wide variety of data sources.

Garman (1990) points out an additional factor that comes into play when we view the goal of data collection as capturing student and teacher thinking: the development of thinking over time. Data collection currently is almost always accomplished by the observation of a single period of instruction.

> [A] lesson generally means an episodic event taken out of context within a larger unit of study. It is time to consider the unfolding lesson as a major concept in clinical supervision. We must find ways to capture how a teacher unfolds the content of a particular unit of study and how students, over time, encounter the content (Garman 1990, p. 212).

By collecting data over longer periods of instruction, we would be likely to obtain a much more complete picture of both teacher and student thinking. We would also capture a much richer portrait of the teacher's view of how the discipline should be represented for students. Although it might at first seem that collecting data over several periods of instruction requires additional time for observation by the supervisor, this is not necessarily the case. When the teacher becomes a collaborator in the process, and multiple data collection techniques are used (e.g., videotapes, student homework, student tests), the supervisor need not be present for every period of instruction during which data are gathered. The teacher can take primary responsibility for much of the data collection and then meet with the supervisor to jointly interpret and discuss the meaning of the data.

Greater Balance Between General Concerns and Content-Specific Issues and Questions

Given the renewed emphasis and research on content-specific learning and teaching, the focus of supervision should shift from total emphasis on general concerns to the inclusion of content-specific issues and questions. This does not mean that we should exclude general behaviors. To do so would clearly be a mistake because process-product research has been successful in identifying some behaviors that seem to transfer across content (Gage and Needels 1989). However, as Shulman (1987) has pointed out, excluding content-specific strategies from the supervisory process has also been a mistake. We need to balance content-specific issues and general issues.

On the surface at least, this need to expand the focus of supervision poses a dilemma for many schools. Principals, who supervise teachers in many different content areas, carry out the much of the supervision that takes place in schools. The question is whether a generalist can be an effective supervisor when the supervisory process focuses not only on general concerns but also on content-specific strategies and methods. Given the new supervisory mindscape, we believe it is possible.

If the supervisor is viewed as a collaborator whose primary task is to help teachers reflect on and learn about their own teaching practices through the collection and interpretation of multiple sources of data, and the teacher who has content expertise is allowed to direct the process, it seems reasonable to think that content-specific issues could be addressed through supervision. In addition, if supervision is viewed as a function—not merely a role—to which many people in a school can contribute (Alfonso and Goldsberry 1982), it would also be possible to use a process of group supervision, peer coaching, or colleague consultation to help address content-specific issues, provided the peers have the appropriate preparation and skills.

Whatever personnel are used to carry out the process, the scope of supervision needs to be expanded to include questions such as these: What content should be taught to this group of students? Are the content and the instructional approaches being used compatible? What beliefs about the content and its general nature are being conveyed to students by the teacher's long-term approach to the subject matter? Are students acquiring the thinking and learning strategies that are most important for long-term success in the discipline?

Emphasis on Group Supervision

Just as students seem to benefit when they are placed in groups to cooperate with each other in the learning process, teachers seem to benefit when they are allowed to work together in groups to help each other learn about and refine the process of teaching (Little 1982). Teachers learn by watching each other teach. In addition, the new roles they take on and the perspectives they gain promote higher levels of thinking and cognitive development (Sprinthall and Thies-Sprinthall 1983). This benefits students because teachers who have reached higher cognitive-developmental levels tend to be more flexible and better able to meet individual student needs (Hunt and Joyce 1967). Collaborative practices have been endorsed and employed in staff development circles for several years; however, supervisory practice, which also aims at professional development, typically continues to occur on a one-to-one basis between supervisor and teacher.

We concur with Fullan (1990), who pointed out the necessity of linking collaboration to norms of continuous improvement:

> There is nothing particularly virtuous about collaboration per se. It can serve to block change or put students down as well as to elevate learning. Thus, collegiality must be linked to norms of continuous improvement and experimentation in which teachers are constantly seeking and assessing potentially better practices inside and outside their own school (p. 15).

Similarly, group supervision must be viewed as an activity whose primary aim is learning about and improving teaching. Teachers are sometimes uncomfortable when they are asked to confront tough questions about their own teaching. Collaboration and mutual support from colleagues can be vehicles for enabling teachers to risk facing those tough questions. However, there is a danger that collaboration can be wrongly viewed as meaning to support one another without rocking the boat or causing any discomfort. When this happens, collaboration can degenerate into a mechanism for skirting tough questions through unwarranted assurances that things are just fine. To avoid this degeneration, all participants must understand that learning about the instructional process and improving student learning are the primary goals of group supervision. Collaboration is a means to an end, not an end in itself. It is a mechanism for providing support as teachers engage in the sometimes disquieting, uncomfortable process of learning.

Given the research on cooperative learning and teacher collegiality, we hypothesize that if supervision were carried out as a group process in which the supervisors and teachers were interdependent in achieving group and individual goals, the process of supervision would become more effective in helping teachers learn about and improve their teaching. In addition, enabling those teachers who may be less committed to growth to work together in groups with colleagues who are more committed to the process may be an effective strategy for creating shared norms that are supportive of the supervisory process. In discussing the concept of collaborative cultures, Hargreaves and Dawe (1989) eloquently describe what supervision might become when it is viewed as a cooperative group process. "It is a tool of teacher empowerment and professional enhancement, bringing colleagues and their expertise together to generate critical yet also practically-grounded reflection on what they do as a basis for more skilled action" (p. 7).

What we have labeled "the changing mindscape on learning and teaching" demands a new mindscape on supervision, a mindscape grounded in the following principles and beliefs:

♦ The primary purpose of supervision is to provide a mechanism for teachers and supervisors to increase their understanding of the learning-teaching process through collaborative inquiry with other professionals.

• Teachers should not be viewed only as consumers of research, but as generators of knowledge about learning and teaching.

• Supervisors must see themselves not as critics of teaching performance, but rather as collaborators with teachers in attempting to understand the problems, issues, and dilemmas that are inherent in the process of learning and teaching.

• Acquiring an understanding of the learning-teaching process demands the collection of many types of data, over extended periods of time.

• The focus for supervision needs to be expanded to include content-specific as well as general issues and questions.

• Supervision should focus not only on individual teachers but also on groups of teachers who are engaged in ongoing inquiry concerning common problems, issues, and questions.

These principles and beliefs are not completely new. They closely parallel the principles of clinical supervision as endorsed by Cogan (1973) and Goldhammer (1969). Unfortunately, these principles have not been widely adopted. We believe that the changing perspectives on learning and teaching provide a powerful impetus for putting these principles of supervision into practice. When these concepts begin to touch the mainstream of supervisory practice, supervision is much more likely to have a positive impact on teacher thinking, teacher behavior, and student learning.

References

Alfonso, R.J., and L. Goldsberry. (1982). "Colleagueship in Supervision." In *Supervision of Teaching*, edited by T.J. Sergiovanni. Alexandria, Va.: ASCD.

Anderson, L.M. (1989). "Classroom Instruction." In *Knowledge Base for the Beginning Teacher*, edited by M.C. Reynolds. New York: Pergamon Press and the American Association of Colleges of Teacher Education.

Blumberg, A., and R.D. Jonas. (1987). "Permitting Access: The Teacher's Control Over Supervision." *Educational Leadership* 44, 8: 12–16.

Brandt, R. (1988–89). "On Learning Research: A Conversation with Lauren Resnick." *Educational Leadership* 46, 4: 12–16.

Brandt, R. (1989–90). "On Cooperative Learning: A Conversation with Spencer Kagan." *Educational Leadership* 47, 4: 8–11.

Bransford, J.D., and N.J. Vye. (1989). "A Perspective on Cognitive Research and Its Implications for Instruction." In *Toward the Thinking Curriculum: Current Cognitive Research*, edited by L.B. Resnick and L.E. Klopfer. Alexandria, Va.: ASCD.

Brooks, J.G. (1990). "Teachers and Students: Constructivists Forging New Connections." *Educational Leadership* 47, 5: 68–71.

Buchman, M. (1984). "The Priority of Knowledge and Understanding in Teaching." In *Advances in Teacher Education. Vol. 1*, edited by L.G. Katz and J.D. Raths. Norwood, N.J.: Ablex.

Cochran-Smith, M., and S.L. Lytle. (1990). "Research on Teaching and Teacher Research: Issues That Divide." *Educational Researcher* 19, 2: 2–11.

Cogan, M. (1973). *Clinical Supervision*. Boston: Houghton-Mifflin.

Dewey, J. (1902). *The Child and the Curriculum*. Chicago: University of Chicago Press.

Fullan, M. (1990). "Staff Development, Innovation, and Institutional Development." In *Changing School Culture Through Staff Development. The 1990 ASCD Yearbook*, edited by B. Joyce. Alexandria, Va.: ASCD.

Gage, N.L., and M.C. Needels. (1989). "Process-Product Research on Teaching: A Review of Criticisms." *Elementary School Journal* 89, 3: 253–300.

Garman, N.B. (1986). "Reflection: The Heart of Clinical Supervision: A Modern Rationale for Professional Practice." *Journal of Curriculum and Supervision* 2, 1: 1–24.

Garman, N.B. (1990). "Theories Embedded in the Events of Clinical Supervision: A Hermeneutic Approach." *Journal of Curriculum and Supervision* 5, 3: 201–213.

Goldhammer, R. (1969). *Clinical Supervision: Special Methods for the Supervision of Teachers*. New York: Holt, Rinehart, and Winston.

Hargreaves, A., and R. Dawe. (1989). "Coaching as Unreflective Practice." Paper presented at the Annual Meeting of the American Educational Research Association, San Francisco.

Henry, G. (1986). "What Is the Nature of English Education?" *English Education* 18, 1: 4–41.

Hunt, D.E., and B.R. Joyce. (1967). "Teacher Trainee Personality and Initial Teaching Style." *American Educational Research Journal* 4: 253–59.

Joyce, B., and B. Showers. (1988). *Student Achievement Through Staff Development.* New York: Longman.

Lampert, M. (1990). "When the Problem is not the Question and the Solution is not the Answer: Mathematical Knowing and Teaching." *American Educational Research Journal* 27, 1: 29–63.

Little, J. (1982). "Norms of Collegiality and Experimentation: Workplace Conditions of School Success." *American Educational Research Journal* 5, 19: 325–340.

Perkins, D.N., and G. Salomon. (1989). "Are Cognitive Skills Context-Bound?" *Educational Researcher* 8, 1: 16–25.

Putnam, R. (1990). "Recipes and Reflective Learning: 'What Would Prevent You from Saying It That Way?'" Paper presented at the Annual Meeting of the American Educational Research Association, Boston.

Resnick, L.B., and L.E. Klopfer. (1989). *Toward the Thinking Curriculum: Current Cognitive Research.* Alexandria, Va.: ASCD.

Schlechty, P.C. (1990). *Schools for the 21st Century.* San Francisco: Jossey-Bass.

Schön, D.A. (1983). *The Reflective Practitioner.* San Francisco: Jossey-Bass.

Schön, D.A. (1989). "Coaching Reflective Teaching." In *Reflection in Teacher Education*, edited by P.P. Grimmet and G.P. Erickson. New York: Teachers College Press.

Sergiovanni, T.J. (1985). "Landscapes, Mindscapes, and Reflective Practice in Supervision." *Journal of Curriculum and Supervision* 1, 1: 5–17.

Shulman, L.S. (1987). "Knowledge and Teaching: Foundations of the New Reform." *Harvard Educational Review* 57: 1–22.

Shulman, L.S. (1990). "Transformation of Content Knowledge." Paper presented at the Annual Meeting of the American Educational Research Association, Boston.

Slavin, R.E. (1989–90). "Research on Cooperative Learning: Consensus and Controversy." *Educational Leadership* 47, 4: 52–54.

Sprinthall, N.A., and L. Thies-Sprinthall. (1983). "The Teacher as Adult Learner: A Cognitive Developmental View." In *Staff Development. 82nd Yearbook of the National Society for the Study of Education*, edited by G.A. Griffin. Chicago: University of Chicago Press.

Wilson, S.M., L.S. Shulman, and A.E. Richert. (1987). "150 Different Ways of Knowing: Representations of Knowledge in Teaching." In *Exploring Teachers' Thinking*, edited by J. Calderhead. London: Cassel.

4

Teacher Empowerment and the Development of Voice

Andrew Gitlin and Karen Price

Based largely on the work of Freire (1972, 1985) and Giroux (1983, 1985a, 1985b, 1986), an empowerment perspective has begun to emerge in the area of teacher evaluation.* At the center of this perspective is an emphasis on human agency. As opposed to changing schooling by tightening guidelines and developing sanctions, this perspective is based on the assumption that change is best accomplished when individuals and groups are free to look critically at what they are doing. Rather than pitting one actor against another, however, evaluation processes should help participants join together in a quest for an understanding of teaching. To develop this understanding, Freire (1985), Shor (1980), and others (Gitlin and Goldstein 1987) suggest that dialogue can play an important role and include both "how to" questions and their relation to a wider moral discourse. Within this process of mutual inquiry, or dialogue, the people being observed are no longer "objects" of evaluation, but "critical subjects" who "add . . . to the life they have the existence they make" (Freire 1985). It is this involvement in making history, as opposed to watching it, that enables individuals and groups to more powerfully act on and change teaching and schooling.

Although promising, the empowerment perspective recently has been criticized for not addressing such questions as: Empowerment for what? What is the role of the person "doing" the empowering? and Doesn't the emphasis on agency ignore the fact that without alternative structures little is likely to change at the level of school practice? By addressing these questions, we hope to not only build on and provide a

---

*In this chapter, we use the term *evaluation* as the equivalent of *supervision*.

more detailed description of the empowerment perspective, but also expose the prejudgments that inform our view.

Empowerment as "Voice"

Empowerment, as we are using the term, is linked to the notion of voice. When fully developed, voice is an articulation of one's critical opinions and a protest (Hirschman 1970)—not simply a gripe but a challenge to domination and oppression. Though domination and oppression cannot be defined in a universal manner (Giroux 1989), they are likely to include an unjust use of power. In such cases, particular individuals or groups dole out sanctions and rewards or assert pressures of one sort or another that disenfranchise, silence, and unnecessarily limit the opportunities of others. The ability of groups to assert such pressures and the likely responses of others to them are influenced in dramatic ways by school structures.

For example, a state-mandated core curriculum that specifies the objectives teachers must cover clearly shifts the power between district administrators and teachers toward the district. Although the result of this shift is never guaranteed and often is contested to one degree or another, the district assumes the authority to make certain types of claims about the nature of the curriculum found in the school.

The development of voice, therefore, should make it possible to see and challenge the structures and events that lead to an unjust use of power. Voice may begin as an individual undertaking, but it is most effective when groups who share a common view act in concert.

When we define empowerment as voice, it becomes less of an instrumental process that can serve an array of ends, and more a political process for contesting domination and oppression. In a school context, empowerment perspectives would address some of the most consistent and glaring inequities in our schools, such as those involving patriarchy, racism, and class distinctions. Because this view of empowerment centers on relations of power, those involved must be self-reflective about their role in the process. In an evaluation context, for example, it matters if an evaluator is one who can decide what your salary is or determine the nature of your work. Power relations are also shaped by structures such as district-imposed curriculums, tracking, classroom size, and the organization of school decision making. The influence of these structures can limit the voice of disenfranchised groups.

Unfortunately, most evaluation schemes found in our schools do little to embrace the ideals of an empowerment perspective. For the most part, evaluation is a ritualized tradition in which teachers put on a show to achieve a positive assessment (Gitlin and Smyth 1989). Why evaluation has taken on such a meaning is very much related to the assumed purpose of evaluation.

Traditional Administrative Supervision

Because teaching is thought of as a women's profession (Laird 1988), teachers are treated quite differently from people in male-dominated occupations. Teachers are treated as if administrative supervision is necessary to ensure proper behavior. The cliché "Those who can't do, teach" is a reflection of the low status of teachers and women in our society (Apple 1986). Given this widely held disdain for the work that teachers do, it is not surprising that evaluation has been narrowly constructed as a form of control. In traditional administrative evaluation, teachers have little or no say in determining the standards for good teaching; instead, they are forced to behave in ways that at best reflect only one notion of good teaching. Within this type of evaluation, teachers are viewed as deficient, and their personal knowledge is ignored. Others—nonteachers—determine which teaching behaviors are valued (Gitlin 1990).

In this chapter, one of our objectives is to explore what these typical evaluation schemes do to teachers and how they differ from an empowerment perspective. The next section includes a personal narrative by Karen Price, who is a special education teacher in an elementary school. Price describes her experiences with both a standard form of evaluation and one that explicitly attempts to embrace the empowerment ideal. We draw on her experiences to look more closely at the underlying assumptions of the process and analyze how these assumptions structure notions of good teaching, the teaching role, and teachers' relations with others.

Karen's Experiences in Administrative Supervision

Having entered teaching late in life, I was sensitive to wanting to look the part and to be technically credible in diagnosing and prescribing effective strategies for the students with disabilities in my charge. Fortunately, my administrative evaluations were quite positive. This assessment, however, did not completely quiet my intuitive doubts about the process of evaluation. These doubts became full-blown fears when I saw what happened to the teacher next door. This teacher had given 25 years of his life to teaching; as far as I could see, he was quite personable and liked kids. It did not appear that there were any severe disparities between us as teachers, except that my room was neater and more organized. And yet this teacher's evaluations were handled quite differently from mine; he was observed for a longer period of time and received pages of "documentation" on what were perceived as deficient areas of his teaching. After one such evaluation, the evaluator poked his head in my classroom and noted, "This guy is really a mess."

As I closed my door on my classroom, I thought, "When will my turn come?"

When I tried to befriend this teacher who was under daily attack, my principal told me that I seemed like a capable person and that if I wanted to be successful I should align myself with successful teachers. Evaluation not only seemed arbitrary, but also acted to isolate the supposedly good teachers from those who were viewed as deficient. Over time the fears lessened as I gained confidence in myself and successfully accomplished the "evaluation show." Only my "self-talk" honestly addressed the relief I felt when the principal did not come to see my everyday classroom struggle.

My current evaluation system is one of the best in my fifteen years of teaching. The principal is compassionate, trusts teachers tremendously, and provides many opportunities for feedback. Essentially, this is what happens. The principal supplies each teacher with a packet that outlines the formal observation procedures and the district-approved and -mandated observation process. In particular, the district forms ask the principal to comment on elements of lesson design, motivation, retention, transfer, reinforcement, learning environment, human relations, thinking skills, learning styles, and so forth. I use these forms as a kind of crib sheet to firm up lesson plans and make sure they fit the identified items on the list.

The first step in the observation process is to fill out a preobservation form, on which teachers are required to provide written statements on lesson plan objectives and to identify teaching competencies and possible students who are experiencing difficulty. When this form is completed, the teacher signs up for a time to be observed. The timing of the observation seems very important to many teachers. Commonly, for example, teachers comment on the relation of their observation to others. "I sure don't want to be observed after teacher X; that would be a tough act to follow." And when the time for the observation arrives, it is not unusual to see some teachers trading students to help ensure a more favorable assessment.

When the evaluator comes into the room, nothing is said to the students, but almost all know what is going on. As the lesson proceeds, the principal writes down specific student and teacher responses without engaging in any verbal dialogue with the students or teacher. At the end of the observation, the principal leaves as unobtrusively as possible.

When scheduling permits, usually two or three days after the observation, the principal gives the teacher feedback on the lesson. The teacher is typically asked to provide additional information on the strengths and weaknesses of the lesson in relation to the predetermined objectives outlined on the district form. The time allotted for this feedback is fifteen to twenty minutes. Then the principal presents the teacher a copy of the written report and makes friendly comments as the conference is brought to a close.

Reflections on Administrative Supervision

This type of typical teacher evaluation builds on several fundamental assumptions:

• Evaluation is a process that compares a set of predetermined standards (established by experts residing outside the evaluation process) with a set of practices (performed by the teacher).

• Evaluation is a one-way process—from the evaluator to the observed teacher. Although the teacher can comment and add to the principal's analysis of strengths and weaknesses in the post-observation conference, she must do so in terms of the preestablished criteria. Further, the observed teacher has no opportunity to suggest an alternative meaning to those posited by the evaluator. The teacher cannot, for example, argue that the evaluator mistakenly thought a student was off task because there is no opportunity to make such an argument. Even if there were such an opportunity, the evaluator is assumed to be expert and doles out rewards and sanctions; therefore, such challenges could negatively affect the teacher's work life.

• Evaluation reflects the ahistorical and technical nature of knowing. The evaluator must assume that he can know what is going on in the classroom without considering either the classroom history or the personal histories of teacher and students. This ahistorical perspective gives an inflated importance to the events observed, limits the types of explanations offered, and obscures the roots of particular occurrences or patterns that may be emerging over time. Because the predetermined criteria are technical in nature, the feedback also ignores a range of important moral, political, and ethical concerns.

• Administrative evaluation assumes an individualistic, competitive view of evaluation. Not only is evaluation a private undertaking between a supposed expert and a teacher, but teachers clearly view themselves in competition with each other.

In sum, traditional, administrative evaluation procedures posit a technical view of good teaching that is arbitrary in many regards. This view strengthens the notion that the role of teachers should be limited to the act of teaching The teacher is seen as a nonexpert, whose knowledge of teaching can be pushed to the side or ignored entirely. Teachers clearly resist this influence by learning to give the evaluator what is expected and by manipulating the situation. But this resistance enhances neither human agency nor a sense of common interests. Instead, administrative evaluation schemes allow teachers to continue teaching in their accustomed styles, silence those working in the classroom, and leave in place the bureaucratic hierarchy of the school.

It is the aim of empowering forms of evaluation to challenge these outcomes and, as we articulated earlier, to develop teachers' voice. The next section includes another personal narrative by Karen Price, in which she illustrates her experiences with an empowerment approach to evaluation, called "horizontal evaluation" (Gitlin and Goldstein 1987). Our objective here is to understand the ways in which empowerment approaches may and may not overcome the limitations of traditional approaches.

An Empowerment Approach: Horizontal Evaluation

Horizontal evaluation is a process in which teachers start out by collaboratively analyzing the relationship between their teaching intentions and their practices in ways that point to "living contradictions" (Whitehead and Lomax 1987). Teachers search for the gap between what they desire to do in their teaching and what they actually end up doing. And when no mismatch is found between intention and practice, teachers think through why it is they want to achieve the particular ends they have identified, as opposed to unquestioningly accepting them. Intentions can be stated in advance or can emerge from discussion. When stated in advance, they become a text for analysis.

For example, a teacher might have the intention of having all students obey the rule, "Raise your hand before speaking." Instead of simply observing the extent to which actual practice reflects this intent, participants should discuss why the rule is important, and under what conditions and when it might be most appropriate. Once issues like this can be clarified, their desirability can be examined and debated in relation to a normative framework.

In illuminating the relationship between educational means and ends, horizontal evaluation draws primarily on the work of Gadamer (1975) and Habermas (1976), who have helped shape three methods: "communication analysis," "historical perspective," and "challenge statements." These methods, along with a consideration of alternative practices, are used to enhance and deepen the dialogue between the teacher and observer.

Communication Analysis. Participants use this analytical process to understand how the prejudgments they hold about teaching frame their teaching and shape behavior. For example, if a teacher believes that chaotic student behavior is caused by the low abilities of the students, the question, "What do you mean by 'low abilities'?" could be posed. Implicit values that lie behind statements and practices like this can, therefore, be made explicit and thus reconsidered by the participants. Reconsideration of these values can amount to a transformation in the way teachers daily make and remake school reality. If teachers realize that the labeling they use is inappropriate because it is based on an undisclosed view of the socioeconomic status of the students, then they can reorganize classroom structures and pedagogy to reflect a more egalitarian view.

Historical Perspective. Adopting an historical perspective allows teachers to see apparently commonsense notions and actions not as natural and immutable, but rather as choices that are part of an historical tradition. For instance, if a teacher regards teaching as a process of depositing information in the heads of students, adopting an historical perspective can encourage discussion about what factors have historically encouraged this kind of pedagogy. The interests embedded within such a view can then be more fully analyzed.

Challenge Statements. Sometimes discussions about in-class activity between a teacher and a colleague become stilted or bogged down and cannot go beyond clarifying values and prejudgments. At such times, either person can initiate a challenge statement designed to get discussion moving again. For example, if a teacher holds to the view that students should obey her classroom rules in all circumstances, questions can be raised about students' and teachers' rights, and about the role and purpose of adult authority. The resulting conversation might seek to investigate the legitimacy of adult authority and the implications this holds for the education of students in a democracy.

Alternatives. Horizontal evaluation asks participants to link the insights gained through dialogue to the realization of alternative teaching practices. The chosen alternative is a turning point for further discourse on the relation of intentions to practice. In other words, while the dialogue may end with a suggested alternative, this alternative then becomes part of a new set of practices that are examined by the participants. Alternatives are an important part of the dialogue process because new insights can be linked to practice.

Karen's Experiences in Horizontal Evaluation

As part of my master's program at the University of Utah, I had the opportunity to experiment with horizontal evaluation. A first step in this process was to explore what might be called "local histories." To fulfill this requirement, I wrote a personal history that focused on the journey that led me to choose a career in teaching. Then I wrote a school history, which explored the school's political framework, including organizational structures and priorities. With these "texts" as a backdrop, I began to focus on the next steps.

At this point, however, I was a somewhat reluctant participant. I saw the process as a tedious assignment that I just had to get over with. Preparations to leave my classroom seemed to be a hurdle. My team member was at a different school, and our chances to get together were thwarted by schedules and other teaching priorities. Horizontal evaluation, as was true of administrative supervision, didn't seem to offer much of value in terms of teaching—but I did agree to give it a try.

The next step was to choose a colleague to team with. The goal of horizontal teaming was to participate in at least three evaluation "laps," in which each lap allowed both participants to be observer and teacher. For each lap, my colleague and I held a conference about the observations and recorded each conference on an audiotape. We then transcribed the audiotapes and analyzed the content. The resulting text replaced the traditional evaluation sheets and rating scales used in administrative approach.

During the second lap, when my colleague and I decided to meet at her home to do the post-observation conference, my attitudes about the process started to change. For the first time, I began to view evaluation as something more than a process of control. What I found, despite my initial hesitancy, was that the process helped identify some reoccurring themes, frustrations, and annoyances that were common to both of us.

Clearly, I was not alone in my worries and concerns. What was unique about the process was that the observer could be an advocate rather than a judge or a censor. Together, we were able to appraise the situation and consider a wide array of problems and concerns. In my personal history, I proclaimed that as a public servant, I desired a less isolated existence in the workplace of public education. Horizontal evaluation provided a small step in this direction.

The themes that emerged from our post-observation conferences were diverse, yet common themes kept coming up for reexploration. It was as if each of us had a kind of broken record that identified the struggles and dilemmas that emerged out of our personal intentions and teaching practices. We approached these concerns from both thinking and feeling levels as we tried to articulate whose interests were being served by our teaching practices. Often, *communication analysis* provided a method to unearth these important concerns. For example, we analyzed the following parts of our dialogue concerning how to encourage students to make decisions: (*T* refers to the Teacher being observed, and *O* refers to the Observer):

> *T*—Yes, sometimes I feel a little like "Mary Cheerleader" with some of these kids. . . . You know. Trying to work for even bits and parts of things that I can compliment them on because, as you probably noticed, there were a number of other things going on. . . . It's something I work on every day—about how to find the things they're doing that are approaching what I'm asking them to do.

> *O*—I heard you use the word *decisions* a lot. So you seem to turn the problem back to them and say, "Okay, that's your decision." Is that what you do purposely?

> *T*—Yes, I'm really trying to focus on the kids being in charge. . . .

> *O*—Tell me more about "being in charge." Why do you think kids should be in charge?

Other concerns were also illuminated through our articulation of the tremendous gaps between intention and practice. On a day-to-day basis, I strive to address "success" in a rather routinized way. There is an element of justification when I look at my intentions. I must reluctantly admit that when I was asked to state my intentions, they were often designed to indicate the rightness of my practices. For example, as a special education teacher, I have been trained to be a behaviorist, someone who must obtain tangible results. Although these concrete outcomes would clearly be accepted by my special education peers, when I asked what interests are served by the emphasis on these results, I have blanks in my dialogue.

Initially, our dialogue remained on the level of comparing intentions and practices; but over time, as trust developed, we began to use a more historical perspective. We talked about the histories of our classrooms, job descriptions, schoolwide programs, and personal histories.

O—Do you agree with the behavior modification kind of philosophy?

T—Oh, I really struggle with it. I think that the district certainly supports it, and a lot of special education teachers use approaches like behavior modification out of a certain need, I guess. I am fighting something tangible. But it's . . . it can be a trap. . . . I try to put it on the kids, about their knowing where they stand, and what they earned, so it isn't some mysterious person giving them permission for something good or something bad. That they have some control in it. So I use it for a shaper, I guess. A shaper of behavior.

O—As a teacher, what issues about control do you struggle with? Is there something about control historically that you struggle with?

T—Yes, that is an excellent question. I think I have struggled with various issues of control for a long time.

At this point we also started to feel more comfortable in posing *challenge statements*. As our relationship got stronger, we focused on illuminating understanding rather than on making hierarchical judgments on arbitrary standards of "worth." These challenge statements, in turn, often led to the identification of *alternative practices*. For example, in one interchange about what to do about students who tattle on each other, I learned about the other teacher's use of an anonymous "tattle box."

O—[When] those two boys challenged each other over the points they received, you said, "You're on your honor now!" Do you care to comment on "honor"?

T—I just said that as a spur-of-the-moment idea . . . and I guess it was more like a gesture on my part that I could trust them just to see what would happen. . . .

O—The final thing I noticed about those two boys was that when they were bumping into each other, you directed them to solve the problem themselves. I noticed the rules on your wall, and one of them was "No Tattling."

T—Well, there isn't anything that drives me up the wall worse than "Teacher, so and so did this. Teacher, make him stop." It just irritates me. So, it is one of those things that I've been trying to indoctrinate into my students!

O—I like the idea of giving it back to them and saying "Here, have this problem," but sometimes they have to have something to do with it.

T—I feel that it's a power struggle, because . . . if I take sides with one person who is having a problem, then that creates problems with other students. . . .

O—I don't know if you noticed that in my room I have a little wooden box. . . . It's just a recipe box, and my students just write a little note and stick it in the "tattle box"; and periodically we see what's in it. . . . not as a "tell you what to do," but as another way of handling it.

T—That's a neat idea. It's nice to know that it has reduced tattling for you. I never thought of that, and you are right about the "need to put the information somewhere." It seems like a more natural way to disengage from the power struggle.

In sum, horizontal evaluation has pointed out to me that I view teaching as a compromise. The compromise often occurs because what I expect from my students is often vague and unclear to me. It is no wonder that the practices do not often match my vague notions of success. As I continue to identify this concern, I am going to strive for more personal clarity on what it means to be successful so that I can fill in some blanks in my professional dialogue.

Reflections on Horizontal Evaluation

This type of teacher evaluation builds on a vastly different set of assumptions from those of the administrative model:

• The horizontal approach assumes that evaluation proceeds by analyzing standards, in the form of stated intentions, and their relation to practice. Teachers have a say in determining these standards, and the assessment process centers on how the standards are met in practice.

• In horizontal evaluation, both participants work together to understand teaching, through collective reflections and actions.

• The horizontal approach also assumes that history plays an important part in understanding the slice of life captured in a particular observation. This process focuses on the historical relations, norms, and structures found in the school, as well as the teacher's beliefs and experiences related to schooling.

• This evaluation approach assumes that it is important to assess the ethical, political, and moral implications of strategies and practices in schools and consider effective alternatives.

These assumptions suggest that good teaching involves the examination of both aims and practices and their relationship. Good teaching is a process of considering and reconsidering what one does and how this relates to a set of intentions that are examined and reexamined. The role of the teacher, as a consequence, includes setting goals and determining purposes. And because teachers work together on this process, there are more opportunities to break down the isolation that obscures common interests and limits collective actions. Finally, teachers' knowledge becomes an important part of the evaluation process.

Karen's experiences suggest both the possibilities and limits of an empowerment approach. One limit is that teachers' involvement with traditional forms of evaluation is likely to color the way they initially approach alternative models. It takes time, experience, and trust between participants to see the benefits of an empowerment approach. Participants need the opportunity to remake their evaluation history. Some school structures, especially those that are taken for granted, also may not be discussed immediately, especially if no attempts are made to expand the dialogue beyond the individual pairs of participants. Only when dialogue becomes a wider collective effort can others have an opportunity to "see" what may be overlooked by the original pair of participants. It is also clear that dialogue itself does not ensure that teachers will see or protest forms of oppression and domination. Though the teachers in the narrative example did raise issues of power and control, these concerns did not become focused in a way that led the teachers to protest in any fundamental way their relation with students or the wider influence of schooling on students. Finally, an empowerment approach is time consuming and costly in the sense that substitutes need to be hired to enable teachers to observe one another. If this approach is to have a collective moment, permanent ways must be found to relieve teachers from their already busy schedules (Apple 1986). Implementing empowerment approaches to evaluation, without addressing the fact that most teachers have little or no time even for a cup of coffee, is to severely limit the possibilities of this approach.

On the other hand, this empowerment approach helped the teachers in our example escape what might be called the "control-resistance cycle," where teachers transform the process into a game of pleasing the evaluator. The teachers not only valued the process but—after trust developed—welcomed critical insights. This empowerment approach also challenged teacher isolation. This challenge is important in building the collegial relations that enable teachers to share ideas and discuss educational issues. As opposed to the administrative model, which leaves teachers silent, this approach helped teachers tell their stories and have their "plots" examined. The teachers in our example were able to see problems typically taken for granted; develop their understanding of a wide range of issues, including moral concerns; and use this understanding to make alterations in their practice. These teachers also changed the way they saw the classroom. As part of this process, they addressed relations of power that can lead to oppression; and they began to develop a voice.

* * *

The experiences in horizontal evaluation that we have presented suggest that evaluation need not silence teachers. It can use and examine what they know to alter practice. Though it is true that the ideal of empowerment in terms of the development of voice was not achieved in this one example, the process of expanding the teachers' role was begun. Such an expanded role for teachers includes a moral discourse that focuses on the aims of education and confronts the historical limits of those working in what is often referred to as a woman's profession. Finally, alternative forms of evaluation create the possibility that teachers and others can take a more active role in challenging the way traditional schooling "disadvantages" particular groups.

References

Apple, M. (1986). *Teachers and Text: A Political Economy of Class and Gender Relations in Education*. New York: Routledge and Kegan Paul.

Freire, P. (1972). *Pedagogy of the Oppressed*. Harmondsworth: Penguin Books.

Freire, P. (1985). *The Politics of Education*. South Hadley, Mass.: Bergin and Garvey.

Gadamer, H. (1975). *Truth and Method*. New York: Seabury Press.

Giroux, H. (1983). *Theory and Resistance in Education: A Pedagogy for the Opposition*. Amherst, Mass.: Bergin and Garvey.

Giroux, H. (September 1985a). "Intellectual Labor and Pedagogical Work: Rethinking the Role of Teacher as Intellectual." *Phenomenology and Pedagogy* 3, 1: 20–32.

Giroux, H. (May 1985b). "Teachers as Transformative Intellectuals." *Social Education* 49, 5: 376–379.

Giroux, H. (January 1986). "Critical Pedagogy and the Resisting Intellectual." *Phenomenology and Pedagogy* 3, 2: 84–97.

Giroux, H. (1989). *Schooling as a Form of Cultural Politics: Toward a Pedagogy of and for Difference*. New York: State University of New York Press.

Gitlin, A. (Summer 1990). "Understanding Teaching Dialogically." *Teachers College Record* 91, 4: 537–563.

Gitlin, A., and S. Goldstein. (Winter 1987). A Dialogical Approach to Understanding Horizontal Evaluation. *Educational Theory* 37, 1: 17–27.

Gitlin, A., and J. Smyth. (1989). *Teacher Evaluation: Educative Alternatives*. London: Falmer Press.

Habermas, J. (1976). *Communication and the Evolution of Society*. Boston: Beacon Press.

Hirschman, A. (1970). *Exit, Voice and Loyalty*. Cambridge: Harvard University Press.

Laird, S. (November 1988). "Reforming Women's True Profession: A Case for Feminist Pedagogy in Teacher Education." *Harvard Educational Review* 58, 4: 449–463.

Shor, I. (1980). *Critical Teaching and Everyday Life*. Boston: South End Press.

Whitehead, J., and P. Lomax. (January 1987). "Contradictions in 'Action Research and the Politics of Educational Knowledge.'" *British Education and Research Journal* 13, 2: 175–190.

II

The Practice

5

Restructuring in a Large District: Dade County, Florida

Gerald O. Dreyfuss, Peter J. Cistone, and
Charles Divita, Jr.

A cross the United States today, states and school districts are adopting various models of restructuring as a strategy to qualitatively improve the viability and competence of educational systems and schools as organizations. Advocates of school restructuring argue that quality control and quality improvement in education cannot occur without a fundamental transformation in the institutional culture of schools and in the roles, relationships, and interactions of individuals within them.

In his analysis of leadership as managed cultural change, Schein (1985) states that "we simply cannot understand organizational phenomena without considering culture both as a cause of and a way of explaining such phenomena" (p. 311). Culture is pervasive and complex, he explains, and it affects virtually all aspects of the organization—strategy, structure, processes, reward and control systems, and daily routines.

The traditional dominant organizational culture of schools is manifest, among other ways, in highly formalized and bureaucratic structures. Such structural arrangements are embedded in patterns of basic assumptions and beliefs that affect organizational functioning. Great emphasis is placed on the specification of procedural rules and regulations, on hierarchical control systems, and on centralized decision making. Thus, Mary Ann Raywid (cited in Timar 1990) observes:

> At levels too fundamental to be challenged, many of those in schools have accepted that there must be differential status and authority assignments, fixed roles, clearly divided responsibilities and accountability measures, and written rules governing interactions. . . . Such

understandings, and the interaction patterns they produce, yield a school's social order. This "order" determines the way in which its constituents "do" school, and this, in turn, generates the school's climate (p. 58).

These distinctive features, particularly the preoccupation with normative structure over behavioral structure, led Bennis (1959) to describe such systems as "organizations without people."

Those who advocate school restructuring, on the other hand, hold to a different conception of organizations and the actual and proper relation of individual participants and groups to organizations. They view organizations as "organisms" (Morgan 1986) and stress the importance of informal and behavioral factors over formal structure. Their model emphasizes interpersonal and small-group behavior in organizations. In contrast to the bureaucratic mode, formal authority relationships are minimized, as are procedural rules and regulations, to enhance interaction and participation in decision making. Likewise, there is an equalizing of the distribution of power, as consensus and collaboration are accepted as norms in place of bureaucratic direction and control. Basic to the idea of school restructuring is the expectation of creating a professional work environment for teachers, principally through collegial and collective management at the school-site level.

Context of Reform in Dade County

As with the United States as a whole, education reform in Dade County, Florida, Public Schools (which include those in Miami) has gained strong momentum and enjoyed high visibility during the past several years. The vigor and success with which a broad range of strategies has been implemented have placed the system—the fourth largest in the United States—at the cutting edge of the national education reform movement. Indeed, many observers regard developments in Dade County as the most significant reform movement in America's public schools today, with primary emphasis on the professionalization of teaching and on the restructuring of the system by which schools are governed and decisions are made.

Conceptual Foundations

Educators in Dade County discern and practice supervision within the context of a fundamental transformation in the institutional culture of schools—and in the roles, relationships, and interactions of individuals within them. Several premises undergird that thought and practice:

1. Large, urban, multicultural/multilingual school systems, if not all school systems, face a host of educational issues that can best be defined, analyzed, and addressed at the local school-site level.

2. Given the wide diversity of problems, potentials, perspectives, and resources associated with these schools, no singular approach to supervision is likely to provide an adequate framework for assisting school districts in their restructuring and empowering initiatives.

3. A multiplicity of supervision methods, techniques, and devices must be conceptualized and drawn upon in a manner that respects each school's unique mission and goals and that simultaneously maintains the unity and integrity of the school system as a whole.

4. It is unlikely that the plethora of supervisory practices and innovations which evolve in a district undergoing restructuring flow deliberately and systematically from a priority framework. However, an examination of characteristics common to practices and innovations generated and found to be successful may reveal an underlying genesis in contemporary research and theory.

On the basis of these premises, the Dade County Public School System has developed an array of supervisory programs and activities. Yet, despite the variety of methods, techniques, and devices that has been applied at all levels of the school system, there is an underlying set of principles and values around which these diverse initiatives coalesce. These organizing principles and values are derived from some of the most influential literature concerned with organizational renewal. Research and theory in the fields of quality improvement, adult learning, reflective practice, human motivation, and organization development have been particularly influential in developing effective supervisory practices supportive of restructuring. Figure 5.1 shows the fields of research and theory that have had the most potent influence in Dade County's restructuring initiatives.

Quality Improvement Theory

Perhaps the most widely recognized set of principles related to the concept of restructuring has been advanced by W. Edward Deming, in whose name the most coveted business prize in Japan, if not in the world, has been designated—the Deming Prize. Deming urges those committed to improving quality to apply fourteen points to their improvement efforts (Walton 1986).

Figure 5.1
Conceptual Foundations of Dade County Public Schools' Supervisory Policies and Practices

An examination of the experience of the Dade County Public Schools suggests that the values, principles, concepts, and models embodied in the literature of quality improvement substantially underlie many of the successful supervision initiatives launched by the district in its effort to restructure schools (Ouchi 1982, Peters and Waterman 1982, Naisbitt and Aburdene 1985, Fitzgerald and Murphy 1982, Byham 1989, Crosby 1979). Figure 5.2 presents Deming's fourteen points and suggests how each may be applied to the process of educational supervision.

Figure 5.2
Application of Deming's Fourteen Points to Supervision

1. *Create constancy of purpose for the improvement of product and service.*

    Redirect supervision's role from "checking on teachers" to a primary role of continually stimulating research, innovation, improvement, and developing strategies for maintaining quality standards once improvements are instituted.

2. *Adopt a new philosophy.*

    For all associated with the supervision process, inculcate and reinforce a sense of values devoted to excellence in workmanship and service.

3. *Cease dependence on mass inspections.*

    Shift supervisory attention from inspection of school system products for defects and "required re-cycling" to improvement of the process that is responsible for the observed results.

4. *End the practice of awarding business on price tag alone.*

    Develop long-term relationships with individuals and agencies that can supply the best quality supervisory support. Awarding contracts to lowest bidders too often equates to the lowest quality of materials and services' being available to support supervision processes.

5. *Improve constantly and forever the system of production and service.*

    Management, and all others involved in the supervision process, must be dedicated to the search for improving quality. This will require a long-term commitment to supervisory resources, to promoting the stature and visibility of the supervision process, and to adequately recognizing accomplishments that the supervisory process yields.

6. *Institute job training and job retraining.*

    Provide effective linkage between supervision and staff development activity.

7. *Institute leadership.*

    Conceptualize the role of supervisors as facilitators, leaders, helpers, and diagnosticians rather than tellers, checkers, or punishers and provide training to improve supervisors' skills in these areas.

8. *Drive out fear.*

    Promote personal and professional feelings of security among school staff. Eliminate punishment, retribution, and other forms of threat. Promote an open, respectful, and appreciative supervisory environment.

Figure 5.2—*continued*
Application of Deming's Fourteen Points to Supervision

9. *Break down barriers between staff areas.*	Resolve interdepartmental, interschool competition. Establish collaborative and mutually supportive and complementary goals. Build a team approach to problem solving and quality improvement.
10. *Eliminate slogans, exhortations, and work force targets.*	Avoid "top down" slogans and admonitions. Let these adornments surface from within grass roots groups if they so choose. Likewise, performance targets should be set by these groups.
11. *Eliminate numerical quotas.*	Avoid tying supervisory judgments of performance to satisfaction of minimal quotas. Performance judgments should be derived not from numbers but from quality and effective application of sound methods of practice.
12. *Remove barriers to pride of workmanship.*	Supervisors should strive to ensure that school personnel have the guidance, tools, equipment, materials, and support services required to do an "excellent job." The supervisor should be vigilant of opportunities to remove barriers to these requirements.
13. *Institute a vigorous program of education and retraining (focused on quality).*	All participants in the supervisory process, including management, must be provided with the insights and skills required of a comprehensive quality improvement effort. For example, education and training devoted to quality improvement concepts and philosophies, team building, statistical procedures, problem solving, and decision making is essential.
14. *Take action to accomplish the transformation.*	A well-prepared (representative, experienced, and skilled) supervisory infrastructure must be formed to provide overall direction and support to the systemwide improvement effort. Long-range goal setting and action planning by this participatory group is essential.

Adult Learning Theory

Given that effective supervision is fundamentally a growth-inducing (learning) process, the literature on adult learning is particularly instructive in terms of how to relate to adults (be they parents, teachers, or administrators) involved in the process of supervision. Knowles (1980) provides four assumptions that he maintains should direct the efforts of those who facilitate adult learning. These assumptions and their application to supervision are shown in Figure 5.3.

Figure 5.3
Application of Adult Learning Theory to Supervision

1. *Self-concept*	Supervisory processes should recognize adults as autonomous and self-directing.
2. *Experience*	Adults have rich backgrounds to be tapped through supervisory processes. Supervision can elicit individuals' expertise and bring it to bear, in a collective fashion, on pressing educational issues.
3. *Readiness for learning*	Adults' readiness for learning is determined by the unique circumstances they encounter in their professional practice. Supervision must be sensitive to the actual and perceptual reality of all involved in the supervisory process.
4. *Time perspective*	Adults' involvement in developmental activities will vary according to the immediacy of application of newly acquired abilities and insights. Adults will be committed to supervision that can yield desirable results in the near-term future. Adults must see how supervisory initiatives relate to their current professional lives.

Dade County's evolution of supervisory practices to support restructuring has adhered closely to the assumptions advanced by Knowles.

Reflective Practice Theory

Argyris and Schön (1974) suggest that professionals, through inter-action, create a design for their behavior and come to hold a theory of their practice—a theory-in-action. Such a theory includes values, strategies, and underlying assumptions that govern the behavior of professionals in terms of what they say and do. At one level, a professional articulates an "espoused theory" to justify actions or to seek social acceptability. At another level, a professional has a "theory-in-use," which is revealed by the person's overt behavior and which may not be in keeping with the individual's espoused theory. Theories-in-use can be revealed, examined, tested, modified, and replicated only through a process of reflection on one's practice. Depending on the nature of the "governing variables" (values) of the theories-in-action, professional behavior can be seen as one of two types: Model I or Model II.

Model I Behavior. This type of behavior is characterized by striving to achieve organizational purposes as the individual sees them, maximizing winning and minimizing losing, minimizing the eliciting of negative feelings and behaving rationally with minimal emotionality. Model I professionals take actions to gain control over aspects of the environment that they perceive personally affect them and to unilaterally protect themselves and others from being hurt. Model I professionals and their associates may seem defensive and very narrow in terms of the range of choices they envision or are willing to risk undertaking. Model I behavior seldom leads to any public testing of theories-in-use and often leads professionals to concentrate only on learning and actions that eliminate pain but that fail to remove the underlying cause (Schön 1987). Model I behavior does not enable professionals to examine their practice strategies. Argyris and Schön (1978) refer to this phenomenon as "single-loop learning."

Model II Behavior. This type of behavior places a premium on gaining access to valid information, making free and informed choices, and being committed to constantly evaluating and implementing choices. Professionals with Model II values focus on actions that address causes, not just those that minimize pain. They view their professional opportunities, effectiveness, and satisfaction as being jointly controlled with colleagues. Protection of self and of others is recognized as a mutual rather than individual responsibility and process. Model II behavior is characterized by minimum defensiveness; value on learning; and high degrees of freedom of choice, commitment, and risk-taking. Professionals operating from a Model II perspective are receptive to continually generating hypotheses; examining their values, assumptions, and resultant actions (double-loop learning); and publicly testing and disclosing their findings (Schön 1987).

The process of restructuring a district is largely one of moving people's value orientation—both individual and systemwide—from a Model I perspective to that of Model II. Supervisory practices must promote a climate in which it is both safe and encouraged for areas that were formerly private and off limits to discussion to become public and subject to discussion. In such a climate, change and improvement become more highly prized than constancy and predictability; and single-loop learning gives way to double-loop learning. Obviously, these shifts in orientation are not accomplished easily.

Human Motivation Theory

The field of human motivation is instructive to those interested in transforming traditional supervisory processes. Three of the most noteworthy—by Herzberg and Associates (1959), McClelland (1961), and Vroom(1964)—are reviewed here.

Herzberg and his associates (1959) would have modern supervision processes attend to both the "motivation and hygiene needs" of persons associated with the system. Motivation needs are concerned directly with the job of schools, whereas hygiene needs focus on surrounding circumstances. Translated to the process of supervision, motivation needs include gaining a sense of achievement, advancing professionally in terms of competence and career, being recognized for achievement, retaining control over decisions affecting one's professional practice, and being engaged in meaningful and interesting work. Hygiene needs include comfortable and appropriate working conditions, satisfying interpersonal relations, high-quality supervision, and supportive and appropriately formulated policies. Districts undergoing restructuring should be certain to address both motivation and hygiene needs wherever possible in the supervisory process.

Like Herzberg, McClelland (1961) believes that supervision should provide opportunities for involved participants to meet their needs for achievement. In addition, he has called attention to needs for power and needs for affiliation. Empowering of persons in school improvement projects must be a major consideration of restructuring. Participants must both sense the new power they have and gain satisfaction from it. Affiliation needs can be addressed through supervisory mechanisms that help participants not only to interact with others but also to develop a sense of group identification, shared interests, mutual support, and common goals and values. Unless districts are careful to attend to the essence of affiliation, they may find the affiliation structures they initiate (e.g., quality circles) to be ineffective, dysfunctional, or even harmful to school improvement efforts.

Victor Vroom's research and theory (1964) suggests that participants in the supervisory process will be motivated as a function of "valence" and "expectancy." Valence refers to the degree of positive affect participants in the supervision process hold for school improvement initiatives. Expectancy refers to the degree of confidence participants have that their efforts will yield desired consequences. If districts effectively address individuals' needs, participants in the supervisory process will likely have a positive attitude toward the school improvement agenda and will be confident of their ability to bring its goals to fruition (Owens 1991).

Organization Development Theory

Concepts, principles, and lessons learned from organization development (OD) research and theory are in keeping with the supervisory implications derived from the literature reviewed thus far. Districts successful in implementing and diffusing supervisory innovations are characterized by a problem-solving orientation and by an internal impetus to change. Furthermore, flexibility and adaptability to local circumstances are conducive to adopting innovations, whereas rigidity and control are not. Continuous planning and evaluation, ongoing opportunities for learning that flow from participants' needs, ready access to technical and consultative services, an ongoing and internally directed search for solutions, and overt support and recognition by key leaders are essential factors in achieving long-term change in schools. As shown in Figure 5.4, Owens (1991) presents ten concepts that characterize a successful OD process. Supervisory practices in Dade County are consistent with Owens' formulations.

Exemplary Supervisory Practices

The preceding research and theoretical foundations substantially undergird supervision in Dade County. The sixteen programs and practices shown in Figure 5.5 illustrate the district's perspective on supervisory practices that support restructuring.

Figure 5.4
Application of Organization Development (OD) Processes to Supervision

1. *The goals of OD*	Supervisory processes should contribute to generation and evolution of school improvement goals and to communication, understanding, and widespread adoption of them.
2. *Self-renewal*	Supervision must develop the district's internal capacity for improvement.
3. *A systems approach*	Supervision must concentrate on generating changes in all aspects of the system.
4. *Focus on people*	Supervisory actions must be based on the requirements of people in the system—the system's greatest resource. "People issues" need to be addressed before task, structure, and technology issues.
5. *An educational strategy*	Supervision should foster participants' growth and be sensitive to learning needs, styles, and resources. Inservice programs should concurrently address participants' needs and school improvement goals.
6. *Learning through experience*	Supervision must promote learning opportunities that are integrally related to job performance, including on-the-job training, experimentation, mentoring, action research, coaching, performance analysis feedback, team learning, and reflective practice discussions.
7. *Dealing with real problems*	Supervision must help participants identify and assign priorities to improvement opportunities.
8. *A planned strategy*	Supervision should be driven by declared goals and by a design for achieving the goals. Plans must be sensitive to the "customers" of the supervisory initiatives.
9. *Change agent*	Those giving guidance to the supervisory process must be carefully selected. These agents need to be viewed by participants in the system as credible and competent.
10. *Involvement of top-level administration*	Supervision must ensure that administrators of the district and bargaining units are actively involved. Passive endorsement is not sufficient. Leaders must be visible in the supervisory process, participate in it, and demonstrate an ongoing commitment to restructuring. Actions being asked of people at lower levels also should be pursued by those at higher organizational levels.

Figure 5.5
Dade County Supervisory Practices

Major Initiatives

- School Based Management and Shared Decision Making
- Satellite Learning Centers
- Dade Academy for the Teaching Arts
- Quality Instruction Incentives Program

New Directions

- Landmark Teachers' Contract
- Shared Decision Making in Feeder Patterns
- Feeder Pattern Councils
- Lead Principals
- Feeder Pattern Technical Assistance

New Roles for Teachers

- Principal/Assistant Principal Selection
- Facilities Planning
- Lead Teachers, Teacher-Directors/Coordinators

Professional Development

- Teacher Education Center
- Teacher Peer Intervention and Assistance
- Leadership Experience Opportunities
- Administrators' Professionalization

Major Initiatives

Though the seeds of professionalization in Dade County were planted in the early 1970s, visionary development and growth of the program took hold in 1986. The four initiatives described here focus on decentralization of the school system to improve the quality of instruction. These initiatives range from work-site decision making to schools at the work place.

SBM/SDM. The centerpiece of reform in the Dade County Public Schools is school based management/shared decision making (SBM/SDM). Approved in principle by the school board in April 1987, SBM/SDM represents a fundamental restructuring of the processes and practices of educational governance. As conceived and implemented in Dade County, SBM/SDM decentralizes decision making and devolves responsibility to school sites within an explicit framework of both autonomy and responsibility. It is intended to enhance the leadership of school-site administrators and promote the empowerment of teachers so as to make the school a more satisfying work place and productive learning environment. This school-level, "bottom-up" strategy thus makes the school, rather than the district as a whole, the focus of change and the point of intervention for organizational renewal.

Satellite Learning Centers. In addition to school based management, the professionalization of education in Dade County encompassed numerous related initiatives. A satellite learning center is operated by Dade County Public Schools in a facility constructed and paid for by a host corporation. The first such center in the United States opened in 1987 to serve the kindergarten-age children of employees of American Bankers Insurance Group's corporate headquarters in Miami. The program quickly expanded to grade 1, and in 1989 to grade 2.

Since then, two more satellite learning centers have opened: one at Miami International Airport for the children of airport employees; the other at Miami-Dade Community College (North Campus) for children of employees, as well as for students who attend the college. In addition, several new agreements with companies throughout Dade County are now being developed. Interested employers range from hospitals and banks to an industrial park complex of more than 50 private-sector firms, which has expressed interest in constructing an entire satellite learning school for children of their employees.

A lead teacher is in charge at each satellite learning center and works with the principal of a nearby (host) school. Children at the center participate in school assemblies and other activities with students at the host school.

For the school system, the satellite helps ease transportation costs and overcrowding while improving student integration by reflecting the commonly heterogeneous population of parents' work environments. It also encourages better communication between parents and teachers. For employees, satellites alleviate many challenges working parents face, such as transporting children to school, having time to become more involved in school activities, and spending more quality time with their children. Employers have already documented a substantial decline in absenteeism, tardiness, and the turnover rate among parents whose children are enrolled in these centers. Satellite learning centers represent the ultimate business-school partnership, fostering teacher empowerment and providing numerous benefits for taxpayers, businesses, schools, parents, and children.

The Dade Academy for the Teaching Arts (DATA). This nine-week program of seminars and clinics is designed to provide secondary school teachers with time to conduct research projects, develop creative teaching plans, and trade instructional strategies. One of DATA's unusual characteristics is that the program is planned and operated exclusively by teachers for teachers. The employee responsible for the DATA project is not an administrator, but a teacher-director. The teacher-director concept, which also is used in the Teacher Education Center, is being continued and expanded. Ten "resident" teachers in six disciplines (mathematics, social studies, learning disabilities, foreign language, English, and science) act as mentors to seventy colleagues (externs) during the year.

Quality Instruction Incentives Program (QUIIP). This voluntary awards program provides financial incentives to individual schools that compete for and receive meritorious status. To become a "merit school," a school must show a dramatic improvement in its students' intellectual and physical development. A smaller number of "educational excellence" schools are selected from the "merit school" list, and a final list of "E" schools demonstrate the most outstanding projects in the district for improving student achievement. What makes this program distinctive is its cooperative development and focus on student achievement. Dade County Public Schools and the United Teachers of Dade successfully negotiated the QUIIP program for inclusion in the teachers' contract. That, in itself, was a national first.

New Directions

The current teachers' contract builds on professionalization efforts initiated in prior years, while continuing to move toward school empowerment throughout the district. Pilot programs include steps to streamline middle management, at both area and district levels. Central to the district's restructuring efforts are the decentralization of decision making to individual feeder pattern, schools, and classrooms and completion of a comprehensive profile for identifying school improvement needs. This profile is being cooperatively developed, along with a plan for implementing recommended strategies for turning around particularly difficult schools.

Landmark Teachers' Contract. Committed to teacher empowerment, the district is determined to make teaching the profession it deserves to be. Attracting and retaining the best teachers continue to be high priorities, because excellent teachers are critical components for quality educational programs and outstanding student achievement. Hailed as progressive, far-reaching, and precedent-setting by the media and educators across the country, the new pact includes an entire article on Professionalization of Teaching. Contract highlights include:

1. Teacher involvement in planning/designing new educational facilities, and in the selection and, at certain schools, assessment of principals and assistant principals.

2. Continuation and expansion of SBM/SDM.

3. Development of a pilot Career Achievement (Career Ladder) Program for Teachers, based on superior performance, professional growth and development, and economic incentives.

Shared Decision Making Extended to Entire Feeder Pattern. In an effort to further reduce bureaucracy and increase broad-based representation in decision making at the school level, an entire geographic area of schools and their administration have been organizationally restructured. The pilot organizational structure includes fewer middle-management positions and the reassignment of area personnel to feeder patterns. It also comprises new governing bodies and leaders for each of the six feeder patterns in the area.

Feeder Pattern Councils. Feeder patterns refer to geographic school enrollment patterns in which students are generally placed in appropriate-level schools, based on where they live.

The primary purpose in establishing Feeder Pattern Councils is to enhance networking and strategic planning among schools in the same feeder pattern. Each council develops and uses a shared-decision-making model for identifying issues of mutual concern, such as educational goals, programs, and strategies. Under district guidelines, broad school and community representation is ensured in each council. Participants include a lead principal, other principals, area and central office technical assistance advisors, teachers from each grade level, and PTA/PTSA members. Also included are the chair of the Feeder Pattern Advisory Committee, an area business/community member, and a student from the feeder pattern high school.

Lead Principals. To effectively coordinate the feeder pattern councils and to assist their colleagues throughout the feeder pattern, the new role of lead principal has been initiated. These high-performing principals carry out a number of major responsibilities outside their own schools, including:

• Coordinating planning, problem-solving, inservice training, and other technical training assistance.

• Identifying and developing a network of community support.

• Planning and implementing a peer supervision and evaluation system for principals.

• Designing strategies to achieve and maintain faculty and student desegregation.

Feeder Pattern Technical Assistance and Support Model. Another program designed to further decentralize district and area administration and, at the same time, increase resources to schools and feeder patterns, is the Feeder Pattern Technical Assistance and Support Model. Initiated in 1988–89, this pilot is intended to improve the delivery of instruction at each school.

Technical assistance and support teams, composed of district and area office administrators with expertise in elementary and secondary education, vocational programs, student services, alternative education, and curriculum design, have been assigned to the Feeder Pattern Council or lead principal for each of the school system's twenty-four feeder patterns. Team members serve as primary contacts for each school in their feeder pattern in dealing with issues related to their specialty area.

New Roles for Teachers

One of the central issues in professionalization is attracting the best and brightest candidates into teaching. The continued professional emphasis in Dade County encourages outstanding teachers to stay in the classroom while enhancing their own career goals, as well as those of their peers.

Principal and Assistant Principal Selection. Programmatic and philosophical continuity are key components in the operation of any school. The promotion or retirement of a principal or assistant principal can dramatically affect a faculty's performance. As part of the collective bargaining agreement, teachers are now permanent members of school-site administrator selection teams. When a vacancy occurs for a Dade County principal or assistant principal, two teachers from the affected school are elected to sit with appropriate district and regional administrators to interview and hire the new administrator.

Facilities Planning. Teachers now also play a critical role in planning the future instructional use of school buildings in Dade County by participating on structural design committees for new and existing schools. Drawn from a pool of teachers that crosses all academic disciplines and grade levels, teacher appointees are involved in the review of various design stages of school construction. The most important innovation in this area is inclusion of teacher input in the preliminary design stage.

The effect of this provision takes on added significance in Dade County because of the 1988 passage of a record-setting $980 million school bond referendum. That money is being used to construct 49 new schools and to renovate the 259 schools already on line. Less than a year old in practice, teacher input already has dramatically changed several school efficiency and safety features, resulting in important modifications of school facilities, work areas, placement of science and home economics laboratories, and other pertinent considerations.

Lead Teachers, Teacher-Directors, and Teacher-Coordinators. New personnel classifications are a growing part of the Dade County landscape. In the county's satellite learning centers, schools at the work place, lead teachers now supervise the program's operation in cooperation with their host school's principal.

A new position of teacher-coordinator has been established for programs of districtwide scope. The first teacher-coordinator is supervising the Future Educators of America chapter program. All secondary schools in the district and nearly all elementary schools have established Future Educators of America chapters. Teacher-directors also remain part of the teachers' bargaining unit. They assume even more responsibility than do lead teachers by working under a county-level administrator and being exclusively responsible for the programs they direct, including the Teacher Education Center and the Dade Academy for the Teaching Arts.

Professional Development

Many programs in Dade County's professionalization movement are designed to help teachers reach higher levels of excellence and ultimately to help students gain a superior education. Several professional development initiatives focus on these goals.

Teacher Education Center. The district's Teacher Education Center (TEC) is governed by a council composed of teachers and administrators and administered by a teacher-director. The TEC provides the most recent research-based techniques in teaching, helping teachers to grow professionally and renew their certificates. A very special project falling under the auspices of the TEC is the Educational Research and Dissemination program, which trains teachers how to use research data in their instructional program. A unique aspect of this project is the involvement of the American Federation of Teachers (AFT). AFT provides such teacher training in collaboration with the union's local affiliate and the school district.

Teacher Peer Intervention and Assistance. The involvement of individuals in setting standards for their own performance is another touchstone of professionalism. In Dade County, the school system and the teachers' union cooperatively developed a diagnostic, prescriptive assessment process, which has been in place since 1982-83. Called the Teacher Assessment and Development System (TADS), it has paved the way for greater involvement in peer evaluation procedures, viewed to be essential in a professionalized environment.

Leadership Experience Opportunities (LEOs). Although opportunities for expanding professional horizons are increasing for classroom teachers, hiring qualified administrators remains an essential ingredient to the success of Dade's professionalization movement. Encouraging teachers to become administrators is yet another component in Dade's educational reformation process. The Leadership Experience Opportunities program for Teachers (LEO-T) provides qualified teachers a semester of administrative training experiences at each of two schools in the district.

Administrators' Professionalization. As the district pursues restructuring of education and teacher empowerment through the Professionalization of Teaching Task Force, a corollary group, the Administrators' Professional Development Committee (APDC), examines issues and makes recommendations regarding the professional development and evolving roles of school-site, area, and central-office administrators. APDC initiatives already underway include professional development programs and incentives, career ladder models, and more equitable managerial classification and compensation. Professional growth is provided through a number of leadership opportunities and internships, such as Leadership Experience Opportunities (LEO) programs, which provide professional development experiences for high-performing leaders—principals, assistant principals, and area and district administrators.

The district also offers Associate Executive Training Programs to prepare qualified principal and assistant principal candidates, as well as a Management Academy, which offers an extensive array of administrative professional development seminars and workshops.

Classifying and compensating all Dade principals at the same executive level (a national "first") supports the research on "effective schools," which shows that the single most important ingredient for an effective school is the able and visionary leadership of an effective principal.

* * *

School restructuring in Dade County is centered on school based management/shared decision making and on the professionalization of teaching. The intent is to achieve a fundamental and pervasive change in school structure and organization and a concomitant transformation in the institutional culture of schools. Supervision in Dade County has seen a fundamental transformation of the institutional culture of schools—and in the roles, relationships, and interactions of individuals within them.

Though the array of programs and policies may seem overwhelming or bewildering, Dade County's supervisory structure is built on sound theory and practice in many fields related to management and education. As stated earlier, one of the most influential of these forces was the recent emphasis on quality improvement in industry, both in the United States and in other countries. As a result of school restructuring in Dade County, empowered professional educators are finding schools to be more satisfying work places and more productive learning environments for children.

References

Argyris, C., and D.A. Schön. (1974). *Theory in Practice: Increasing Professional Effectiveness*. San Francisco: Jossey-Bass.

Argyris, C., and D.A. Schön. (1978). *Organizational Learning: A Theory of Action Perspective*. Reading, Mass.: Addison-Wesley.

Bennis, W.G. (1959). "Leadership Theory and Administrative Behavior." *Administrative Science Quarterly* 4: 259–301.

Byham, W.C. (1989). *Zapp: The Lightning of Empowerment*. Pittsburgh: Development Dimensions International Press.

Crosby, P.B. (1979). *Quality Is Free*. New York: Mentor.

Fitzgerald, L., and J. Murphy. (1982) *Installing Quality Circles: A Strategic Approach*. San Diego, Calif.: University Associates.

Herzberg, F., B. Mausner, and B. Snyderman. (1959). *The Motivation to Work*. New York: Wiley.

Knowles, M.S. (1980). *The Modern Practice of Adult Education: From Pedagogy to Andragogy*. New York: Cambridge Books.

McClelland, D.C. (1961). *The Achieving Society*. Princeton, N.J.: Van Nostrand.

Morgan, G. (1986). *Images of Organizations*. Beverly Hills, Calif.: Sage.

Naisbitt, J., and P. Aburdene. (1985). *Reinventing the Corporation*. New York: Warner Books.

Ouchi, W.G. (1982). *Theory Z*. New York: Avon.

Owens, R.G. (1991). *Organizational Behavior in Education*. 4th ed. Englewood Cliffs, N.J.: Prentice Hall.

Peters, T.J., and R.H. Waterman. (1982). *In Search of Excellence: Lessons Learned From America's Best Run Companies*. New York: Harper and Row.

Schein, E.H. (1985). *Organizational Culture and Leadership*. San Francisco: Jossey-Bass.
Schön, D.A. (1983). *The Reflective Practitioner*. New York: Basic Books.
Schön, D.A. (1987). *Educating the Reflective Practitioner*. San Francisco: Jossey-Bass.
Timar, T. (1990). "The Politics of Schooling Restructuring." In *Education Politics for the New Century*, edited by D.E. Mitchell and M.E. Goertz. New York: Falmer Press.
Vroom, V.H. (1964). *Work and Motivation*. New York: Wiley.
Walton, M. (1986). *The Deming Management Method*. New York: Dodd, Mead.

6

Peer Assistance in a Small District: Windham Southeast, Vermont

Susan James, Daniel Heller, and William Ellis

For the past ten years, our school district, the Windham Southeast Supervisory Union (WSESU), has been attempting to improve our supervision and evaluation practices. We devoted considerable time to Madeline Hunter's model of supervision and her research on teaching and learning. We also studied various models of summative evaluation. During the past five years, administrators frequently discussed supervision and evaluation and attended conferences on the subject.

Out of these discussions came a sincere dedication by all administrators to create effective procedures in supervision and evaluation. This unusual climate of receptivity and motivation, which was shared by all administrators, was viewed as a rare opportunity for the district. Central office administrators made it possible for a committee of teachers and administrators to collaborate on an assessment of district procedures in supervision and evaluation and on a pilot project in peer supervision.

This chapter describes two district projects that operated independently of each other for some time. First, the supervisory union high school English Department's Peer Assistance project, an approach to peer supervision, was developed over a two-year period by local teachers. Second, the Staff Support Group, a joint teacher/administrator committee discussing evaluation and supervision, met for several months and then adopted Peer Assistance as a district pilot project for the following school year. Peer Assistance became an official district program in 1989, and voluntary participation has grown. It has evolved into a redesign of the district's model for evaluation and supervision. Though ours is a small district, we believe our efforts can be instructive to others in similar situations and with similar needs.

Our district, the WSESU, is located in the southeastern corner of Vermont. The five small towns comprising the supervisory union have a combined population of 19,850. The WSESU includes elementary districts in the towns of Brattleboro, Dummerston, Putney, Vernon, and Guilford; a middle school for 7th and 8th graders; and a union high school.

A total of 3,200 students are served by the WSESU District. There are 285 certified teachers, 200 classified staff members, and 25 administrators. Six independent school district boards and one supervisory union board govern the five town elementary schools, the middle school and the high school district, and the supervisory union. The next section describes the peer assistance program that began at the high school.

A Grass Roots Effort from the English Department

Each spring, at the last meeting of the Brattleboro Union High School English Department, staff members set a theme for the following school year. In June 1986, we decided that *evaluation* and *supervision* were long overdue as subjects for our investigation.

When the year began the following September, we embarked on what was to become a major project in teacher empowerment and professional growth. Immediately we differentiated between supervision, a process of professional growth, and evaluation, a process of judging competence for employment status decisions. We knew that we needed more supervision. Our department consisted of sixteen teachers and one department head. The department head was responsible for evaluation, budget, program development, curriculum, and scheduling—along with supervision. He also taught two classes. Obviously, through no fault of his own, the time available for substantive, clinical supervision was minimal.

A department member suggested that we might observe each other teach as a means of mutual aid. The idea of peer supervision was born. The idea intrigued all of us. Weren't we trained professionals? Couldn't we learn from each other? Did we not have the necessary expertise to help each other with professional issues? We could be a department of sixteen supervisors. All was not that simple, however.

Peer supervision placed all of us in new roles. How did the department head fit into this project? There were conflicts over this issue from the start, but I am happy to say that we did resolve them. We reasoned that if supervision were to be a purely helpful, growth-oriented process, then its purpose would be compromised by the involvement of an evaluator. The department head was not a peer of other English teachers. There seemed to be an inherent contradiction in going to one's evaluator with a problem such as lack of classroom control. Wouldn't going to another teacher be more comfortable? Furthermore, aren't teachers qualified to deal with and solve their own problems? On the other hand, the department head had to be intimately involved in the project. Who was going to get us the time, money, substitutes, and support services to allow the experiment to work? This was a difficult new role for the department head: active support without direct involvement.

The new roles for teachers were equally uncomfortable. What should we do when we entered each other's classroom? Who were *we* to pass judgment on our peers? Who should observe whom? How does one do an observation? How should the observation be reported? Many of us feared being observed.

Despite the fears, we decided that we would all try peer observations at least once as observer and once as observee. The department set a date by which these observations should take place, and the department head provided some substitute support to free us from classes. After this first round, we came together as a full department to discuss what had happened. There was nearly universal enthusiasm for the idea of peer supervision.

We learned some practical lessons from our first experiences. Two stand out:

• Department members decided to form groups, thus reducing the logistical nightmare we had created. With the teachers in a group, we had a clearer picture of whom we were working with. Members of a group could cover classes for each other to allow one teacher time to observe another. A sense of closeness and commitment grew within groups because of their natural intimacy.

• A simple structure emerged that greatly facilitated our efforts. Each observation included a preconference and a post-conference. The preconference established the practical points of time and place, but more important, the *what* and *why* of the observation. At this conference, teachers would decide on the purpose and method of the observation. The post-conference ensured that something would happen as a result of the observation.

At this point, we were proceeding well. We had eliminated the possibility of evaluation from our peer supervision project, thus maintaining it as a process of professional guidance, help, and growth. We had imposed a nonrestrictive structure that allowed tremendous creativity and flexibility within the project. We needed leadership. Because of the conflicts mentioned earlier, we did not want the department head to run the program. Part of what made the project particularly valuable to us was its grass roots nature and teacher ownership. This provided focus and organization. Someone could now run meetings, collate efforts, and organize the project in general.

Other problems emerged, however, that were not so simply resolved. Peer supervision, especially with three-part observation cycles, takes time. Time usually means money—we essentially had neither. We needed to develop the leadership aspect of the project while not offending the official administration of the school. We were walking a fine line here; needing administrative support but fearing administrative control. Role conflict continued. The question of voluntarism emerged. Some of us, in our enthusiasm, wanted to insist that all department members participate; but we learned that the nonevaluative nature of the program demanded that participants be volunteers. You cannot force someone to give or take help.

We needed training in observation and conference techniques. In keeping with our philosophy of teacher ownership and professionalism, we largely trained ourselves. Department members would read, experiment, or go to workshops and then share their new knowledge with others. The money finally came, after much effort, from district special project funds and local industry. The time came from a noninstructional paraprofessional financed with these funds. Teachers could sign up for the paraprofessional to cover noninstructional duties such as study hall. Thus, we traded nonprofessional time for professional time.

Other issues included confidentiality and documentation. Because we were nonevaluative in nature, we agreed that all peer observations were strictly confidential, the business only of those teachers involved. The observed teacher had the prerogative to disclose the facts of the observation. All this helped to encourage participation and experimentation. Documentation was trickier. Several teachers were loath to have anything committed to writing. The group decided to leave the issue and method of documentation to the discretion of individual participants. However, we still had to document our efforts if we were to sell the program to the school board. We did this through statistical questionnaires, videotapes of the process at work, and personal anecdotal records written for publication.

The program grew in scope as it fed teacher empowerment. We were seeking control of our own professional growth. English Department members were conducting inservice programs for other departments, other school systems, and national conferences. We began to realize our potential as professionals. The program developed our self-esteem and a sense of personal worth and importance. Cycles of observation led to long-term professional and personal relationships. People who hardly knew one another were becoming close colleagues. We began to perceive our English programs as a continuum. Middle school teachers were working closely with senior high teachers. Cross-discipline work also began to emerge.

Having avoided too rigid a system for observation paid off. The program naturally expanded into other forms. Teachers served as guest lecturers for each other. We conducted some research projects. There were incidents of team teaching and teachers' exchanging teaching assignments from time to time. We were having the time of our lives and expanding our talents at the same time. Teachers exchanged materials as well as advice. Some classes shared literature experiences by writing to each other. The program was limited only by our imaginations. Peer supervision is fun.

There were any number of reasons why the program worked. I think the most important was the sense of teacher ownership and control. We were working for ourselves. We were helping each other because we wanted to. Our professional expertise was validated each time one colleague asked another for assistance. We were filling the need for supervision that the system's design would not permit. We had no desire to take anyone's job. The department head could do as much supervision as he could find time for, but we were going to supplement those efforts with efforts of our own. Our success led to a condition of continuous inservice when the program was working at its best. At any given time, about 20 percent of the teachers were taking a course, reading some professional publication, or participating in a workshop. Through peer supervision, we were more often in positions to share our expanding knowledge with each other.

The system as we conceived it was devoid of threat. The observed teacher invited the observer. There was no possibility of evaluation. All observations were strictly confidential; the process was based on trust and encouraged risk taking, for without risk there is no growth. Colleagues developed new concern and respect for each other. We were developing a learning community. Students saw us going in and out of each other's classrooms, learning from each other, and not being afraid to ask for help or give it. In one project involving students from different classes who worked with each other, several students remarked that they found asking their peers for help was easier than asking the teachers. This was our point exactly.

The primary purpose of peer supervision is to maximize one's expertise by sharing it with others. Peer supervision breathes life into a school system. It makes professionals. It is exciting. It works.

The next section outlines the development of peer assistance throughout the district.

Instructional Improvement Through the Years: A Collaborative Approach

1987–88 School Year

In 1987, administrators were increasingly frustrated with their inability to provide effective supervision to teachers because evaluation, which rarely improves instruction, consumed so much time that little was left for productive supervision. In addition, the hierarchical relationship between evaluator and teacher understandably created defensive barriers between the two people. It was difficult to take risks with a supervisor who was also the evaluator. Change requires risk and struggle before it occurs.

A committee of eighteen interested volunteers formed the Staff Support Group (SSG). Although initiated by administrators, the group was not to be dominated by them. The SSG membership was half teachers and half administrators. The Assistant Superintendent of Schools facilitated the meetings until February 1988, when the SSG work required considerable time outside of meetings. The SSG then elected a new chair from their ranks.

The purpose of the SSG was to find an effective and nonthreatening process to help teachers improve their professional performance. The group hoped to separate supervision from evaluation so that research, exploration, and risk taking could flourish. They also wanted to assist administrators focus more time on those teachers who desired and needed assistance from them.

The SSG met once a month. We wanted to meet when we were free to work for two hours or longer without other pressures or interruptions. The district paid for half-day substitutes for the teachers. We began in October 1987 and soon realized this was a long-range project requiring considerable commitment. Consistent attendance was a problem for half the year, but lessened as the year progressed and the SSG gained momentum and direction.

Our major challenges were to overcome communication and trust barriers and to persevere until we found a clear direction. The SSG was a diverse group of administrators and teachers from elementary and secondary schools, general and specialized teaching disciplines, and special education and Chapter 1. Many had not worked together before. This diversity fueled considerable discussion. It was necessary to bring all members to the same level of knowledge to develop productive working relationships. We needed common definitions and a shared purpose, both of which take time and tolerance to develop.

The SSG devoted the fall meetings to discussing and defining supervision and evaluation and surveying all district employees. We asked employees to tell us how they were evaluated and supervised, to assess the strengths and weaknesses of these processes, and to provide suggestions for improvement.

In January 1988, an SSG subcommittee tabulated results of the survey. Responses indicated that district employees were dissatisfied with the time and depth devoted to the supervision and evaluation they were receiving. There was a variety of suggestions to provide professional assistance in ways other than traditional evaluation and supervision models. Most of these ideas were based on peers' helping each other. The most frequent suggestion was for the committee to provide information and opportunity to learn about the Peer Assistance program being conducted by the English Department in our district high school.

Our meetings in January and February of 1988 concentrated on educating ourselves about supervision and evaluation issues of interest to the SSG and the district staff. We read many articles and shared information. (See the Bibliography for a list of useful resources.)

We then discussed our district's process for evaluation and supervision, examining strengths and weaknesses with increased knowledge about alternatives and the beliefs of other district employees. We explored models that separated evaluation and supervision, and we brainstormed possibilities. This was a difficult time for the SSG, because a clear direction was still not obvious. The more we learned, the more overwhelming this challenge became—despite our clear dedication to succeed.

Evaluation is charged with emotional overtones and produces tension and defensive behavior, especially in a committee of teachers and administrators. There were disagreements, misunderstandings, and frustrations as we struggled to communicate with each other. We learned the importance of separating evaluation and supervision, and of concentrating on only one of these at a time. Gradually the SSG began to develop trust, communicate effectively, and clarify its purpose.

At the end of March, Carl Glickman presented a two-day workshop in our district on supervision and evaluation, attended by forty district employees including administrators, teachers, counselors, and paraprofessionals. Participants worked in small groups and wrote ten Action Plans aimed at improving supervision in the district; some plans also included evaluation.

The workshop proved to be pivotal for the SSG. In April, we reviewed the ten Action Plans. Many paralleled our work, but many of these plans gave us new ideas for improving supervision. Most helpful was the variety of ways the workshop organized the implementation of participants' goals. This structure helped us clarify our plan and gave us confidence in our previous ideas. We decided to conduct a district-wide pilot project on Peer Assistance during the 1988–89 school year. This project was based on the peer supervision project of our secondary English Department, discussed earlier.

In the spring of 1988, the SSG wrote an Action Plan. Our decision to put evaluation aside until the project was completed allowed us to focus on one pressing need expressed by all employees: peer supervision. Key teachers in the English Department's Peer Assistance program were invited to become members of the SSG and help us specify our Action Plan. This plan is summarized as follows:

• *Goal*: To establish a supervisory process for all staff members in the district, which will encourage both professional growth and enhance learning.

• *Definitions*: *Supervision* = a nonevaluative process for the purpose of improving instruction; generally, it is an ongoing process occurring every year. *Evaluation* = professional judgment on a staff member's competence for the purpose of determining job status.

• *Mission Statement*: We believe a supervision process leads to professional growth and enhances learning. Staff members will use the expertise of their colleagues and the services of the community. We believe that growth occurs by taking risks within a supportive, professional network. The supervision process is collaborative but not evaluative.

The timeline of the Action Plan ran from May 1988 to August 1989. It specified communication with district employees through writing and oral presentations, training, project completion, SSG recommendations, and initiation of study of evaluation procedures.

1988–89 School Year

The beginning of the 1988–89 school year was devoted to education and motivation of district employees regarding the Peer Assistance pilot project.

On August 31, all teachers met in the high school auditorium for various presentations. One of these was by an active member of the English Department's Peer Assistance program. She spoke to the teachers about Peer Assistance, describing what it is, how it works, why it works, and why the English teachers were so excited about it.

On September 2, the SSG sent a short memo to all principals and department heads, telling them that an SSG member would be asking them for time to discuss the pilot project with teachers and paraprofessionals. Also in the memo was information concerning the administrators' role in the Peer Assistance pilot project. Administrators could also consider volunteering; Peer Assistance is not limited to teaching behaviors. Administration support would be needed in helping project participants find time and class coverage to carry out the project.

Administrators were also told that they would not be directly involved in the work of volunteer pairs, unless a pair requested it. Administrators would still be responsible for evaluation of teachers, which may also include supervision by the administrator. This would be completely separate from the Peer Assistance pilot project. There was clear support from all administrators.

The SSG then divided the district's schools and departments among its members and gave additional short, informal presentations to small groups during September.

The presentations included a list of responsibilities for volunteers working in pairs. These included:

- Attend fall training and follow-up workshop.
- Write an Action Plan during training.
- Complete at least one full clinical supervision cycle.
- Read *Techniques in the Clinical Supervision of Teachers*, by Keith Acheson and Meredith Gall (New York: Longman, 1987).
- Participate in project evaluation.

Soon after the presentations, the SSG collected names of volunteers for the pilot project. There were 100 volunteers, one-third of our teaching staff, representing every school in the district. Though we were excited so many had volunteered, we would have to make some adjust-ments to our Action Plan. Because the district did not have enough money or substitute teachers to hold the training during school hours, training was held from 4 to 9 p.m. at school expense. An additional training session was held for those who could not attend the first session. Training was conducted by an English teacher, who was an active Peer Assistant participant.

The majority of those trained were teachers, but administrators, counselors, and paraprofessionals also participated. Communication and collaboration were begun not only between close colleagues, but also between some who worked in different buildings and with differing content and age groups.

Short presentations on the pilot project on Peer Assistance were given to the districtwide school board by the assistant superintendent and the SSG chair. School board members offered support and interest.

In January 1989, we held a two-hour workshop for Peer Assistance project volunteers. In preparation for the workshop, volunteers com-pleted a questionnaire soliciting their desires for the workshop content and asking them what problems and successes they were experiencing as Peer Assistance participants. In the workshop, small groups shared specific activities that worked well and problems they were experienc-ing. Some suggestions emerged for solutions for these difficulties. The major problem Peer Assistance participants encountered was finding the time. This was also a problem for the project organizers. There was never time to conduct support groups for project volunteers in the individual schools. These small groups would have helped uncertain volunteers solve problems and share ideas.

In March, when the pilot project ended, a summary questionnaire was sent to everyone who attended the Peer Assistance training in the fall. The questionnaire results were as follows:

• About half of those who received Peer Assistance training com-pleted the entire project.

• All the volunteers believed the pre- and post-observation confer-ences were valuable for focusing observation and providing specific strategies for the observed volunteer.

• In addition to clinical supervision cycles, Peer Assistance volun-teers attended other workshops, team taught, collaborated on curricu-lum and specific students, shared professional literature, and visited teachers outside their team.

• All participants said Peer Assistance was an excellent means of clarifying and solving problems and increasing collaboration and communication between colleagues. All said they would like to continue their involvement.

In early spring 1989, the SSG evaluated these results and designed a plan for expansion of Peer Assistance in the next school year, 1989–90. There was no money available to hire a district Peer Assistance coordinator, even part time. The committee members believed it important to move the Peer Assistance coordination from the district level to each school and department. In each school and department, Peer Assistance volunteers would form a committee to share knowledge and to encourage participants. The committee would select a leader to coordinate activities they chose to undertake.

Each Peer Assistance leader would be part of a district Peer Assistance Steering Committee, with the purpose of keeping Peer Assistance active and facilitating communication between schools and departments. In May 1989, representative Peer Assistance volunteers from each building or department, along with the SSG chair, met to review and refine recommendations of the SSG for expansion of the Peer Assistance project. The Peer Assistance representatives decided to meet again in early September to get the Peer Assistance Committees started and to arrange training sessions for new participants. The SSG chair would then let the district and school Peer Assistance Committees take over the project coordination.

In May, the SSG sent a letter to district employees, containing the results of the pilot project and the recommendations for expanding Peer Assistance in 1989–90. In addition to the commencement of district and school Peer Assistance Committees, recommendations were also made in the following areas: training of new participants, time to participate in the project, variations of Peer Assistance, recertification credit, and a mentor program for new teachers.

Both committees, the SSG and the Peer Assistance representatives, agreed that administrative support was crucial to the survival of the project. Administrators could not pressure employees to participate in Peer Assistance, but administrators must willingly help participants find time and release money and personnel for training and class coverage.

At a meeting in June 1989, all administrators, including the superintendent and the assistant superintendent, agreed to commit time and money for 1989–90 for three clinical supervision cycles for each Peer Assistance participant and for training of new participants. There were not enough resources to provide teachers with release time for all Peer

Assistance activities; but it was critical that enough time, money, and moral support be committed to the project by administration so that the project would have the opportunity to thrive.

1989–90 School Year

At the beginning of the 1989–90 school year, all district teachers and administrators attended a lecture and discussion by Carl Glickman. He encouraged participation in Peer Assistance. Glickman also met informally with the SSG and Peer Assistance representatives from all district schools to assist in the expansion of Peer Assistance.

In two early fall meetings, the SSG and Peer Assistance representatives from each school planned implementation. Peer Assistance leaders held information meetings in their schools. In October 1989, twenty additional volunteers were trained in the Peer Assistance clinical supervision techniques.

As in the previous year, Peer Assistance participants expanded the model and used a variety of techniques to assist each other. The district Peer Assistance Committee met monthly to discuss ways to help Peer Assistance teachers and to encourage new participants. The district committee strove to define its role.

Though Peer Assistance activity grew during 1989–90, especially in the elementary schools, participation was not as great as we anticipated. The district suffered two serious blows that diverted considerable energy and time from the program. First, negotiations for teachers' contracts were prolonged and difficult and remained unsettled until late fall. Second, in November, the district lost its superintendent of fifteen years to a sudden heart attack. In addition, one school had a major building project, and three schools were undergoing state approval, which requires almost all staff's nonteaching time. Survival of Peer Assistance during this difficult year was a major accomplishment. Peer Assistance was alive but still fragile. We realized it would require careful nurturing and a more comprehensive look.

Two years before, in 1988, the SSG had discussed a cyclical evaluation model, creating considerable interest in investigating this model for possible adoption in our district. Under this system, summative evaluation for most professional staff members would occur every three years, with the two years between evaluations devoted to supervision. When involved in supervision, teachers, or other professional staff members, would choose one of several supervision activities, one of which is Peer Assistance, and design their individual Professional Development Plan for the year.

In the winter of 1990, the district was ready to discuss evaluation in depth. After two years of concentration on Peer Assistance, it was clear our annual evaluation procedures must be redesigned to allow peer supervision room to grow and to improve instruction in more classrooms. A few district schools successfully experimented with cyclical evaluation in the 1989–90 school year. A committee of administrators met regularly to define the model. All professional staff members in each school held discussions about cyclical evaluation.

The goals of our cyclical evaluation model are:

• To allow professional staff members the freedom to *actively pursue* professional improvement, to collaborate with colleagues, and to take risks without fear of evaluation.

• To improve instruction and learning.

• To allow evaluators more time to concentrate on assisting fewer staff members in more depth in any one year.

1990–91 School Year

The district has a new superintendent who supports the growth of Peer Assistance and the new cyclical evaluation/supervision model. We decided to use our new cyclical evaluation/supervision model with all professional staff members in all district schools for the 1990–91 school year and to assess its merits in the spring. We believed that Peer Assistance could grow and succeed if it were carefully integrated into our new evaluation/supervision model. Because the focus was concentrated on each school or department rather than on the district, the struggling district Peer Assistance Committee became unnecessary.

In November 1990 Pam Robbins gave a two-day workshop on Peer Coaching to thirty teachers representing each district school. It successfully expanded thinking about what Peer Assistance can be. We recognize the need to improve our communication skills so that collaborative teams and pairs can be as productive as possible. This will also influence the success of other district projects in curriculum, instruction, and restructuring.

In the spring of 1991, administration and professional staff members evaluated our new cyclical model of evaluation and supervision. There was overwhelming support for the new system and agreement that it is better than traditional annual evaluation for all professional staff members. The level of personal commitment to professional development seemed to increase. A wider variety of projects was undertaken, many of them involving Peer Assistance and collaboration.

To assess the value of Peer Assistance and our cyclical evaluation/supervision system, we must complete a full three-year cycle. Our first year of integrating Peer Assistance with our new supervision and evaluation program has been very encouraging. Is this resulting in an improvement in instruction and learning? We believe it is, but we must monitor it for two more years to be certain.

* * *

Peer Assistance participants are convinced that continuation is not only valuable but essential in our schools. A major benefit of the program is its positive influence on the climate of the school. It creates a spirit of cooperation and collaboration among staff members. It is a springboard to open discussions of education and helps educators generate ideas for curriculum projects, professional development, and school improvement. Peer Assistance participants can risk change, because risk is shared with colleagues who have similar jobs and who do not evaluate each other.

Some critical challenges that face public education demand immediate attention and creative solutions. Peer Assistance will not solve these problems, because it is intended to improve specific instructional practices of participating teachers. But if Peer Assistance is widely accepted and used in a school or school district, it can stimulate the atmosphere of receptivity, trust, and creativity necessary to solve major problems.

The most significant value of Peer Assistance is to the students. Peer Assistance improves instruction, because teachers are looking at what they are doing and analyzing it with a peer. The same theory underlying teaching students metacognitive strategies as a learning aid is at work in Peer Assistance. If teachers review and evaluate their teaching practices with colleagues, instruction will improve.

The survival of a peer supervision project depends on several critical factors:

1. Peer supervision must be voluntary: it takes energy, dedication, time, and a desire to make it work.

2. Administration must be supportive and understand its own role.

3. The steering committee, in our case the Staff Support Group, should be made up of teachers and administrators.

4. The committee needs to write specific and distinct definitions of evaluation and supervision, so that communication is clear.

5. There should be a facilitator committed to the steering committee and the peer supervision project. The facilitator's task is to organize, coordinate, and communicate, which requires considerable time and perseverance.

Peer Assistance is effective because it is highly variable and adaptable to the individual educator's needs. It is controlled by the person being supervised, not by an evaluator; thus, risks can be taken. Our district's effort has demonstrated that a small school district without the resources to hire a coordinator can create a major program that enhances teaching and learning. It is difficult to become a good educator, and to remain one is exhausting and isolating. Peer Assistance can give more educators the opportunity to excel by learning from colleagues without fear of being judged primarily by mistakes.

Bibliography

Acheson, K.A., and M.D. Gall. (1987). *Techniques in the Clinical Supervision of Teachers*. New York: Longman.

Brandt, R.S. (February 1987). "On Teachers Coaching Teachers: A Conversation with Bruce Joyce." *Educational Leadership* 44: 12–17.

Brandt, R.S. (February 1987). "Learning With and From One Another." *Educational Leadership* 44:3.

Cook, G.E. (February 1985). "Teachers Helping Teachers: A Training Program in Peer Supervision." Paper presented at the 65th Annual Conference of the Association of Teacher Educators, Las Vegas, Nev.

Ellis, E.C., and others. (March 1979). "Peer Observation: A Means for Supervisory Acceptance." *Educational Leadership* 36: 423–426.

Garmston, R.J. (February 1987). "How Administrators Support Peer Coaching." *Educational Leadership* 44: 18–26.

Glickman, C.D. (1990). *Supervision of Instruction: A Developmental Approach*. Boston: Allyn and Bacon.

Goldhammer, R., et al. (1980). *Clinical Supervision*. 2nd ed. New York: Holt, Rinehart, and Winston.

Hunter, M. (1982). *Mastery Teaching*. El Segundo, Calif.: TIP Publications.

Knoll, M. (March 1988). "Does Peer Coaching Leave the Principal on the Bench?" *ASCD Update* 30: 2.

McBeath, M., and D. Carter. (August 1981). "Staff Development Program Evaluation Application of a Peer Supervision Program." Paper presented at the Annual Conference of the American Psychological Association, Los Angeles.

McPaul, S.A., and J.M. Cooper. (April 1984). "Peer Clinical Supervision: Theory vs. Reality." *Educational Leadership* 41: 4–9.

Raney, P., and P. Robbins. (May 1989). "Professional Growth and Support Through Peer Coaching." *Educational Leadership* 46, 8: 35–38.

Reavis, C.A. (1978). *Teacher Improvement Through Clinical Supervision*. Bloomington, Ind.: Phi Delta Kappa Educational Foundation.

Rothberg, R.A. (November 1985). "Improving School Climate and Reducing Teacher Isolation." Paper presented at the 10th Annual Meeting of the National Council of States on Inservice Education, Denver.

Sergiovanni, T.J., ed. (1975). Professional Supervision for Professional Teachers. Alexandria, Va.: ASCD.

Sergiovanni, T.J., ed. (1982). *Supervision of Teaching*. Alexandria, Va.: ASCD.

Sergiovanni, T.J., and R.J. Starratt. (1979). *Supervision: Human Perspectives*. New York: McGraw-Hill.

Showers, B. (1985). "Teachers Coaching Teachers." *Educational Leadership* 42: 43–48.

Smyth, W.J. (April 1986). "Peer Clinical Supervision as 'Empowerment' versus 'Delivery of a Service.'" Paper presented at the 67th Annual Meeting of the American Educational Research Association, San Francisco.

Sullivan, C.G. (1980). *Clinical Supervision: A State of the Art Review*. Alexandria, Va.: ASCD.

Wagner, C.A., and J.P. Smith, Jr. (June 1979). "Peer Supervision: Toward More Effective Training." *Counselor Education and Supervision* 18: 288–293.

7

School Renewal in Chaska, Minnesota, Independent District #112

Jean A. King and Carol J. Ericson

In 1989, the National Education Association (NEA) selected Chaska, Minnesota, Independent School District #112 to be part of the national NEA Learning Lab project. The $5,000 award provided a tangible reward for years of work in the district, but more important was the national recognition the district received. The schools in Chaska are actively engaged in renewal that will enable them to better serve the children of their community as they approach the next century. Supervision has played a central role in this process, contributing to the sense of synergy and forward movement many staff members report. The lessons Chaska has learned in the past decade—often the hard way—may prove instructive for other districts interested in effecting change.

The ideas in this chapter come from many people who are participating in the ongoing transformation of District #112—teachers, principals, central office administrators, and school board members. First, we discuss the district's educational context; second, the factors that have affected the ongoing change process; and third, suggestions for supervision based on the district's experience.

The World of District #112

To make sense of the changes the district has experienced requires some awareness of its educational context. Minnesota has long been known as the "Brainpower State," reflecting an historical commitment to quality public education and student learning. Garrison Keillor was not kidding when he said that all the children in Lake Wobegon were "above average"; until recently, standardized test scores gave Minnesota's school community reason for pride. On average, the state supports its schools better than most; and, since the Progressive era, its districts have been known for living on education's cutting edge. Innovations abound: the "Minnesota miracle" of school finance in 1971; educational choice programs, including open enrollment and postsecondary enrollment options; widespread site or school based management; differentiated staffing; and outcome-based education (OBE).

This is not to say, however, that school districts in Minnesota are without problems. The issue of funding equity is so highly contentious that seventy-two districts are currently on opposite sides of a court battle to force some resolution of the issue. A legislative report released in 1989 pointed to slipping standardized test scores and some small districts' being unable to provide the mandated state curriculum. With more than 430 districts still functioning and a new state administration, fears of consolidation loom on the horizon. Increasing numbers of minority students challenge many districts to make good the claim that education can lead to a better future, and underlying concerns about how to eliminate racism and intolerance and how to promote true school integration cannot be ignored.

District #112 represents five diverse communities at the western edge of the Minneapolis-St. Paul "Twin Cities" metropolitan area. The school system serves nearly 4,000 students living within its 80 square miles. Elementary enrollment is growing by more than 10 percent each year; a new elementary school opened in the fall of 1990 to help accommodate the increasing numbers of students. The district's facilities include an Early Childhood Center, housing kindergarten programs; three elementary schools serving grades 1 through 5; a middle school housing grades 6 through 8; and a high school for grades 9 through 12. Commitment to education is high in the District #112 community. The community supported two referendums in three years, as well as approving a bond issue to build the new school. The dropout rate is less than 2 percent.

Teachers and administrators working for the past ten years in District #112 have witnessed a major transformation: a move from a traditional labor-management division of school activities to a unified change effort involving teachers, administrators, and school board members. This effort focused on preparing students for the 21st century. Two events—one constructive, the other traumatic—provided the necessary framework for initiating the change.

The constructive event was the formulation of Project 21st Century, which began in 1982 when a group of community and district volunteers began to meet regularly to discuss what District #112 schools should look like in the next century. The group tackled future-oriented questions like "What if you woke up tomorrow morning and everyone could read?" and "What if everyone suddenly was able to get along with his neighbor?" The futures discussions involved ten to twenty participants and "operated outside of everything else," as one group member noted. Within two years, the group had generated a new philosophy, mission statement, and set of educational goals for the district that were adopted by the school board in 1984.

The other critical event also occurred in 1984 as the Project 21st Century products were nearing completion. The Chaska Education Association (CEA) went on strike for twenty-two days. In the opinion of some who lived through it, this divisive and emotional walkout proved to be a turning point in the eventual transformation of the district. One board member posits that "it is what opened the door to this opportunity" because it released tension that had accumulated in the district and in all likelihood encouraged the retirement of the longtime superintendent. The arrival of a new superintendent, coupled with the newly revised district mission and goal statements and the readiness of many teachers to "put the strike behind them," resulted in change activities that have given District #112 the reputation in Minnesota as a district "on the move."

Enabling Factors in the Process of School Renewal

The experiences of teachers and administrators in District #112 mirror other discussions of school change (e.g., Glickman 1990; Miles and Louis 1990; Sergiovanni 1990) and point to five enabling factors for the renewal experienced during the past decade: (1) a common vision, (2) a superintendent committed to collaborative decision making, (3) a unified district team, (4) time and resources to support the change process, and (5) supervisory "tough love."

A Common Vision

District #112's Project 21st Century, which began as a small group of committed individuals "doing their thing" outside the day-to-day operations of the district, created a "vague vision" of what education needed to look like at the beginning of the next century. The group, including representatives of the faculty, administration, school board, and community, "set aside all that we knew about schools" to bring a clean slate to the planning process. As one person commented, "We had no roadmap. It was by the seat of our pants." But after two years of discussion that included reviews by seventeen community groups, the vision was written down, in its shortest form, as follows: "Interdisciplinary outcome-based curriculum delivered to flexible multi-age groups by teacher-directed instructional teams."

In actuality, the vision comprised two pieces: first, the statement of "essential beliefs and values" and accompanying supports that would form the conceptual base for the transformation of District #112 schools and, second, a process that would lead to this transformation. The list of beliefs included ideas like "Risk takers are respected" and "When in doubt, trust, . . . don't blame." The support list included site based management, staff and curriculum development, and teacher education institutions.

Equally important was the creation of a *process* for change—an open-ended, inclusive process that included all actors in the district, collaborating to solve problems as they arose. One member of the planning group, in reflecting on the completed vision statement, put it this way:

> By that time, we hit the wall of planning, and the question became how to operationalize what we were discussing. . . . The structure and discipline was in place for planning the future. It was one of the tools in the toolkit to get us [beyond the strike].

Both the content of the vision and the process that led to it, then, were essential because people involved in the district now knew the changes they were after and how they would work on making them happen. This "super-vision" continues to guide the entire process of change.

A Superintendent Committed to Collaborative Decision Making

Arriving in 1985, the new superintendent faced a district that had recently survived a divisive teachers' strike, a district that had lived for years with a traditional "us-them" division between faculty and administration. And yet, in the wake of Project 21st Century, this same district had publicly committed itself to creating a different school world. The new superintendent took the district at its word. People agree that her role was critical:

> We all felt when she came that we had the missing piece. She was critical to getting the new mission used, to saying, "This is what guides our decision making."

She had the spirit of the process and would have invented it if we hadn't. . . .

How did the superintendent go about the task? She broadened the base of decision making to include teachers in new ways, and she listened to what they said. She paid personal attention to teachers, speaking directly with them and, according to one board member, "caring about them as professionals and colleagues."

Within a month after the superintendent arrived in the district, meetings began among CEA leaders, school board members, and administrators to build a base for new relationships. Fifty-four conflict issues were identified, categorized, and discussed; and action plans were developed for their resolution. Follow-up sessions later in the year tracked progress toward the mutual goals. As contract negotiations again approached, association and school board leaders were trained in collaborative bargaining techniques. The resulting contract included a proposal by the teachers' association to mutually create a staff development and evaluation plan for the district.

New opportunities that acknowledged the experience and professionalism of teachers were created. Several teachers moved into district program coordination roles in the areas of language arts, gifted and talented, and parent liaison. For the first time, teachers were added to the management team, which met twice monthly to guide operations of the district. Later, as the district increased its commitment to decentralized management, teachers in two schools took direct administrative roles in addition to their teaching responsibilities. Throughout it all, the superintendent's door was always open. She listened and responded to the human needs generated by increasing change.

In the fall of 1986, all teachers received a personal copy of the Carnegie Report, *A Nation Prepared: Teachers for the 21st Century*, with a cover letter from the superintendent and presidents of the Chaska and Minnesota Education Associations urging their response to this challenge. By December, teachers in each school had thoroughly discussed the report. A districtwide synthesis of teacher reaction and input resulted in 1986 in the commission of what is called the *Chaska Productivity Study*, using a business perspective to identify ways in which teachers thought they could increase their professional productivity (Dahl & Associates 1987). All 200 faculty members contributed data for the study that resulted in the identification of avenues through which restructuring might occur—for example, by decreasing the time teachers spent on nonteaching tasks. These data, from teachers themselves, brought restructuring front and center in the district, and the study was even reported in *Education Week* (June 17, 1987). No longer were change efforts "off to the side"; both the rationale and roadmap for reform had come directly from classroom teachers.

With the direct connection made, the superintendent's supervisory focus, in an important sense, included every teacher in District #112. Teachers commented:

> [The superintendent] established connection with teachers. They believed her, trusted her, and were willing to listen. . . . If she said [something], they would consider it and wouldn't completely dismiss it.

> Teachers have so little belief that they can do it themselves [i.e., make decisions, changes], they need to have their decisions respected. The superintendent's acceptance was critical.

> [The superintendent] allowed all these things to happen. . . . You create a milieu where teachers can produce ideas, then you get out of the way and let them try them out.

This role for the superintendent was not without risks. As one administrator noted: "The chain of command is kind of muddied now—it used to be cleaner." The district's six principals face new challenges when teachers they supervise sometimes know more about district-level change activities than they do. For this reason, the superintendent needs to work closely with building administrators. Some people wonder, too, if such direct working ties could exist between superintendent and teachers in a larger district. Finally, the question of what will happen next—since this superintendent moved to a nearby district (June 1990)—worries those who remain behind. In a "simple association," some people "have tied the [change] process" to the superintendent and worry that, with her gone, the process will end.

Others are not concerned:

> I was really down when I heard about [the superintendent's] leaving, but now I think it's going to be fine. She's enabled us to stand on our own feet. We won't allow any superintendent to go back. There'd be open revolt. [The superintendent] says, "*You* are the masters of change. *You* control your future."

> [The superintendent's] gift to us is to give us our freedom.

A Unified Team of District Personnel and Community Members

The teachers' strike pitted teachers against administrators in a classic enactment of the conflict between labor and management. Those who cling to "this old tape, the us-them view"—whether they are teachers or administrators—can effectively block the school renewal process. The Chaska experience emphasizes that districts must move beyond such thinking before real change can take place. One teacher put it succinctly:

> Everybody has to be willing to give up a bit of the glory for the sake of the team. . . . It's impossible for individual teachers to do school renewal alone in their classrooms. We can only do it if we unite with other teachers, administrators, parents, and students.

With District #112's students as the continuing focus, change activities seek to meaningfully involve all appropriate stakeholders in the schools' future. The organizational structure is "not a top-down system, but a flattened-out model." At best, principals and union leadership work together, on an ongoing basis, with the central office, teachers, school board, and the community. A teacher compared his image of the professional change "team" to a district athletic team that recently made it to the state championships. The team had no exceptional individual players, but it did have five or six good plays and exceptional teamwork. The coaches worked together collaboratively, without placing blame, and concentrated on what the players did well.

For example, in 1988 teacher and administrative members of the management team reviewed restructuring proposals from thirteen teacher teams comprising more than fifty faculty members. Using external funds the district had received, the team awarded summer planning grants for new delivery systems to one-year projects in one middle and three elementary schools. Central office administrators facilitated training for the teams and did the legwork to provide research and other resources teachers requested. Within the teams themselves, many of which had never worked together before, teachers took a division-of-labor approach, using the Myers-Briggs (1976) analysis of individual team members' strengths to increase their knowledge and appreciation of each other's talents.

Each program addressed differentiation of roles and increased parental involvement. Teachers tapped into parent resources through preschool goal-setting conferences, during which they listened to parents provide information about their children, their families, and their educational goals. This approach effectively solidified the parent-teacher team and resulted in increased home-school communication throughout the year and a higher incidence of parent-initiated communication, especially regarding family issues likely to affect the child's learning. The district's smallest elementary school, lacking a certified principal, forged a site-based-management agreement with the school board and formed a management council of parents and staff. The parents have proven to be a source of encouragement and ideas; mutual respect among educators and parents is reportedly high.

When teamwork doesn't materialize, the process can stall. On the one hand, principals can block the process by stopping questions, limiting teacher decision making, and "perpetuating the open secrets in a building." On the other hand, teachers can refuse to take part in what they may see as one in a continuing line of change efforts. Some people in District #112 remain distrustful of administrators.

> One person confirms that when teachers make decisions, they don't get blamed as much as a principal who might make the same decision. . . . Teachers need to see that administrators and teachers are each working toward the same goals of improving education for kids.

Team spirit has grown in District #112 in recent years. The school board has "supported the process," according to one teacher, but, being an autonomous group aware of its policy-setting role, has not tried to control it. Some fear that the "CEA doesn't trust the process." But others sense that the association, moving far from the confrontation embodied in its earlier strike, "is now leading changes." And what of the teachers who are taking part in deciding what their schools and teaching roles will become?

Clearly there are tensions between the classroom-focused role of traditional teaching and the more individualized, decision-oriented role that many District #112 teachers are experimenting with. As part of the broader district "team," teachers experience this tension:

> Teachers are told that as teachers we're all the same—same pay, same load, same hours; but people know that's not true. Yet the system is set up to celebrate sameness and discourage differences. . . . The comfort of the profession is an opiate.

> People out on a limb are ostracized by the group. They've betrayed their tribe. . . . You're not supposed to do things that make them [other teachers] look bad, like working extra hours to make a new approach work.

As one person commented, "The [change] process was not tainted by the strike; it got tainted when certain teachers were identified as elite, separate from everyone else." The fact is that *everyone* who participates in renewal activities—teachers, principals, central office administrators, and board members—is at risk and must be open to "learning new tricks."

"Sometimes you just get tired and wish you could do things without changing the rules," lamented one principal, noting the importance of strong self-concepts for both teachers and administrators who alter their traditional roles.

Time and Resources for Adult-to-Adult Communication and Change-Related Activities

The following comment captures the emotion of a career educator confronting the change process:

> We tell teachers to get out of boxes [i.e., traditional roles], then give them no time, no resources to do anything different. . . . Teachers feel overwhelmed, overworked, and underappreciated.

People *can* engage in school renewal before students arrive in the morning, after they leave in the afternoon, and on evenings and weekends; but if, over time, those are the only hours available for such work, frustration is a likely by-product. As another teacher put it, "Yes, kids come first, but you need to have time to plan." In District #112, a state grant in 1985 was important because it "freed up planning time when we had reached the limit of where we could go without money. . . . Many pieces had been done, but we needed to pull things together." Since that time, the district has aggressively sought outside funding to release teachers from classroom activities so they can participate in development projects. In an important sense, grant money has funded change in the past five years.

Cray Research underwrote the Chaska Productivity Study, and First Bank System funded teacher productivity training. Later, Cray made an additional grant for the district to plan the role of teacher interns within differentiated teams. Two years of funding from the State of Minnesota initiated an alternative delivery system pilot, and Medtronic Foundation grants supported the evolution of the project for two more years. A state grant was awarded to the district for a teacher mentorship demonstration project. A companion grant to Augsburg College, Minneapolis, from the State Board of Teaching helped cement a partnership between Chaska and the college. This partnership resulted in the creation of a year-long teacher internship prior to certification, as well as other improvements in teacher induction. The research and development function is fully integrated into the central office, and a full-time coordinator generated eight proposals for outside funding in the 1989-90 school year.

Though releasing teachers during the school day is an important step, the obvious problem that has now arisen stems from the fact that they are periodically absent from their classes, and students either have substitutes or a study hall. One District #112 board member reported "taking a lot of flak from parents" because teachers are often out of their classrooms. To the extent possible, one solution is to build such work into certain teachers' schedules to guarantee time on a regular basis for change activities.

If District #112's experience is indicative, supervision in the form of personal support may prove to be a critical resource during the change process:

> Teachers are taking tremendous risks, but are naive about the fact that change hurts. You can't always control change. Teachers think people should be safe, shouldn't get hurt.

> The new roles are disquieting, discomforting for teachers *and* principals. . . . Give us permission to be angry or scared, anxious, to question anything . . . in a framework of respectful dialogue. We all need someone to say it's okay to be down.

Part of the superintendent's success stemmed from her ability to provide this support both to district teachers and administrators. As one person put it, "The organization has to be set up for that kind of personal interaction; it worked here."

Supervisory "Tough Love"

The traditional roles of accountability and evaluation continue in the district because state and school board mandates—and good practice—require that they must. At the same time, in developing working relations among staff and creating the unified district team, the superintendent in some areas moved beyond a hierarchical model of authority to an inclusive, collegial model. The side-by-side existence of these approaches has made teachers and administrators alike uncomfortable. People agree: The superintendent demonstrated "tough leadership."

> She was willing to make tough choices, which is part of why people trust her. She created belief. The message is, "Be competent." If you're competent, there are many opportunities. We'll pay attention to what you say.

As discussed before, people also agreed that the superintendent cared. Teachers trusted her, knowing that she listened carefully to what they said. The challenge was to convince teachers that they "have real power should [they] choose to exercise it," to give them the confidence to change in dramatic ways, but to help them see that, in the process of change, they must maintain high levels of professional performance.

This "tough love" approach to supervision has confused some because "people don't believe you can be tough and caring at the same time." One person noted two responses to unpopular decisions:

They say, "She [the superintendent] couldn't do that" and blame someone else [typically another administrator]; or they say she's two-faced. We haven't learned how to be honest with people.

If teachers are to participate in supervising their colleagues, they need extensive training, noted one teacher: "It's like the family of an alcoholic; teachers may be highly critical of an incompetent peer, but it's kept in the family." Making teachers responsible for working with that individual will require new skills in collaboration. A related problem comes from teachers who become complacent when they interpret positive feedback as support for the status quo. How can administrators and teachers make their colleagues feel comfortable with existing classroom practice, but simultaneously motivate them to improve?

In summary, then, five factors enabled District #112 to move from a highly traditional school system to a system preparing itself for education's future by experimenting with innovative roles and structures. A shared vision, a superintendent supportive of collaborative decision making, team building, time and resources for change-related activities, and high expectations delivered with care each contributed to the success of the decade-long effort that continues to this day.

Making Sense of Supervision for School Renewal

The success of any change effort may well lie in the eye of the beholder. Some Chaska teachers and administrators continue to wonder whether "anything we've done has really changed things for kids." Others are highly optimistic and predict with enthusiasm, "Given all the information, teachers and support staff will come up with the best decisions for children." The reality probably lies somewhere between these extremes. Teachers and administrators eager to support school renewal can learn three lessons from the experience of District #112.

First, a *shared vision of the desired outcome*—a successfully "renewed" school—is the sine qua non of the renewal process. Faculty and staff—from the central office to the individual school—must hold before them an image of a supportive learning environment for children working with teachers and other staff, however that might be translated in local terms. Supervisors play a critical role in initiating district, school, or program vision-making and, at best, guide an inclusive planning process to ensure the meaningful involvement of key stakeholders in the school community.

Second, supervisors must create a *climate for collaboration*. Whereas the changes made must ultimately prove important for children, equally important initially are the changes required of adults. By their actions, supervisors can support collaborative decision making and make it a part of the renewed school culture. Their own decision making should model the desired process, building over time the districtwide team of school and community representatives that works as a unit to put the collective vision into place. Supervisors can jointly set role-expanding tasks with teachers and then provide staff development to teach requisite skills, resources to release people during the school day to work on change-related projects, and support at a personal level throughout the process. The range of potential activities should be broad and creative.

Given the vision and the climate for collaboration, the third lesson from District #112 is the importance of *holding the course*—committing to the process of change for a number of years and not yielding—because school renewal will not happen overnight. A long-term perspective is mandatory. It is no surprise that the traditional roles of teacher and administrator create a major challenge to change within many school districts. One board member reported that "many teachers are unable to adopt the responsibilities of leadership." Others noted that some choose not to become involved in the change process, preferring instead the roles for which they were prepared.

Supervisors must therefore take the long view and work actively to engender trust and openness, even recognizing that false starts and missteps are likely. They must also hold people accountable for results once they have taken on responsibilities for change.

As mentioned earlier, the superintendent discussed in this chapter has recently moved to another district, as have at least two other individuals important to the change process. The major question now facing District #112 is how to sustain the renewal process of the past decade in light of personnel changes and a troubled state economy. The progress made to date, coupled with the NEA's teacher-centered learning lab model, provides the structure for continued efforts. One teacher summarized the feelings of his colleagues in noting, "If you define school renewal as a process of being open to change, of experimenting to find a better way, we're doing that."

References

Dahl, T., & Associates. (1987). *Performance Improvement in Chaska: The Next Steps*. White Bear Lake, Minn.: Tor Dahl & Associates.

Glickman, C.D. (September 1990). "Pushing School Reform to a New Edge: The Seven Ironies of School Empowerment." *Phi Delta Kappan* 72: 68–75.

Miles, M.B., and K.S. Louis. (May 1990). "Mustering the Will and Skill for Change." *Educational Leadership* 47: 57–61.

Myers-Briggs, I. (1976). *Myers-Briggs Type Indicator*. Palo Alto, Calif.: Consulting Psychologists, Inc.

Sergiovanni, T.J. (May 1990). "Adding Value to Leadership Gets Extraordinary Results." *Educational Leadership* 47: 23–27.

8

A View from the Central Office

Edward F. Pajak

R ecent events in Europe have captured the attention and interest of people all over the world. The collapse of communism in Eastern Europe, symbolized so dramatically and powerfully by the destruction of the Berlin Wall, is suddenly behind us. Just ahead lies the equally significant unification of the twelve-member European Community in 1992. The restructuring of the economic and political institutions of Eastern and Western Europe is an exciting and challenging endeavor that is, however, fraught with uncertainty.

A major issue that Europeans are grappling with today is the question of balance between what is best for Europe and what is best for individual countries and nationalities. In the United States, the proper balance between central control and local autonomy, between integration and independence, between uniformity and diversity, and between coordinated effort and local initiative has been disputed for more than 200 years by states' rights advocates and supporters of a strong national government.

The question of balance between what is best for the whole and what is best for the parts that compose it, is also an educational issue today, as U.S. educators and policymakers struggle with the problem of restructuring schools. From the 1950s through the 1970s, public education in the United States became increasingly bureaucratized as decisions shifted away from teachers and principals to district offices, state education departments, state legislatures, and the federal government. The intended outcomes of centralized bureaucratic organization, as well as the purposes sought by educational reformers from the 1950s onward, are increased efficiency and improved equity. Some characteristics traditionally associated with bureaucracy are the following: a hierarchical chain of authority, a specialized division of labor governed by rules and regulations, and an impersonal orientation.

Sometime in the mid-1980s, however, educators and policymakers in the United States became aware that instead of making schools more efficient and equitable, bureaucratic organization was actually creating obstacles to school success. These obstacles include the following:

- A lack of communication and cooperation between teachers and administrators
- An absence of teacher participation in decision making
- Restricted autonomy for principals and teachers
- Organizational rigidity
- Isolation of teachers from their colleagues
- Low morale
- Expensive evaluation systems that had little relevance or impact on what happened in classrooms and schools

During the late 1980s and continuing into the present decade, an alternative to what might be termed the "bureaucratic system" began to emerge. This alternative—let us call it simply "emerging practice"—is characterized by decentralization, shared decision making, school based management, the notion of the principal as instructional leader, and teacher empowerment.

The emerging practice in U.S. schools is an expression of the restructuring movement in American education, which is redefining roles and responsibilities in schools. Many principals are exercising greater autonomy and authority; and leadership teams composed of teachers, administrators, and sometimes community members collectively make decisions based on what they believe is in the best interest of students. In many schools, mentor teachers and peer coaches are inducting new colleagues into the profession and are improving teaching through frequent observation and feedback in one another's classrooms.

This chapter describes the emerging definition of school organization as it relates to supervision and discusses the implications of this redefinition for the role of central office supervisor of curriculum and instruction. The new definition reflects a movement away from bureaucratic monitoring and standardization and toward tolerance and facilitation of diversity in schools and classrooms. My intention is to outline concepts regarding central office supervision by contrasting how supervisory practice might be enacted differently within the bureaucratic tradition and recently emerging models of school organization.

I have purposely described the bureaucratic and emerging paradigms in extreme terms, as polar opposites, to highlight differences between the two perspectives. There is little chance that either position, as outlined, accurately reflects the reality of any existing school district. Most schools lie somewhere between the two extremes, displaying a more bureaucratic orientation for certain dimensions of supervision and less for other dimensions.

I am indebted to several different sources of information about current practices in supervision:

1. Two recently completed studies of successful district-level supervisors that were conducted at the University of Georgia (Pajak 1989a, Smith 1990).

2. Conversations spanning several days in June 1990 among a nationally representative group of educational practitioners and scholars at the annual meeting of the Education Commission of the States.

3. The members of the Department of Curriculum and Instruction in Clarke County, Georgia, with whom I have been working on the problem of redefining the mission and roles of central office supervisors in an increasingly decentralized school district.

In contrasting the bureaucratic tradition and the emerging decentralization of school organizations, I refer to twelve dimensions of supervisory practice that were recently identified in a research project sponsored by the Association for Supervision and Curriculum Development (ASCD) (Pajak 1989b, 1990). The dimensions were derived from an extensive review of research literature and supervision textbooks that was aimed at locating and verifying knowledge, attitudes, and skills that are most closely associated with outstanding supervisory practice. I present the dimensions in order of their importance to supervisory practice, as indicated by a survey of more than 1,000 educational leaders in the United States and Canada who have reputations for being outstanding practitioners:

- Communication
- Instructional program
- Motivating and organizing
- Curriculum
- Service to teachers
- Community relations
- Staff development
- Planning and change
- Observation and conferences
- Problem solving and decision making
- Personal development
- Research and program evaluation

Dimensions of Supervisory Practice

These twelve dimensions may be thought of as organizational processes that support the improvement of teaching and the professional growth of educators. The dimensions can be enacted, however, in a manner that is more consistent with *either* a bureaucratic or a more decentralized approach. Recognizing that reality is always much more complex than any dichotomy can adequately represent, I think it is useful to show how the two approaches differ for each dimension of supervisory practice.

Communication

Bureaucratic System. Information in a highly bureaucratized system flows between the central office and local schools along official channels. Communication is most often initiated at the top and flows downward. Information flowing upward is limited to what the central office wants to know and is submitted in the form of written reports. The reports from schools are compiled into one district report.

Emerging Practice. In school systems that encourage decentralized communication, open dialogue occurs between the schools and the district office. Information flows freely in both directions, from the top down and vice versa, as well as horizontally throughout the district. Communication can be initiated at any level; such communication contributes to the construction of a common vision and district mission. Good ideas and unique perspectives can emerge at any level. Communication is inclusive, allowing all involved to participate, understand, and commit themselves to the mission.

Staff Development

Bureaucratic System. Under bureaucratic organization, staff development is driven by needs assessments conducted by central office staff members, who identify priorities for the district. Inservice for teachers is planned at the district office, with little participation from teachers. Teachers are a passive audience who are expected to attend a fixed number of inservice sessions per year.

Emerging Practice. The need and demand for staff development increases with emerging supervisory practice as teachers become more involved in decisions about curriculum and instruction and in peer supervision. Teachers actively participate in identifying needs and planning inservice sessions at the school level. As members of a com-

129

munity of learners, they often make presentations to their colleagues instead of relying on outside consultants.

Instructional Program

Bureaucratic System. In schools that operate according to the bureaucratic paradigm, instructional programs are designed and practices are planned by experts at the district office level. These programs and practices are then passed down as requirements to teachers at the classroom level, and the teachers function as isolated technicians.

Emerging Practice. In schools that take a more decentralized approach, instruction is planned by groups of teachers who share the same students, subject, or grade level. Teachers function as professionals who are experts concerning their classrooms. Coordination is achieved by establishing networks of people who are involved in similar efforts and who engage in frequent discussions about teaching.

Planning and Change

Bureaucratic System. In a bureaucratically organized school district, people at the top of the hierarchy establish goals and implement changes. Goals thus formed may not be widely shared or understood by everyone. Schools and classrooms are expected to adopt these goals and changes as policies. Teachers and principals are discouraged from initiating innovations that depart from policy. The purpose is to make the current system run more efficiently.

Emerging Practice. In many schools today, the culture of the school district is value driven. A clear vision of the mission of the district exists. Goals that are congruent with the district mission are identified at each school by teams of teachers, administrators, and sometimes community members. Innovation, experimentation, and risk-taking by teachers and principals are encouraged. The purpose is to rethink and redesign the way things are done.

Motivating and Organizing

Bureaucratic System. Governance is from the top down and autocratic in a bureaucratically oriented school system. Teachers and principals rely primarily on written job descriptions and contracts to determine the behavioral expectations for their jobs. Supervisors in the hierarchy evaluate the performance of individuals, with uniform criteria expressed in observable and measurable terms. The administration distributes rewards to individuals according to the degree of their conformity with prescribed behaviors.

Emerging Practice. With the emerging approach to motivation, everyone is encouraged to participate in developing a shared vision and to work toward the achievement of collective aims. Performance is evaluated according to outcomes achieved using multiple measures of success. Accomplishments of groups are recognized. Leaders perceive themselves as resources who model the values of the organization, not as monitors or rule enforcers.

Observation and Conferences

Bureaucratic System. In systems with a bureaucratic approach, principals make most of the classroom visits; and these visits are primarily to evaluate teacher performance. Such classroom visits are infrequent, except for beginning teachers and teachers who are having difficulty. Central office staff visit occasionally to "show the flag"—or may be called on to observe teachers who are having chronic difficulty in order to secure further documentation for their dismissal. Most teachers view their classrooms as "sacred ground" and resent intrusions from outsiders.

Emerging Practice. In many schools today, observation and conferences take a much different form. Teachers engage in peer coaching and visit each others' classrooms often, to help improve instruction. Beginning teachers are paired with master teachers, who serve as mentors. Less competent teachers are able to learn from observing others and may feel subtle pressure from their peers to improve classroom performance.

Curriculum

Bureaucratic System. In systems with a bureaucratic orientation, subject-matter specialists at the district level write the curriculum, which is then implemented by teachers in the classroom. Curriculum revisions are conducted at predetermined intervals of three to five years. Teachers feel little ownership for the guides they are given, and the content of the guides has little relation to what actually gets taught.

Emerging Practice. In schools with the emerging approach to supervision, teachers participate actively on subject-area and grade-level committees and develop curriculums that are best suited for the needs and interests of students. The implementation of new curriculums is closely linked to staff development. Curriculum is viewed as a relevant, vital, and never-ending process, rather than as a document that sits on a shelf.

Problem Solving and Decision Making

Bureaucratic System. In bureaucratically oriented districts, problem solving and decision making are viewed as processes that are best handled by experts at the top of the district organization. Rules, regulations, and procedures are formulated in an attempt to anticipate and prescribe an answer for every problem or decision that teachers or principals may encounter.

Emerging Practice. In many schools and districts today, problem solving and decision making are recognized as best handled by teachers and principals who are closest to the problems of practice. With autonomy and flexibility, local staff deal with problems as they arise. Schools are encouraged to experiment, inquire, learn, and renew themselves.

Service to Teachers

Bureaucratic System. When support is provided at all in schools with a bureaucratic orientation, additional materials and resources are made available to individual teachers who are perceived as in need of remediation. Deficits in performance based on district or state criteria have greatest priority.

Emerging Practice. With the emerging systems, the district provides support to groups of teachers who are interested in improving their instruction. These groups locate and obtain materials and resources to help the teams achieve the agendas that they have established for themselves. Successful schools are given maximum freedom to set and pursue their own courses of action. Teachers rely on networks of peers to both give and receive assistance.

Personal Development

Bureaucratic System. Personal development is a matter that is largely left up to each individual in a bureaucratically oriented school, based on personal career goals and interests. At the district level, staff make efforts to ensure that everyone is familiar with the rules, regulations, and policies that govern the organization.

Emerging Practice. With the emerging paradigm, individuals and groups reflect on their values, beliefs, and practices. Growth is continuous, as staff members redefine their roles, responsibilities, and relationships within the school. The district and the schools provide resources and information that challenge school teams to move beyond current practices.

Community Relations

Bureaucratic System. In schools within a bureaucratic system, community relations is a matter of public relations. A primary objective is to keep parents and taxpayers happy by telling them what they want to hear. The system excludes the community from many decisions that are considered the domain of professionals.

Emerging Practice. In many schools today, educators make an effort to educate parents and taxpayers about what is happening in the schools and to involve them directly in decisions at the local school level. Participants work to develop a consensus from a diversity of viewpoints and constituencies.

Research and Program Evaluation

Bureaucratic System. In a bureaucratically oriented school system, evaluation is top down: people who are uninvolved with the implementation of programs evaluate these programs on the basis of narrowly defined outcomes. Success is measured solely by student performance on standardized achievement tests. District-level staff monitor and compare the performance of students from different schools, but consequences rarely follow. Data are often inaccessible to teachers and principals.

Emerging Practice. With the emerging approach to program evaluation, educators at all levels view schools and classrooms as centers of inquiry. Multiple indicators of success are used at the school level for measuring student achievement. These indicators, which may include standardized tests within a broader context of assessment, are consistent with the mission and goals of the district. Information is used to inform and is accessible to teachers to make changes in instruction and curriculum to teach students more effectively. Teachers develop new knowledge through action research about what works best for the students in each individual school.

There Are No Panaceas

During the 1980s, a few individuals proposed total decentralization of public education as a solution to the unresponsiveness of public education to demands for improvement. More reasoned voices have recently cautioned, however, that decentralization should not be viewed as a panacea (Murphy 1989). Indeed, unbridled decentralization might very well have the same catastrophic effect on public education that deregulation has had on the American airline and banking industries.

The chaos occurring in the Soviet Union is another example of the result of too rapid and uncoordinated decentralization.

Many local schools are likely to flounder if they are suddenly cut loose and told to chart their own courses, because the bureaucratically oriented system has never prepared them for autonomy and self-governance. Principals may be reluctant to share the power entrusted to them with school based management, and a few might even be tempted to abuse it. Teachers unaccustomed to collaboration may lack the confidence and skills they need to participate productively in shared decision making. Parents and community members may press for mandatory prayer at the beginning of each school day or contact football for elementary school children.

A school district organized closer to the emerging practices described in this chapter is also likely to experience problems, such as an increase in "noise" within the system as competing factions clamor to be heard. At the very least, without an infusion of encouragement, new ideas, and resources from outside the school, faculties may quickly plateau in their efforts or focus solely on issues of school management without ever getting to the touchy question of improving teaching in their own classrooms.

A solution to the dilemma faced by many schools and districts—in both bureaucratic and emerging practices—may be found in what Jerome T. Murphy calls "integrated decentralization," involving *both* strong central coordination *and* strong local diversity (Murphy 1989). This notion is consistent with the findings of Lawrence and Lorsch, who studied many different types of organizations during the 1960s and found that the most successful displayed *both* high integration of effort *and* high differentiation among their component parts (Lawrence and Lorsch 1969).

Murphy suggests that the central office can maximize the benefits of integrated decentralization by shifting away from monitoring and enforcing policy and toward providing services, facilitating, and coordinating. Central office staffs should attend most closely to those schools that have problems and unrealized potential, he believes, whereas schools that are already successful should have maximum freedom to pursue their own courses (Murphy 1989).

Supervision and Bureaucracy

As the decade of the 1990s unfolds, educators and policymakers in the United States are beginning to recognize that restructuring of education cannot stop at the schoolhouse door (Anderson 1989). Vertical as well as horizontal restructuring is needed throughout the educational enterprise to ensure that innovations initiated at the building level survive and flourish. The district office must do more than simply grant permission for site based management and shared decision making, followed by benign neglect.

Research on effective schools that includes the central office supervisor as a focus of study confirms the importance of the district level position (Wimpelberg 1988). Most of the available evidence indicates that instruction in many schools is not likely to improve without leadership from the district office that can forge linkages between schools and the central office, among schools, and among teachers within schools (Burch and Danley 1980, Fullan 1982, Wimpelberg 1988, Pajak 1989a). Simply stated, the central office must take a proactive position toward restructuring.

Unfortunately, central office supervisors can easily become mentally trapped in the bureaucratic model, which prevents them from serving the needs of principals and teachers. Supervisors can easily become psychologically fixed on issues of control, monitoring for compliance with policy, and enforcing uniformity of practice. When this occurs, teachers and principals not only miss the support that they need from the central office, but they come to resent visits from district-level staff as intrusions on their autonomy. Teachers may even perceive curriculum development and staff development as things that are done "to them" instead of "with them." A highly bureaucratic system encourages passivity and dependence, it seems, with resources flowing most readily to those who do not raise questions or rock the boat.

Supervision and Emerging Practice

Effective central office supervisors of curriculum and instruction have always avoided the bureaucratic mind trap and have played a key role in facilitating the achievement of integrated decentralization within their districts. They accomplish this end in many ways, most of which are consistent with what successful central office supervisors have done all along (Pajak 1989a).

How can central office supervisors help to achieve the ideal of integrated decentralization as their districts become involved in restructuring? Here are some ideas to consider:

• Take the initiative in developing a clear expression of core values, beliefs, and goals that reinforces a district culture characterized by student learning, professional growth, diversity, innovative practice, and risk taking.

• Provide opportunities for broad-based participation in the development of collective aims to encourage ownership and a sense of obligation to work toward those aims.

• Communicate, represent, and interpret the core values, beliefs, and goals widely to people within and outside the organization.

• Work cooperatively with the local business community to garner support.

• Present district policies as values and guidelines instead of narrow prescriptions to allow a wide range of goals and sufficient flexibility to accommodate local agendas.

• Help teachers write meaningful school philosophies that are congruent with the district mission, establish priorities to avoid being all things to all people, and set achievable instructional goals.

• Facilitate school autonomy and shared governance by seeking out information that school teams need and by coordinating activities in pursuit of common goals.

• Be willing to negotiate discrepancies and inconsistencies between district goals and school goals.

• Facilitate problem solving and decision making by helping teachers identify "nonnegotiable" areas and find ways to get waivers and exemptions from state policy.

• Anticipate increased conflict and develop problem-solving strategies that are inclusive and collaborative.

• Provide technical assistance, information, staff development, additional resources, and time to help teachers and principals reshape their roles and rethink their responsibilities.

• Model the importance of collaboration, collegiality, trust, caring, asking questions, listening carefully, and nurturing leadership in others.

• Promote open and honest communication within the district to encourage the sharing of successes and failures so that schools can learn from one another. (Autonomy should not mean isolation.)

• Provide training to teachers in areas such as classroom observation and conferences, problem solving and decision making by consensus, team building, interpersonal communication, conflict resolution, and other areas that are relevant to self-governance.

• Coordinate staff development training when the needs identified by several schools overlap.

• Keep school action plans focused on student learning, instruction, and curriculum and provide school teams with special content expertise.

• Reassess and redefine central office roles and functions individually and as a team.

* * *

Local schools may briefly flourish when the constraints of district rules and regulations are lifted, but an ongoing infusion of new ideas and resources is also necessary to maintain the process of improvement. The available evidence suggests that a balance between central coordination and local autonomy is needed in every organization to maximize performance.

As school districts embark on restructuring efforts, discussion should begin fairly early about which aspects of supervision will be coordinated by the central office and which will be handled by the local schools. Each of the twelve dimensions of supervisory practice presented in this chapter can be viewed as a continuum that can serve as a focus for deliberation and negotiation.

The ideal balance between central control and local autonomy is likely to differ somewhat from one district to another, and within the same district from one time to another, for each of the twelve dimensions. Multiple definitions of empowerment, shared decision making, and school based management are both possible and desirable because they allow for local definitions that can evolve as conditions change.

The challenge of achieving a workable balance of integrated decentralization is before us—as educators, as citizens, and as members of the international community. Taking time to achieve the right balance to begin with is essential; then revisiting our decisions periodically will ensure that the proper balance remains.

References

Anderson, B.L. (June 1989). "Reformation of the Full Education System." Unpublished working paper. Denver, Colo.: Education Commission for the States.

Burch, B.G., and W.E. Danley. (May 1980). "The Instructional Leadership Role of Central Office Supervisors," *Educational Leadership* 37, 8: 636–639.

Fullan, M. (1982). *The Meaning of Educational Change.* New York: Teachers College Press.

Lawrence, P.R., and J.W. Lorsch. (1969). *Organization and Environment: Managing Differentiation and Integration.* Homewood, Ill.: Richard D. Irwin.

Murphy, J.T. (June 1989). "The Paradox of Decentralizing Schools: Lessons from Business, Government, and the Catholic Church," *Phi Delta Kappan* 70, 10: 808–812.

Pajak, E. (1989a). *The Central Office Supervisor of Curriculum and Instruction: Setting the Stage for Success*. Needham Heights, Mass.: Allyn and Bacon.

Pajak, E. (1989b). *Identification of Supervisory Proficiencies Project*. Alexandria, Va.: ASCD.

Pajak, E. (September 1990). "Dimensions of Supervision," *Educational Leadership* 48, 1: 78–81.

Smith, R.G. (1990). "The Importance of Twelve Dimensions of Effective Supervisory Practice Derived from Educational Literature as Perceived by Selected District Level Supervisors." Doctoral diss., University of Georgia, 1990.

Wimpelberg, R.K. (1988). "The Dilemma of Instructional Leadership and a Central Role for Central Office," In *Instructional Leadership: Concepts, Issues, and Controversies* (pp. 100–117), edited by W. Greenfield. Boston: Allyn and Bacon.

III

The Preparation

9

Collegial Support by Teacher Mentors and Peer Consultants

Nancy L. Zimpher and John E. Grossman

The trauma experienced by beginning teachers can be traced to several sources. In particular, new teachers are often placed in difficult instructional settings once occupied by veteran teachers who have now achieved more manageable assignments (Schlechty and Vance 1983). Further, there is little collaboration between veteran and novice teachers (Adams 1982), and what collaboration there is often dissolves into simple mimicry of veteran practices. Beginning teachers tend to make practical, survival kinds of decisions to ease the anxieties of their early years of teaching (Joyce and Clift 1984). They are often left to fend for themselves without the support of the teacher education faculty who helped them move through the preservice program (Yarger 1982). In addition, they are faced with inadequate time for planning, reflection, and further growth, as well as a lack of powerful teacher models to help them achieve expertise in teaching (Howey, Bents, and Corrigan 1979).

This profile of the beginning teacher is well codified in many studies on the problems experienced by beginning teachers (Veenman 1984) and the modest effects of initial teacher preparation in assisting beginners with the complexities of the classroom (Howey, Matthes, and Zimpher 1987). It is no wonder, then, that attrition during the early years of teaching is remarkably high. Several years ago, accounts of the beginning teacher exodus were documented (Morris 1982): 50 percent of new teachers in the United States will not be in the classroom five years later. Haberman (1987) places this figure at closer to three years for entering teachers in urban districts.

More convincing than the obvious problems confronted by beginners has been this crisis in the teacher dropout rate. It has undoubtedly been the impetus for many legislative initiatives to provide assistance to entering teachers. State regulations that mandate beginning teacher assistance programs are now evident in thirty-six states (American Association of Colleges for Teacher Education 1988), though few of these promulgated standards carry the necessary appropriations to effectively fulfill the mandates. Nonetheless, entry-year program designs are essentially becoming commonplace in the professional education landscape.

These state mandates have several characteristics in common. Most state-level programs require that all beginning teachers become engaged in district-level programming to assist in their initial teaching needs. These programs rarely invoke assistance from higher education. Rather, districts must assume primary responsibility for ensuring that each novice teacher is provided some form of assistance from a veteran teacher mentor. Teacher mentors must be engaged in district-level preparation, although special certification for teacher mentors is not typical. Further, regulations do not specify the amount of time the mentor spends with the inductee; amount of release time; special stipends for service; or associated selection criteria, such as years of teaching experience, classroom competence, or preparation for assuming the role of mentor teacher. Rather, districts are expected to resolve these issues locally to stay in compliance with state mandates.

In contrast to the evolving roles of teacher mentors in entry-year programs, an alternative approach has arisen—"peer assistance and review" (PAR) programs, first designed by the Toledo Public Schools in 1981 (Toledo Public Schools 1988). Similar programs have been developed in Rochester, New York (Gillet and Halkett 1989), and in two other Ohio cities, Columbus (Foster 1985) and Cincinnati (Johnson 1988). These PAR programs provide initial assistance to beginning or *intern* teachers through consultant teachers, who also make recommendations to a review panel regarding contract continuation for beginning teachers. In addition, PAR programs offer assistance and assessment to veteran *intervention* teachers—those who are experiencing considerable difficulty in the classroom.

Though the intervention aspect of the PAR program is especially provocative, we will not discuss it in this chapter because it is not comparable to the focus of most mentoring programs, with which PAR is being compared.

This chapter describes the two models, including commonalities, unusual features, and problems and issues associated with each design. We compare and contrast these two opposing but complementary approaches to beginning teacher assistance; in our discussion, we hope to characterize the nature of emerging versions of "the new supervision"—that is, teacher-directed, collegial supervision.

What separates these two roles is the distinction made between assistance and assessment, one we would like to highlight throughout this chapter. Contemporary mentor designations include the following:

- Coach, positive role model, developer of talent, opener of doors, protector, sponsor (Schien 1978).
- Trusted guide, counselor, teacher-guardian (Galvez-Hjornevik 1986).
- Colleague teacher, helping teacher, peer teacher, support teacher (Borko 1986).

In contrast, the PAR consultant offers the same kinds of assistance as would a mentor, while also providing periodic assessments that ultimately factor into a review panel's decision to retain the beginning teacher on a regular contract.

In many ways, these two roles exemplify a dilemma present in the supervision literature over time—that is, the degree to which the roles of formative assistance and summative evaluation can or should be manifested in the same individual. Sergiovanni and Starratt (1988) directly address the issue:

> Evaluation is an integral part of supervision, and this reality cannot be ignored by supervisors and teachers. Indeed, attempts to mask evaluation aspects of supervision by not using the term or by denying that evaluation occurs or by declaring that evaluation is reserved only for the annual administrative review of one's teaching will not be convincing. Despite the rhetoric, everyone involved knows that evaluation is part of the process of supervision (pp. 350–351).

Oliva (1989) discusses two views of supervision:

- Nonevaluative supervision consists of helping teachers improve instruction through giving feedback from classroom observations—a form of consultative or formative review.
- Supervision with evaluation includes administrative assessments for the purpose of making personnel decisions and determining contract renewal, merit pay, assignments, and placements on career ladders. This approach separates staff authority (formative assistance) from line authority (evaluative review), separating "the helping relationship from the administrative dimension" (p. 54).

Our view is that new constructs of teachers supervising teachers attempt to achieve these same separations, however successfully. That is, mentors give formative assistance and should not be engaged in assessment. PAR consultants, alternately, give summative assessment; thus, their "assistance" is suspect. The controversy surrounding the PAR approach was apparent in a recent, heated debate in the Ohio General Assembly (Schmidt 1990) between the two state affiliates of the American Federation of Teachers (AFT) and the National Education Association (NEA). The issue was over whether teachers engaged in the assessment of their colleagues (typical of the PAR programs in Toledo, Cincinnati, and Columbus) were in fact violating fair labor practices, with employees assessing employees, thus leaving union members without union job protection. According to Schmidt, the Ohio NEA (OEA) affiliate believed that the responsibility to renew teacher contracts should be left to the school administration:

> "Our position is that teachers who evaluate other teachers should do so for the purpose of improving the performance of the teacher being evaluated." . . . [The affiliate] assert[ed] that teachers who know that their evaluators could eventually recommend their discharge will be less likely to discuss the difficulties they are encountering (Schmidt 1990, p. 22).

Schmidt's article closes by acknowledging that OEA's largest local, the Columbus Education Association—in its fifth year of a peer review program—strongly opposed its parent organization (in this case, the OEA) in this debate.

Thus the seeds for this chapter. Our first treatise is that variations on the old theme of instructional supervision are emerging and are fueled primarily by teachers' assuming a more direct role in supervisory practice.

Our second treatise reflects a divergence in opinion and practice regarding the separation/integration of formative and summative supervision, that is, the potential blending of assistance and assessment. These, we suggest, are the inherent ends of a supervision continuum illustrated by a mentoring model (assistance) and a PAR consultant model (the merger of assistance and assessment) of teacher-directed, collegial supervision.

A Mentoring Model

The evolution of the mentoring project described here is well documented in the myriad progress reports and other summaries required of federally funded projects from the U.S. Department of Education's Office of Educational Research and Improvement (Zimpher 1988). Because this project is reasonably representative of many mentoring programs, we profile it here as a model on the "assistance" end of the supervision continuum.

The Franklin County/Ohio State University (OSU) Induction Year Program was a three-year collaborative effort between The Ohio State University and five local school districts in the adjacent county area. The University enlisted 100 dyads of mentor teachers and beginning teachers during the first year of the project and then two additional groups of beginning teachers and newly trained mentors in the remaining years. The project began through conversations with superintendent representatives and local teachers association presidents in the five participating districts. These districts formed local coordinating councils that currently oversee the established entry-year programs, now that federal funding has expired.

Two groups were critical to this project: the beginning teachers and the mentors. To stimulate as much involvement in the project as possible, the planners defined the terms *inductee* or *new teacher* as broadly as possible:

1. Teachers assuming a first-year teaching assignment, typically immediately following graduation and serving under a provisional teaching certificate.

2. Teachers with some teaching experience who had been on leave from teaching for several years and who, upon returning to the classroom, may have experienced some reentry problems.

3. Teachers assuming major new substantive assignments as a result of recertification or significantly new teaching assignments, such as teachers new to a district, new to a building, or new to a grade level or subject area.

Project planners described the mentor teacher as an experienced teacher who is "a master of the craft of teaching and personable in dealing with other teachers; an empathetic individual who understands the needs of the mentorship role" (Zimpher and Reiger 1988). Planners also took special care to ensure that the mentor role was *not* that of an evaluator and that the mentor had no part in personnel decisions. Thus the teacher mentor was viewed as a supportive advocate for the beginning teacher.

Mentor teachers were chosen in one of three ways: (1) by administrators, (2) by administrators and teacher representatives who selected the teachers collaboratively, or (3) by teachers' directly volunteering. Mentors and inductees were matched as much as possible by subject area, grade level, building assignment, and other common grounds for affiliation. As well, project planners developed guidelines for mentor service, including the nature of support and facilitation, interpersonal support, assistance with classroom management, planning and teaching concerns, time management, community orientations, materials development, and weekly sharing and feedback sessions. However, resources were not available for release time to allow the dyads to work together during school hours; nor were mentors provided additional stipends or other contractual support.

Finally, mentor teachers participated in a year-long program of professional development offered by OSU to help the teachers more effectively serve in their mentoring roles. Beginning teachers also participated in a professional development course during the first year. However, during the subsequent two years, a select group of teacher mentors sought to fulfill even more challenging leadership roles for the project, and in turn became mentor trainers (members of a teacher leadership cadre) for the remaining participating mentors, who in turn provided direct instruction and support for the participating beginning teachers. Ultimately, project staff determined that it was equally effective to provide assistance to inductees almost exclusively through the vehicle of the mentor teacher as through direct university instruction (Stallion 1987).

A PAR Consultant Model

As noted earlier, the Toledo Public Schools initiated a peer assistance and review program in 1981 that has since become a template for successful programs in Rochester, Cincinnati, and Columbus. Initially, the Toledo Federation of Teachers negotiated with the administration a new approach to teacher evaluation, offering assistance and assessment to two groups of teachers. According to McCormick (1985), the Toledo plan uses "a controversial, but apparently effective, combination of rigorous evaluation, training for new teachers, remediation for veteran teachers, and peer review in an effort to sweep the faculty clean of incompetents" (p. 19). By the school district's account, "the Toledo Plan provides a formula for professional development of beginning teachers and an evaluation system that detects and screens out those who show little aptitude for the classroom" (Toledo Public Schools 1988, p. iii). We have used elements from the Ohio and New York programs to show characteristics of this approach to peer assistance. Typically, teachers are selected for participation as PAR consultants

through an application and selection process. This and other administrative aspects of the program are guided by a PAR panel. In Columbus,
for instance, this panel includes three central office administrative
representatives and four teacher representatives. All decisions of the
panel must be by a two-thirds vote, so the members must strive for a
cooperative relationship. The chair of the PAR panel rotates annually
between the union president and the superintendent's designee. Ultimately, all reviews and recommendations to continue contracts for
intern or intervention teachers are directed to the PAR panel, which
makes the final decision about renewal. This process bypasses traditional patterns of building principals' determining contract renewal. (In
Ohio, however, state law requires that termination or contract renewal
recommended by the PAR panel ultimately reside with the superintendent and the school board.) Through both negotiated agreements and
consensual agreement, at least in Columbus and Toledo, either party to
the agreement can recommend withdrawal of the program, in which
event the program would be terminated.

PAR consultants are selected from the active ranks of classroom
teachers. As noted earlier, these consultants serve a three-year term,
with full release from the classroom during those years. As of the
1990–91 school year, PAR consultants in Columbus received an additional stipend of $4,000. In all but the Columbus district, serving as a
PAR consultant is part of a more elaborate career ladder initiative, an
idea that is pending in Columbus, as well. The caseload for PAR
consultants is typically ten to fourteen beginning teachers, with a range
of eight to twenty. In this program, consultants work across five domains of preparation to enhance their effectiveness with the intern and
intervention teachers, as follows:

- Classroom processes
- Instructional supervision
- Adult development
- Inquiry orientations to teaching
- Selected local needs (Howey and Zimpher 1989)

In some instances, particularly in Toledo and Columbus, actual
continuing professional development is extended to beginning teachers
through the efforts of the PAR consultants. In Columbus, the consultants have offered an extended "course" for all beginning teachers in
collaboration with faculty members at OSU. For instance, in the 1989–
90 school year, this course focused specifically on action research as a
vehicle for reflecting on classroom practice, although the focus of

professional development for PAR consultants varies each year. PAR consultants in Columbus have also initiated a "PAR Plus" program, in which consultants also supervise a limited number of OSU student teachers as part of their caseload.

PAR consultants typically observe intern teachers or hold conferences with them at least weekly. It is not unusual, in a difficult case, for a PAR consultant to submit as many as fifty to sixty observation analyses for a single intern. Consultants are matched with interns on the basis of instructional experience (i.e., elementary consultants typically work with elementary level interns) and, where possible, by subject area expertise. In Toledo, as elsewhere, "the evaluation process is one of continuous mutual goal-setting based on detailed observations and follow-up conferences" (Toledo Public Schools 1988, p. vi). Other participating districts have a compilation of forms, as well, that are used in the consultations. Areas of concern in PAR review in Columbus include the following:

- Teaching performance
- Pupil relations
- Management activities
- Overall value to the school program
- Personal characteristics
- Staff relations
- Parent-community relations
- Professional growth

As of 1990, the attrition rate for beginning teachers attributable to the peer assistance and review process is about 5 percent (5.4 percent in Columbus). Many of these teachers (3 percent) make an individual decision to leave the profession after receiving feedback in the PAR program.

A Comparison of the Two Models: Issues and Pitfalls

Fundamental to our discussion are the particular attributes that define emerging supervisory roles that are essentially teacher-directed and collegial in nature—as well as differences between roles that offer assistance only and roles that combine assistance and assessment. Though the issues and pitfalls we discuss are not necessarily "common" for both models, they reflect what we believe to be some important preconditions for programs of collegial supervision to function effectively.

The Assessment-Versus-Assistance Dilemma

From the outset, the Franklin County/OSU effort rejected the notion of incorporating both assistance and assessment, largely because the prerogatives of the teachers associations included no directive on this issue. Before the project began, teachers had not advocated for such an assessment role; nor did they appear to *want* such a role. The only irony worth reporting is that repeatedly, at the culmination of a year's work in a role that was to be strictly assistance oriented, mentors complained about their lack of involvement in the principal's decisions on contract renewal for the beginning teachers in the program (reminiscent of the old saw, "You can't have it both ways").

In contrast, the PAR programs grew out of precisely the dilemma the mentor program sought to avoid. As Dal Lawrence, the president of the Toledo Federation, observed: "We felt that before teaching could become a profession, teachers had to have some responsibility and voice in determining who was good enough to become a practitioner" (Olson 1989). Though this is not a popular viewpoint among all educators, it is squarely the position of the AFT and, more recently, the NEA. Clearly, Keith Geiger, current NEA president, is eager for the membership to assume more direct responsibility for continuing teacher professional development, as evidenced in an annual convention address: "My fellow delegates, for this year and next year and all the years of this decade . . . give us the tools and we will finish the job!" (Geiger 1990).

Implications for the Role of Principals

The school effectiveness literature has placed considerable emphasis on the role of the principal as an instructional leader. Given this emphasis, principals and teachers would naturally need to enter into negotiations as mentoring and PAR consultant roles become more pervasive. In district after district, the reactions of principals have been chronicled, including Adam Urbanski's observations as president of the Rochester teachers association: "What we have here is an attempt by administrators to scuttle this program because of fear that it encroaches on their turf" (Rodman 1987).

In Cincinnati, one central administrator observed, "The process set up the administrative staff to feel like losers. The principals and line staff felt that the board had given away all their authority" (Johnson 1988).

AFT President Al Shanker stated: "If employees are no longer merely told what to do, but are now given responsibility for planning, executing and evaluating their work, it's not surprising to find that the old foreman or plant manager believes that a new scheme just won't work unless he's on top of it all—unless he's supervising it" (Shanker 1987).

Particularly with peer review programs, the role of the principal does in fact shift, in that additional assistance for observations and evaluations for beginning teachers is carried out through the PAR consultant. And, by the contract, the role of the principal is not considered in these review proceedings. In actuality, most PAR consultants in the Columbus program (and, we suspect, elsewhere as well) regularly report consultations with principals. Concomitantly, principals regularly concede that without the presence of the PAR consultant much of the assistance and assessment responsibilities that might otherwise fall to the principal would never get done.

Collegial Relations

In initial studies of teachers serving in peer supervisory roles, Devaney (1987) reported that teachers had difficulty giving critical feedback to their peers. Explanations for this situation derived from long-held views of teacher equality: "A teacher is a teacher is a teacher." Resistance to differentiation of roles came in the form of not wanting to cast one teacher as somehow "better" than another, or, as Futrell once observed about the Carnegie lead teacher concept, "It suggests that some teachers are more equal than others" (Devaney 1987). In Toledo, there was an attempt to avoid these kinds of connotations, particularly emanating from "master teacher" designations. "We didn't want to cause professional jealousy . . . even though [consulting teachers] clearly are exceptional" (McCormick 1985). Thus, the terms *mentor*, *consultant*, or "teachers helping teachers" evolved in the regular lexicon. Much more could be said about the relational differences and the kind of preparation that could be helpful to teachers as they assume these supervisory leadership roles, but these topics are dealt with in more depth elsewhere (Howey 1988, Zimpher 1988).

Selection and Preparation

Collegial relations can be tempered considerably by the degree of specificity associated with the selection and preparation of mentors and consultants. For instance, if some mentors are volunteers, as in the mentoring program described, then levels of expertise are not made clear and questions arise about what qualities separate an exemplary teacher from other teachers. In both mentor and PAR programs, selection criteria could be refined to rule out possible problems with district politics and collegial tensions. In the PAR programs, the criteria are well explicated, although more descriptive and valid measures of the criteria are needed. For example, what is the best way to determine the teacher supervisors' disposition toward effective teaching, their ability to work well in collegial situations, their interest in continuing professional development, or the respect held for these candidates by their colleagues? These issues continually need to be addressed in these programs.

The issue of professional development is also critical to the success of peer review and mentor programs. Surely one criterion for selection as a teacher supervisor ought to be the willingness of candidates to extend their own professional development, but what would be the nature of the preparation program?

Conceptions of Good Teaching

It is difficult to conceive of an assistance/assessment program ultimately achieving instructional improvement among school learners in the absence of a clear conception of effective teaching. As Dal Lawrence ("Teacher Excellence" 1984) acknowledges, "We don't try to tell an intern what is the best technique. The consulting teachers know that their goal is not to make copies of themselves. We present the kinds of things that work in the classroom." Still, "what works" in the classroom is subject to wide interpretation.

A question remains: To what degree can supervisory teachers articulate what constitutes effective teaching and learning in their district? One effort to provide a focus for supervisory practice is exemplified by the Schenley High School Teacher Center in Pittsburgh. At this center, through peer instructional assistance, teachers participate in the Pittsburgh Research-based Instructional Supervisory Model (PRISM). Though this model is derived from research on effective teaching (Wallace, Young, Johnston, LeMahieu, and Beckel 1984) and Madeline Hunter's instructional supervision, it does not address all the complexities of classroom instruction (Mandeville and Rivers 1989). Many peer assistance programs need more of an emphasis on clarifying conceptions of teaching and learning rather than producing the myriad evaluation forms and schedules used in most programs. As peer assistance programs continue to unfold, participants must attend to these instructional issues.

Conditions for Service

What conditions are necessary for a peer assistance program to work? Districts need to work out problems related to resources, time, and placement, among other issues. First, resources to support collegial supervision programs are critical to the effective access of mentors or consultants to beginning teachers. Teachers need time together to observe and discuss each other's instruction. Programs that give the designation without the appropriations to do the job well do a disservice to the whole notion of peer supervision.

Second, finding the "right" combination of teacher time is also an issue. In the PAR programs, teachers serve exclusively as consultants for three years. Thus they are vulnerable to the very criticism lodged at most administrative supervisors—"out of touch with the realities of the classroom." Further, the transition back to the classroom can be traumatic: teachers who have developed considerable skill in instructional supervision find little opportunity to put these new skills to use. The potential of mixing ongoing classroom activity with a partial released-time contract is an appealing way to retain credibility in the program and, at the same time, retain the best teachers partially in the classroom while meeting the needs of beginning teachers.

Third, the effectiveness of mentoring and consultant programs is related to the problems their services are intended to solve. For instance, the problems associated with the beginning years of teaching often result from the less than desirable placements given to new teachers when they enter a district. Thus, PAR consultants, for instance, are expected to help a beginner solve instructional problems that often emanate from poor district placements more than inadequate preparation or ineffectual delivery. Adam Urbanski in Rochester suggests that really the most experienced, veteran teachers—the "Clint Eastwoods of teaching" (quoted by Bradley 1989)—should be placed in the most difficult positions, not novitiates.

Finally, resources will also ultimately determine the degree to which success in these programs has actually been achieved. This is a long-range question about the ultimate impact of these programs on the improved learning abilities of school-aged youth. As the vice president of the Rochester Board of Education observed, "What we need to be able to demonstrate, if we're going to keep all these people supportive, is that we in fact are making incremental progress" (Bradley 1989). This is a critical dimension of any effective supervision program. The effects on student learning most assuredly will spell the demise or future of peer supervision programs. The continual documentation of program effects will be essential as teachers continue to take more direct responsibility for their own professional development.

Bibliography

Adams, R.D. (1982). "Teacher Development: A Look at Changes in Teacher Perceptions and Behavior Across Time." *Journal of Teacher Education* 33, 4: 40–43.

American Association of Colleges for Teacher Education (AACTE). (1988). *Compendium of State Policies*. Washington, D.C.: AACTE.

Borko, H. (1986). "Clinical Teacher Education: The Induction Years." In *Reality and Reform in Clinical Teacher Education* (pp. 45–63), edited by J.V. Hoffman and S.A. Edwards. New York: Random House.

Bradley, A. (December 1989). "This Is Damned Hard." *Teacher Magazine*, 12–14.

Devaney, K. (1987). *The Lead Teacher: Ways to Begin*. New York: Carnegie Forum on Education and the Economy, Task Force on Teaching as a Profession.

Foster, K.G. (December 7, 1985). "Teacher Mentor Program Initiated." *Columbus Dispatch*.

Galvez-Hjornevik, C. (1986). "Mentoring Among Teachers: A Review of the Literature." *Journal of Teacher Education* 37, 1: 6–11.

Geiger, J. (1990). Keynote Address, presented at the Annual Meeting of the National Education Association, Kansas City.

Gillet, T.D., and K.A. Halkett. (March 16, 1989). *An Overview of CIT*. Rochester, N.Y.: Rochester City School District/Rochester Teachers Association.

Haberman, M. (1987). *Recruiting and Selecting Teachers for Urban Schools*. Reston, Va.: Association of Teacher Educators and ERIC Clearinghouse on Urban Education.

Howey, K.R., R. Bents, and D. Corrigan. (1981). *School Focused Inservice: Description and Discussions*. Reston, Va.: Association of Teacher Educators.

Howey, K.R., W. Matthes, and N. Zimpher. (1987). *Issues and Problems in Professional Development*. Elmhurst, Ill.: North Central Educational Regional Laboratory.

Howey, K. R., and N.L. Zimpher. (1989). "Preservice Teacher Educators' Role in Programs for Beginning Teachers." *Elementary School Journal* 89, 4: 437–455.

Johnson, S.M. (June 1988). "Pursuing Professional Reform in Cincinnati." *Phi Delta Kappan* 69, 10: 746–751.

Joyce, B., and R. Clift. (1984). "The Phoenix Agenda: Essential Reform in Teacher Education." *Educational Researcher* 13, 4: 5–18.

Mandeville, G.K., and J. Rivers. (May 1989). "Is the Hunter Model a Recipe for Supervision?" *Educational Leadership* 46, 8: 39–44.

McCormick, K. (July 1985). "This Union-Backed Program Is Ridding Toledo Schools of Incompetent Teachers." *American School Board Journal* 172, 7: 19–22.

Oliva, P.F. (1989). *Supervision for Today's Schools*. New York: Longman.

Olson, L. (September/October 1989). "A Revolution of Rising Expectations." *Teacher Magazine*, 56–63.

Peer Assistance and Review Program. (1986). Columbus, Ohio: Columbus Public Schools, Columbus Education Association.

Rodman, B. (January 14, 1987). "New York Lawsuit Highlights Growing Tension Between Principals, Teachers Over Their Roles." *Education Week* VI, 16.

Schien, E. (1978). *Career Dynamics: Matching Individual and Organizational Needs*. Reading, Mass.: Addison-Wesley.

Schlechty, P., and V. Vance. (1983). "Recruitment, Selection and Retention: The Shape of the Teaching Force." *Elementary School Journal* 83, 4: 469–487.

Schmidt, P. (May 1990). "A Vote for Peer Review." *Teacher Magazine*, 22.

Sergiovanni, T.J., and R.J. Starratt. (1988). *Supervision: Human Perspectives*. New York: McGraw-Hill.

Shanker, A. (January 10, 1987). "Principals' Dual Task Questioned: Teachers Have Leadership Role." *New York Times*.

Stallion, B. (1986). "What Informs an Induction Year Program?" Paper presented at the National Council of States on Inservice Education, Nashville.

Stallion, B. (1987). "Classroom Management Intervention: The Effects of Training and Mentoring on the Inductee Teacher's Behavior." Doctoral diss., Ohio State University.

"Teacher Excellence: Teachers Take Charge. An Interview with Dal Lawrence." (Spring 1984). *American Educator* 8, 1: 22–29.

Toledo Public Schools (1988). "Intern/Intervention Evaluation." In *A Professional Development Plan for Classroom Performance*. Toledo, Ohio: Toledo Public Schools.

Veenman, S. (1984). "Perceived Problems of Beginning Teachers." *Review of Educational Research* 54, 2: 143–178.

Wallace, R., J. Young, J. Johnston, P. LeMahieu, and W. Beckel. (March 1984). "Secondary Education Renewal in Pittsburgh." *Educational Leadership* 41, 6: 73–77.

Yarger, S.J. (1982). "Summary of Analyses for Lack of Recognition of the Importance of Induction in U.S. Teacher Education." Paper presented at the annual meeting of the American Educational Research Association, New York.

Zimpher, N.L. (1988). "A Design for the Professional Development of Teacher Leaders." *Journal of Teacher Education* 35, 1: 53–61.

Zimpher, N.L. (1989). "Using Formative Evaluation to Determine Beginning Teachers' Thoughts About Teaching." In *Shaping Policy in Teacher Education through Program Evaluation* (pp. 73–86), edited by J.J. Denton. College Station: Instructional Research Laboratory of the Department of Educational Curriculum and Instruction, Texas A&M University.

Zimpher, N., and S. Reiger. (1988). *Using Research Knowledge to Improve Teacher Education: Implementation of an Induction Program for Inquiring Professionals*. Final Report (Contract No. 85–0012). Washington, D.C.: Office of Educational Research and Improvement, U.S. Department of Education.

10

Restructuring Student Teaching Experiences

Amy Bernstein Colton and Georgea Sparks-Langer

Today's schools are becoming more and more complex. Just one of the many changes is in the demographics of the student population. Teachers are being expected to work with more students whose language is not English, whose families are poor, and whose cultural backgrounds differ from their own (Kennedy 1991). Another change involves site-based school management; teachers are being encouraged to make more of the major decisions affecting the schools in which they work.

To be successful in such complex situations, teachers cannot simply rely on solutions provided by others. Instead, teachers must be able to make their own judgments based on thoughtful inquiry, analysis, and assessment. We believe student teaching practices need to change to develop a *thoughtful, self-directed professional* who can rise to the many challenges posed by today's schools.

In this chapter,[1] we present a description of the skills and attitudes needed by thoughtful, self-directed teachers. Next we briefly describe a constructivist view of student teaching supervision—an outlook and process that enables student teachers to construct their own meaning out of their teaching experiences. Then, we provide ideas for preparing supervisory teachers[2] for this new role and ideas for restructuring student teaching experiences. Finally, we propose recommendations for future practice in student teaching supervision.

---

[1]We wish to thank Art Costa and Bob Garmston for their comments on an earlier draft of this chapter.

[2]When we refer to "supervisors," we are including both teachers and university personnel who work with student teachers.

The Vision: A Self-Directed Teacher

Given the changes in today's schools, it is clear that universities and schools need to work together to prepare future and current teachers to take on a more active and thoughtful role. The first step involves creating a clear image of the mental skills and attitudes needed by student teachers and clarifying the predispositions and abilities needed by the supervisors who work with them.

We see the teacher of the future as a self-directed person who is intrinsically motivated to analyze a situation, set goals, plan and monitor actions, evaluate results, and reflect on his own professional thinking. As a part of this process, the teacher also considers the immediate and long-term social and ethical implications of his actions. Such a person explores a variety of possible actions—and their consequences—before choosing one. This person is not afraid to take risks and try new ideas. He is also eager and willing to construct new knowledge by sharing ideas and questions with others as a means of growing professionally.

How might this professional behave in a classroom? Let's take an example of a typical classroom situation—two girls talking in the back of the room while the teacher is conducting a class discussion. A teacher might simply conclude that the students are being disruptive and walk to their desks in the hope of stopping the misbehavior. A self-directed teacher, however, might consider several alternative reasons for the behavior before taking action. He might hypothesize that the students are talking because they are confused about the teacher's presentation. He might check out his hunch by observing and listening to the students' interaction more carefully. If the teacher decides the students were confused, he will consider possible actions and mentally play out the consequences of each. Based on this analysis, he may choose to clarify the point the students were discussing. The teacher could then observe the students' reaction and evaluate whether the clarification had the desired result. Further action will depend on what the teacher sees and how he interprets the students' behavior. If the situation does not improve, he might later consult with the students themselves or other teachers to find new ways of thinking about this problem. Finally, he examines his own thinking process—how he framed the problem, chose actions, and interpreted the results. Through these reflections, he may construct new understandings about solving similar problems.

Theoretical Underpinnings:
Construction of Meaning

How do people analyze the events in their environment to construct meaning and plan appropriate actions?

Recent research on cognitive psychology (e.g., Brown, Collins, and Duguid 1989), teacher thinking (e.g., Lampert and Clark 1990), and critical theory (e.g., Van der Veer and Valsiner 1988), points to four ways that teachers construct meaning and make decisions in their daily functioning:

1. *Meaning is created through the interaction between the mind and the surrounding environment.* Teachers develop mental representations—or theories—that enable them to interpret commonly encountered teaching situations. According to Shulman (1987), a teacher's mental representations (or theories) include information about subject matter knowledge, teaching methods and theories, characteristics of learners, and so forth. Teachers also use their life values and morals when interpreting experiences and making decisions for action—for example, conceptions of justice, democratic ideals, and ethics (McLaren 1989).

2. *Meaning is determined by the surrounding cultural context* (McLaren 1989). Teachers must master the tools of their culture to behave in a socially acceptable and effective manner. Shulman (1986) referred to these tools as the *maxims* and *norms* of the environment. Maxims are ideas that have never been confirmed; moreover, they would be difficult to confirm through research. For example, consider this advice commonly given to new teachers: "Never smile before Christmas" and "Never turn your back to your students when writing on the blackboard." Norms identify what in the immediate culture is morally and ethically right; for example, "Don't embarrass a child in front of her peers" and "All students can learn with the proper instruction."

3. *Meaning is constructed through metacognition*—teacher planning, monitoring, and evaluation of thinking processes. The teacher must first be willing to stretch his current understandings in a flexible manner. He will not be content to accept his initial interpretation without first considering alternative interpretations (or "frames," Schön 1987) of a problem. He then internally tests out his options for future action. The teacher is not afraid to experiment to test out new ideas, even if it means risking failure.

4. *Meaning is developed through social interaction with respected others.* This social interaction is crucial to the development of a student teacher. The supervisor's discussions with the student teacher have great potential for helping him become a thoughtful, self-directed teacher. This process of gradually moving a novice to greater levels of competence is called *guided participation* (Rogoff 1990).

Guided Participation

In guided participation, an experienced mentor assesses the level of the beginner and gradually moves him to higher levels of cognitive functioning. This process requires active collaboration, interpersonal skills, the ability to assess another's developmental level, and interactive dialogue.

Through active collaboration, the individual learning the tools of the culture interacts with a supervisor who is more skilled and knowledgeable about the tools. The supervisor builds bridges (or *scaffolding*) from what the student already understands about teaching and the school culture to new understandings and skills. The supervisor provides emotional cues about the nature of the situations, nonverbal models of how to behave, verbal and nonverbal interpretations of behaviors and events, and verbal labels that classify objects and events. This bridging occurs in the "zone of proximal development" (Vygotsky 1978)—the mental "distance" between a person's current problem-solving ability and the ability the person can achieve if coached and supported by a more skilled individual.

A student teacher progresses most effectively through the zone when a trusting relationship has been established with the supervisor. Trust is the main building block for the maintenance of a positive self-esteem (Borba 1989). Without a positive self-esteem, the student teacher will not be willing to try new ideas and take risks. To maintain trust, the supervisor must first actively listen to what the student teacher says. Then the supervisor must take what data she hears and artfully push the student to take risks and try new ideas without asking the student to take on too much. This requires the ability to diagnose where the student is on a developmental continuum.

Initially, the supervisor becomes the conscience for the student—in essence, a "second mind." The supervisor guides the student to consider alternative interpretations and encourages him to take risks in an atmosphere of trust. This guidance includes discussions and modeling of the thinking the supervisor performs in her own planning and decision making. Over time, more and more of the decision making and responsibility are relinquished to the student teacher. At the end of the process, the student has acquired the necessary mental representations to interpret information, set goals, and assess his actions and thinking on his own.

During guided participation, the two individuals often enter the situation with different perspectives. It is the sharing of these perspectives in tandem with the trust established that helps both people refine or change their mental representations about teaching. By engaging in dialogue, both supervisor and student teacher have a chance to share and understand the divergent ideas. Miller (1987) calls this process "argumentation." Argumentation often leads to reinterpretation of the issues at stake. This process might lead to new and creative solutions, resulting in the cognitive growth of both participants.

A Concrete Example

What might this process of guided participation look like? Let's return to the classroom where, this time, a *student teacher* sees two girls talking in the back of the room. The student teacher immediately walks over to the students and asks them to stop. The students stop talking only until the teacher walks away from their immediate area. The supervisor observes this situation and makes a note to discuss it with the student teacher after class.

The supervisor begins the discussion by asking the student, "What were you thinking of when you moved to the back of the room where the two students were talking?"

The student might respond, "I learned in my last education class that when two students are talking, they are not paying attention to your lesson; and the way to stop the talking is to stand next to them."

The supervisor asks the student to describe the result of that action. The student recognizes that it only stopped the misbehavior momentarily and that as soon as he walked away, the talking began again. The student is baffled and not sure what else he should have done. The supervisor follows this up with further questions to assess what ideas are influencing the student's thinking (prior experiences, university course work, personal values, a hunch), and to determine what additional guidance the student needs.

It becomes apparent to the supervisor that the student has not considered anything about the students themselves. He has only thought about what he has experienced and his personal values. The supervisor then asks the student teacher what he knows about the two students in the back of the room—Was talking out of turn a normal behavior for them? The supervisor is thus becoming the conscience for the student teacher by asking the questions it is hoped the student will ultimately ask himself as he makes decisions with his own pupils.

The light goes on in the student teacher's head. The talking is not typical behavior for the two pupils. He realizes there must be something else going on. It dawns on the student teacher that the two disruptive students are best friends, and one of them had been out sick for a week. Perhaps the friend was trying to get the homework assignment. He guesses this is a more probable explanation. This interpretation had not occurred to the supervisor. Together they check out this hypothesis and confirm it with the students. Then they design a system for absent students to get homework assignments.

There are five points we wish to make about this interaction.

1. The supervisor assessed the student teacher's developmental level in the "zone of proximal development" and determined how she could support and guide the student to a higher point.

2. The supervisor never gave the student teacher the answer, but rather guided the student's thinking so that the student would feel encouraged that, with practice, he too could interpret complex situations. The supervisor became the second mind for the student by identifying what mental representations the student teacher was using to interpret the situation and then asking open-ended questions to encourage a "reframing" of the event. Not once was the student asked to take a developmental leap that was too large.

3. The open-ended questions allowed the supervisor to model her own thinking for the student. The student heard first-hand the questions a thoughtful, self-directed professional asks while interpreting classroom events and planning a course of action.

4. Through collaborative problem solving and argumentation, a new interpretation of the situation was discovered. This process can be referred to as "co-construction of meaning" (Miller 1987).

5. Neither individual in the pair would have grown professionally if the trusting relationship had not been well established and maintained.

Professional growth is encouraged through supervisory practices that have proved helpful in a Michigan school district, as described in the next section.

Supervisory Practices

Over the past six years, we have joined with Ann Arbor (Michigan) Public School teachers and Eastern Michigan University faculty to inquire into practices that promote reflective thinking in prestudent teachers, student teachers, and supervising teachers (see Sparks-Langer, Simmons, Pasch, Colton, and Starko 1990). We began our inquiry with courses, seminars, and informal dialogue with supervising teachers (see Colton, Sparks-Langer, Tripp-Opple, and Simmons 1989). These experiences resulted in three insights. We believe supervising teachers need to be able to: (1) become more conscious of their own thinking and become more self-directed, (2) clearly explain their own professional thinking, and (3) promote thoughtful self-directed behavior in others. These became the goals of our training for supervising teachers.

Supervisor Training

As a result of the seminars and inquiry activities, we designed four days of training for supervising teachers. We start with readings and discussion of the characteristics of thoughtful, self-directed teachers and the theoretical underpinnings described previously (see Sparks-Langer and Colton 1991). As we examine these ideas, teachers begin to fit them into their own experiences and modify their theories or mental representations of how people learn. Together, we come to a common understanding of the kind of student teacher we hope to develop.

Next we begin a section on interpersonal skills—a key factor in guided participation. Student teachers are often so tense and self-conscious that they find it difficult to relax and let their minds function flexibly. The course includes communication strategies for building rapport, such as mirroring body language and tone and active listening. We emphasize that maintaining trust is crucial for encouraging risk taking, further movement through the zone of proximal development, and developing or maintaining a positive self-esteem.

In the training, we also share information on self-esteem—what signals low self-esteem, and how to bolster a student teacher's lack of self-confidence. We discuss and practice strategies that can help student teachers to affirm their own worth as they struggle with the many challenges and dilemmas of teaching.

We then focus on how dialogue can promote metacognitive problem solving through engaging mental representations, analyzing cultural norms, and probing personal beliefs. In a "helping trio" activity, teachers work with each other to frame, define, reframe (Schön 1987), and analyze a persistent classroom problem without offering suggestions or solutions. Thus, the idea of stepping back from a problem and examining it from various perspectives is seen as crucial to self-directed professional functioning.

Our model of observation and supervision is strongly influenced by Cognitive Coaching (Costa and Garmston 1988, Sparks 1989). Cognitive Coaching requires the supervisor to ask mediating questions—nonjudgmental, open-ended questions that encourage the student teacher to delve into his professional mental representations and values to try to explain why he acted as he did and why the students reacted as they did. There is a minimum of "supervisor talk" or direct teaching by the coach during the conferences. The intent is to encourage the student teacher to explore his thinking in the interest of becoming more self-directed.

Cognitive Coaching includes a preobservation conference designed to achieve four goals: (1) to model questions a teacher would routinely ask himself about the lesson, (2) to assess what knowledge the student teacher can bring to the situation and identify possible areas for further guidance and problem solving, (3) to guide the student to consider other important information, and (4) to pinpoint a focus for the supervisor's observation. These questions give the student teacher practice in analyzing the thinking and values that led up to his decisions about lesson goals, activities, and assessment. Ultimately, he will automatically ask himself such questions—the essence of a self-directed professional.

In addition to the preconference, we also teach supervisors various observation strategies (Stallings, Needels, and Sparks 1987) so that appropriate, objective data can be used in the discussions that follow. After practicing these instruments in simulated teaching situations, we discuss how to modify them to collect information on various aspects of teaching and learning.

The post-observation conference is taught and practiced next. Again, there are three goals: (1) to model the metacognitive questions of a self-directed teacher, (2) to assess what direction to take as the conference proceeds, and (3) to identify the next steps in the coaching/teaching of the novice. Throughout the conference, probing questions require the student teacher to articulate the thinking behind the decisions he made.

First, the supervisor engages the novice in metacognition by asking how he felt about the lesson, what went as planned, and what the student teacher did that brought about that result. Then aspects that were disappointing are analyzed by the student with prompting and probing—but no judgment—by the supervisor.

After this opening, the supervisor must choose between a more direct style and a continuation of the less direct mediating questions. The choice will depend on the level of trust, confidence, conceptual sophistication, and background knowledge of the student teacher. The more direct approach may include reinforcement of skills or concepts or direct instruction in skills and concepts.

In the less directive approach, the supervisor would invite the student teacher to examine the observation data, using open-ended questions to encourage various interpretations (framing and reframing) of the data, and an awareness of his thinking processes.

As the conference closes, the supervisor and student identify future steps for growth—for example, techniques or ideas that need to be practiced or thought about more deeply. They may also discuss future directions for the next coaching session. Finally, the supervisor asks the student teacher to describe which parts of the conference were especially helpful and if there are any changes that should be made. This helps the supervisor assess her own progress as a coach and provides a model of the teacher as a continuous learner. The conference thus enables both parties to grow and learn professionally.

After the training, monthly meetings allow supervisors to continue to improve as they discuss current challenges, concerns, and needs with other supervisors. Cases are generated and strategies are discussed. A final source of support is provided by the trainer, who coaches the supervisors as they conduct a pre- and post-observation conference. Such coaching helps the supervising teacher hone the new skills and attitudes that promote thoughtful, self-directed thinking in student teachers.

Developmental Activities for Student Teachers

A common shortcoming of many student teaching programs is the lack of (1) a conceptual framework (or theoretical underpinnings) and (2) developmental activities that move the student teacher toward identified goals (Goodlad 1990). We reasoned that student teachers could be guided to construct their own theories and interpretations of their experiences through specific developmental assignments that become progressively more complex.

The assignments we designed are divided into three phases of the fifteen-week student teaching semester. During *the early phase*, the student teacher spends much of his time observing the supervisor teach and listening to the supervisor talk aloud about her thinking and interpretations—for example, what was considered as she planned the lesson and why, what changes were made during the lesson and why, and how she felt the lesson went. Through this process, the student can see that such decisions require a great amount of mental effort and are based on one's own mental representations, personal values, and cultural norms. The student also experiences active collaboration as the pair co-construct meaning out of their classroom experiences.

Also during the early phase, the student teacher helps individual students and takes over the simpler routines. The practice of these routines (e.g., distributing materials) eventually allows the student teacher to perform them with little mental effort, thus freeing his mind to consider some of the more complex aspects of the classroom (e.g., equity in giving students individual attention).

Finally, the student plans a direct lesson (based on Madeline Hunter and Mastery Learning), which is videotaped for analysis. The supervisor's conferencing style may be more directive at this phase if the student has little knowledge, comfort, or experience with which to analyze the events of the day.

An important component of this first phase (and all phases) is the journal kept by the student teacher. We see writing journals as internal dialogue with oneself. The journal is an intermediate step that leads to the development of new mental representations and metacognition.

We have experimented with various approaches to keeping journals, from very structured "reflection journals" to open-ended, free-association logs that are exchanged and responded to by all parties—teacher, student teacher, and university professor. Ideally, students should continue to write in the journals throughout the semester. Their reflections become more focused as the student teachers construct meaning in the social context of teaching through framing questions, experimenting, and pondering dilemmas. It is important that the supervisor review and make comments in the journal on a regular basis.

During *the middle five weeks* of student teaching, the student takes on the teaching of one to three subject areas or class periods. Two formal observations are conducted, one of an inductive lesson, and one of a cooperative learning lesson. The conferencing style now becomes less directive; the student teacher is given more responsibility for interpreting and explaining his thinking about the teaching and learning events of the day. Students write "lesson reflection journals," analyzing why aspects of the lesson were successful or unsuccessful, what conditions and context factors may have influenced the outcome, and what social justice issues or democratic values may relate to the day's events.

In *the final third of the semester*, the student teacher takes on the planning and teaching of the entire curriculum. Journal writing continues as the student teacher becomes more metacognitively aware of what he does. The student teacher plans a unit and is observed teaching a lesson in the unit. Finally, the student teacher videotapes another lesson for analysis and writes a paper that compares and contrasts his behavior and thinking in the first and last videos.

The four formal observations are not the only occasions where the supervising teacher coaches the student teacher. Of course, during the daily operation of the classroom the two confer, share, debate, and reflect as they co-plan, co-teach, and co-construct new meanings. The use of dialogue, metacognition, and problem-solving strategies are prominent during these interactions.

Throughout all phases of the student teaching semester, four themes are stressed: multiculturalism, use of technology, special-needs students, and professional collegiality. Supervisors model the inclusion of multicultural activities and technological tools in their lessons and coach student teachers in these areas. Supervisors also observe their students in special education settings and plan enrichment activities for those who are ahead of the others. Finally, student teachers attend biweekly seminars with other student teachers and go to workshops with their teachers to experience the value of collegial professional learning.

Recommendations and Future Directions

We have learned several valuable lessons during the past six years. First, it is essential that university faculty work closely with teachers in any attempt to improve field experiences. It is, after all, the classroom teacher who has the most contact with the student teacher and who will have the greatest influence on him. Too often, universities take on the responsibility for structuring student teaching with little involvement of teachers. Such innovations rarely get implemented or sustained as intended. Because we worked collaboratively with teachers in reviewing literature, creating a conceptual framework, and designing training and field experiences, more teachers are likely to support the innovations. More important, teachers have become co-inquirers into the process of helping a novice learn to teach. These dedicated teachers are writing about their experiences and what they have learned as we begin to create a case literature about student teaching supervision.

We have also learned four paramount lessons about supervisory practices:

1. Interpersonal skills are crucial to developing a trusting relationship in which the student teacher feels safe to think aloud, express concerns, and take risks. Without trust, it is difficult for the pair to engage in problem solving or planning. This is a gradual process; but all supervisors should have some formal training in communication and rapport-building strategies.

2. By modeling professional thinking, journal keeping, discussion, and small-group problem solving, supervisors can help student teachers develop metacognition. Hearing teachers think aloud as they plan, make decisions, and solve problems is helpful for student teachers.

3. Supervisors and student teachers should discuss specific concepts and ideas in context. If one analyzes generic teaching strategies without discussing the structure and meaning of the content being taught, many valuable lessons are missed. Students should consider (a) the surrounding cultural context, (b) the worth of the instructional outcomes, and (c) the ethical and moral implications of the methods or content.

4. Assessment processes and forms used to evaluate student teachers will need to be changed to reflect this new constructivist view of teaching. Ratings and narratives should include criteria related to the student teacher's capacity for creating meaningful and appropriate interpretations of their classroom experiences. Other criteria might include the propensity for risk taking and experimentation, goal setting, self-analysis, and metacognition.

Supervisory practices ought to move the student teacher along a developmental continuum, starting with less thoughtful, self-directed and effective behavior and encouraging more reflection and more self-directed behavior. We need more research to clearly describe typical patterns in the development of student teachers' thinking and behavior. As we describe this continuum, we will also need to create a framework for diagnosing where the student teacher is in his development. We will need to know more about how big a leap we can ask a novice to take from one spot in the zone of proximal development to another.

Our student teaching assignments are arranged in what we think is a developmental sequence. Yet, some students have whizzed through the stages; and others could barely begin the process. As we continue to study the use of structured field experiences to develop thoughtful, self-directed professionals, we will begin to refine these developmental stages. In turn, we will be able to refine the supervisory practices that can help move a student toward greater effectiveness and success as a teacher.

References

Borba, M. (1989). *Esteem Builders: A K–8 Self-Esteem Curriculum for Improving Student Achievement, Behavior and School Climate*. Rolling Hills Estates: P. Jalmer Press.

Brown, J.S., A. Collins, and P. Duguid. (January–February 1989). "Situated Cognition and The Culture of Learning." *Educational Researcher* 18, 1: 32–42.

Colton, A.B., G.M. Sparks-Langer, K. Tripp-Opple, and J.M. Simmons. (Fall 1989). "Collaborative Inquiry Into Developing Reflective Pedagogical Thinking." *Action in Teacher Education* 11, 3: 44–52.

Costa, A., and B. Garmston. (1988). *Cognitive Coaching Training Manual*. Sacramento, Calif.: Institute for Instructional Behavior.

Goodlad, J. (1990). "Studying the Education of Educators: From Conception to Findings." *Phi Delta Kappan* 71, 9: 698-701.

Kennedy, M.M. (1990). "NCRTL Special Report: An Agenda for Research on Teacher Learning." East Lansing, Mich.: National Center for Research on Teacher Learning.

Lampert, M. and C.M. Clark. (1990). "Expert Knowledge and Expert Thinking in Teaching: A Response to Floden and Klinzing." *Educational Researcher* 19, 4: 21–23.

McLaren, P. (1989). *Life in Schools*. New York: Longman.

Miller, M. (1987). "Argumentation and cognition." In M. Hickman (Ed.), *Social Functioning Approaches to Language and Thought*. San Diego: Academic Press.

Rogoff, B. (1990). *Apprenticeship in Thinking*. New York: Oxford University Press.

Schön, D. (1987). *Educating the Reflective Practitioner*. San Francisco: Jossey-Bass.

Shulman, L.S. (1986). "Those Who Understand: Knowledge Growth in Teaching." *Educational Research* 15, 2: 4–14.

Shulman, L.S. (February 1987). "Knowledge and Teaching: Foundations of the New Reform." *Harvard Educational Review* 57: 31.

Sparks, D. (1990). "Cognitive Coaching: An Interview with Robert Garmston." *The Journal of Staff Development* 11, 2: 12–18.

Sparks-Langer, G.M., and A.B. Colton. (March 1991). "Synthesis of Research on Teachers' Reflective Thinking." *Educational Leadership* 48, 6: 37–44.

Sparks-Langer, G.M., J.M. Simmons, M. Pasch, A. Colton, and A. Starko. (1990). "Reflective Pedagogical Thinking: How Can We Promote It and Measure It?" *Journal of Teacher Education* 41, 5: 11–20.

Stallings, J., M. Needels, and G.M. Sparks. (1987). "Observations for the Improvement of Classroom Learning." In *Talks to Teachers*, edited by D. Berliner and B. Rosenshine. New York: Random House.

Van der Veer, R., and J. Valsiner. (1988). "The Concept of Internalization in Vygotsky's Account of the Genesis of Higher Mental Functions." *Developmental Review* 8: 52–65.

Vygotsky, L.S. (1978). *Mind in Society: The Development of Higher Psychological Processes*. Cambridge: Harvard University Press.

11

Linking Preservice and Inservice Supervision Through Professional Inquiry

Patricia E. Holland, Renee Clift, and Mary Lou Veal
with Marlene Johnson and Jane McCarthy

We've all seen variations on a familiar cartoon. Two hardhatted engineers scrutinize plans and scratch their heads as they stand at ends of completed sections of a highway or a bridge or a railroad that don't meet. This cartoon image is particularly apt these days in describing the relationship—or lack thereof—between what people learn in preservice teacher education programs and what happens when they work as teachers—and are subject to supervision and inservice programs.

Unfortunately, preservice and inservice programs often work at cross purposes. Teachers, especially novices who are at the most vulnerable point in their career, are left to figure out some way to bridge the gap between what they learned about being a teacher and supervisors' expectations that professional development as a teacher is ongoing. It's a lot—and many times, too much—to ask. Teachers (and also some supervisors) who have not been prepared for supervision often see it as something done for teachers who are "in trouble." Not surprisingly, teachers are unwilling to reveal their needs; they protect themselves by engaging minimally in what Garman (1981) has called the "rituals" of supervision.

Contradictions Between Preservice and Inservice Supervision Programs

One way to account for this mismatch between teacher education and supervision is to note the contradictions between what teachers learn in most preservice programs and what is required of them when schools undergo restructuring. Such contradictions reveal fundamentally differing convictions about the nature of teachers' work, about the knowledge teaching requires, and about the process of learning to teach.

Autonomy vs. Collaboration

Teacher education programs continue to reinforce the autonomy that Drebeen (1968) says is one of the earliest things students learn in schools. Students of education are graded for their individual effort and performance. With few exceptions, assignments and tests are solo efforts. The student is expected to relate primarily to the teacher of a given class, and this relationship is encouraged and rewarded through the teacher's power to evaluate and grade. The net effect of this structure may be to produce teachers who can demonstrate a required degree of knowledge and proficiency, but it also conditions students to think that their work in teaching is appropriately done as lone adults responsible for the youngsters in their charge.

This view, however, has continually faced challenge from modern supervision and, now, from advocates of school restructuring. The evolving view of supervision and restructuring is that teachers' professional development is encouraged and enhanced by collaboration with other adult professionals in the school work place. Whether such collaboration occurs between a teacher and someone designated as a supervisor—as in clinical supervision models—involves teachers working together in peer coaching or mentor relationships, or occurs in those few "restructured" schools where teachers have schedules affording them time to plan and teach together, the basic interaction involves adults working collaboratively to improve teaching. These collaborative relationships require of teachers certain skills and attitudes necessary for adults to work with other adults as colleagues. Preservice education, however, does little to encourage students to develop or practice such skills and attitudes; rather, traditional hierarchical roles and relationships are the ones most often modeled and reinforced.

Context-Free vs. Context-Specific Knowledge

Another contradiction between preservice and inservice programs arises from differing notions about the kind of knowledge teaching requires. The focus in most teacher education programs is on knowledge that is context free and is exemplified by generic content and teaching methods. Granted, some exemplary programs and individual teacher educators offer students opportunities to explore the impact on teaching practice of such contextual factors as socioeconomic status, ethnicity, and special needs of children, particularly in contexts that differ from the student's own background and school experience. And, as Shulman (1987) reports, a growing body of research suggests that different subject matter requires knowledge of different teaching strategies. The overwhelming message of teacher education, though, is that knowledge of fundamental teaching methods and of subject matter is uniformly applicable in any school setting.

Little wonder that teachers often criticize their preservice education for not preparing them for the confusing, complex world of schools—particularly urban, multicultural ones. Many novice teachers fail to recognize the influence of preservice training on their practice, and they unquestioningly accept norms of practice that allow them to survive in their particular schools.

In recent years, teacher evaluation models masquerading as instructional supervision have extended into schools the view that teaching requires only technical knowledge. Such models are seductively attractive, with their grand illusion of a uniform set of teaching practices that can be prescribed, taught, evaluated, and rewarded. However, teachers and administrators are growing increasingly frustrated with these models, recognizing that they neither effectively evaluate teachers' overall practice nor provide information that teachers can use to better meet the learning needs of the students in their charge.

Genuine instructional supervision, on the other hand, has continuously affirmed the contextual nature of teaching knowledge and teachers' individual learning needs. Such supervision, grounded in actual events of teaching, assumes that teachers grow professionally when they are aware of how they are actually teaching and have an opportunity to study and modify their practice in the interest of students' learning. Working together, supervisors and teachers determine what information to collect and examine so that classroom teachers can extend their understanding of teaching practices. This process assumes that teachers, as well as supervisors, have learned to identify the important elements of a given teaching context and can decide what information should be used to improve teaching in that context. Unfortunately, many teachers enter schools unprepared to engage in such thoughtful analysis of their practice.

Finite vs. Ongoing Learning

Yet another contradiction between teacher education and supervision resides in the way each envisions the process of learning to teach. Implicit in preservice programs is the sense of a given time frame within which one learns to be a teacher—an end state of knowledge that is reached by graduation. The structure of preservice programs reinforces the notion that coursework and student teaching prepare a student to be a teacher. Once hired, novice teachers often find that conditions in the work place reinforce that assumption. Rarely, for example, do novice teachers find jobs in school districts where university faculty help support and instruct beginning teachers. All too often, novices receive virtually no help. They are expected to teach the same number of classes as experienced veterans, and frequently to teach the most academically needy and difficult students.

In contrast, decades-old assumptions of supervision are now heard again in discussions of school restructuring. These assumptions are that learning to teach is a process continuing as long as one teaches, and that consideration must be given to adapting school structures to meet teachers' learning needs. Behind these assumptions is the intention that teachers continue to increase their professional knowledge and skill through an ongoing study of teaching—their own and others'.

The Concept of Professional Inquiry

Though we may have oversimplified the contradictions between preservice education and inservice supervision, there is no denying that connections between these programs are usually missing. One need only look at the balkanization that exists between programs preparing teachers and those preparing supervisors to see reasons for this lack of connection. There is another conflict: universities continue to reward research for its own sake, and schools are driven by practical needs for change and improvement.

There is an alternative to the bleak prospect that teacher preparation and inservice supervision will continue as unrelated efforts. That alternative is based not on the unrealistic prospect of changing the essential cultures or missions of either universities or schools, but rather on a concept that links both settings in working with would-be and actual teachers. That concept is "professional inquiry."

Professional inquiry suggests a continuous process—perhaps developmental, although that implies a linearity often belied by experience. It suggests a continuum of skills and habits of mind that link preservice and inservice programs. Preservice educators would not only help prospective teachers acquire content knowledge and pedagogical techniques, but would provide them with opportunities for learning to work collaboratively—analyzing contexts of teaching and describing, interpreting, and critiquing events of teaching and learning.

The concept of professional inquiry encompasses what Jonas Soltis (1984) describes as the three major traditions in contemporary views of knowledge creation and use: the empirical, the hermeneutic, and the critical. As common intellectual properties, these traditions serve to define a continuum of teachers' professional development from a beginning point in teacher education through the highest levels of professional practice, as follows:

• *An Empirical Perspective.* Professional inquiry includes a focus on a careful study of actual classroom events and particular teaching methods or practices. From the empirical perspective, accumulating more richly detailed and descriptive information about educational settings is directly correlated with knowledge and understanding of those settings and with teachers' competence, as measured by students' performance. Teachers can increase their empirical knowledge by learning classroom observation techniques that allow them to gather, organize, and depict specific and detailed information about teaching events. Traditionally only supervisors have been trained in such techniques, leaving teachers in a dependent position of having to rely on supervisors' data.

• *A Hermeneutic Perspective.* Hermeneutics involves the interpretive nature of knowledge; that is, meaning resides neither in the events of teaching themselves nor in the data gathered about these events. Rather, meaning—or knowledge—is *created* as these events or data are interpreted by individuals. The process is further influenced by the prior knowledge and presuppositions that individuals bring to their work of interpretation and by the particular focus of a given interpretation. In an oft-cited text on hermeneutics, Palmer (1969) points out that interpretation is not approached with a "blank openness," but is governed by the interpreters' "questioning."

This hermeneutic view of knowledge suggests that knowledge of teaching requires teachers to question and explore their own "educational platforms" (Walker 1971) and the influence these espoused platforms have on their practice and on their interpretations of the practice of others.

• *A Critical Perspective*. In this perspective, the goal of inquiry is to expose existing power relationships in social situations and to address the misuses of power and the exercise of oppressive control over certain members or groups. Smyth (1985) has argued eloquently for the importance of the critical perspective. He contends that supervision must be concerned with how teachers and students can be empowered as active participants in the more democratic creation and use of knowledge. Such critical practices are also advocated for teacher education programs and for educational administration, in which supervision is most often located. However, the application of a critical perspective in teacher education programs—both preservice and inservice—remains marginal, at best. The lack of a critical component in teachers' education suggests that teachers are being inadequately prepared to meet the challenges presented by the growing numbers of students at risk in both school and contemporary life. To remedy this situation, teacher educators and supervisors need to provide teachers with opportunities for examining the relationships between instructional practices and larger economic and political contexts.

Professional inquiry is the conscious development of teachers' own theories of practice. The case has already been made for a theory of practice for supervision that examines teaching from empirical, hermeneutic, and critical perspectives (Sergiovanni 1981). Introducing these perspectives in teacher education programs allows professional inquiry to begin at the outset of students' development as teachers. Professional inquiry thus links teacher education and supervision, providing continued emphasis on the skills and experiences that help teachers grow in their understanding of teaching.

Concepts and Practices that Promote Professional Inquiry

Incorporating professional inquiry into preservice and inservice programs, fortunately, does not have to begin from scratch. There are already concepts and practices that embody the preceding notions of professional inquiry. What these programs need is a wider application of these concepts and practices, and recognition that they inform *both* teacher education and supervision. What is also needed is closer cooperation between teacher educators and supervisors in preparing and supporting teachers to use these concepts and practices. One such concept is Schön's "reflective practice" (1983, 1987).

Reflective Practice

In recent years, the literature in both teacher education and supervision has become replete with arguments for reflective practice and programs based on its principles. The focus, however, has been on how the concept of reflective practice informs the *separate* practices of teacher education and supervision; little attention has been paid to the ways in which reflective practice allows teachers to link their preservice programs with inservice supervision.

The term *professional reflective activity* (Clift, Holland, and Veal 1990) suggests a continuum of reflective practice as an action-oriented connection of preservice and inservice experiences.

Teacher education programs designed to prepare students for professional reflective activity require students to begin developing the ability to interpret and analyze what Schön has called the "messy and indeterminate" nature of actual practice settings and to develop context-specific solutions for the problems encountered in those settings. Such programs also should encourage teachers to recognize that inservice supervision offers continuing opportunities to engage in reflective practice.

Collaboration

Another concept linking preservice and supervision is collaboration. Collaboration can take many forms: teachers in grade level or interdisciplinary teams, teachers and administrators in site based management structures, and teachers and university researchers in field-based studies. These collaborative relationships, in addition to those that have traditionally characterized instructional supervision, provide teachers with opportunities to increase their own knowledge of teaching and to play a larger role in shaping the culture of schools.

Amid growing expectations for collaboration in school settings, preservice efforts to prepare teachers to work collaboratively have emerged. For example, at the University of Wisconsin-Madison, students and cooperating teachers engage in joint research ventures. At the University of Illinois at Champagne-Urbana and the University of Houston, student teachers meet regularly with cooperating teachers and university faculty to consider various issues and problems of practice. Such programs encourage students to regard collaboration as a familiar and useful part of their work in teaching. These preservice programs help students learn to understand collaboration—to distinguish it from mere cooperation and from more subtle forms of organizational compliance—and develop the ability to work effectively with other adults.

Action Research

Action research offers students and teachers another framework for professional inquiry. Its advocates emphasize teachers' roles in exploring and analyzing their work; and they encourage teachers to think of themselves as researchers and of the school as a place for inquiry. As such, action research is again enjoying popularity. Action research incorporates the empirical, hermeneutic, and critical perspectives on knowledge that have been described as characteristic of professional inquiry.

Programs using action research can be found in both preservice and inservice settings in the United States, as well as in England and Australia. These programs stress the value of developing habits of examining and critiquing practice early in teacher training. Noffke and Zeichner (1987) and other researchers have argued that such habits prepare students to enter teaching equipped with attitudes and skills that will assist them in their continuing learning and professional development.

Examples of action research in inservice settings are usually not specifically related to the practice of supervision. However, in terms of the shared objectives of improving practice and the focus on teachers' active role in identifying the focus and means for such improvement efforts, supervision and action research occupy common ground in their approaches to teachers' professional inquiry.

Clinical Supervision

Clinical supervision, which had its origins in the Harvard M.A.T. teacher preparation program (Cogan 1973, Goldhammer 1969), has since been used to supervise teachers in both student teaching and inservice settings. Clinical supervision advances teachers' professional inquiry through its emphasis on trust and open communication about the teacher's practice. So also, clinical supervision supports professional inquiry by encouraging teachers to take an active role in determining the focus of their own supervisory process. Teacher and supervisor agree to concentrate on certain aspects of the teacher's practice, plan together for an observation of the teacher's class, and identify strategies the supervisor will use to collect data that can help the teacher improve her practice. In the conference that conventionally follows a classroom observation, the teacher and supervisor analyze the data collected during the observation and jointly determine what it suggests about the relative strengths and weaknesses of the teacher's practice. On the basis of their analysis, they consider how the teacher can use this information to better understand her practice and to strengthen and improve her teaching.

Unfortunately, clinical supervision's potential as a vehicle for professional inquiry in both preservice and inservice settings remains too often unrealized, for the following reasons:

• Lacking training and skill to make clinical supervision a teacher-centered process, supervisors are judgmental and evaluative of teachers' practice.

• Universities and schools, forced to operate with limited supervisory personnel, find it impossible to allocate the time required for the frequent meetings and observations demanded by clinical supervision.

• The frequent misrepresentation of current teacher evaluation practices as "clinical supervision" causes teachers to view supervision as an unpleasant process serving only bureaucratic ends.

Coaching

Other examples of professional inquiry linking teacher education and supervision are found in various forms of "coaching." The most widely recognized form is that described by Joyce and Showers (1982). Coaching teams—usually two fellow teachers—observe one another try out a particular teaching model they have learned about and have seen demonstrated by others. Team members assist each other as follows:

• They provide feedback on performances of the teaching model in nonjudgmental, informational terms.

• They offer each other emotional support during the difficult process of transferring acquired knowledge of the teaching model into applied knowledge.

• They help each other identify how and when the model can be applied to facilitate student learning.

This form of coaching, labeled by Garmston (1987) as "technical coaching," is one of three varieties used in inservice settings. According to Garmston, the other two are "collegial coaching," which focuses more on reflection and dialogue among teachers about the contexts of teaching, and "challenge coaching," which addresses teachers' particular and persisting problems. These forms of coaching emphasize collaboration among teachers, focus on actual contexts of teaching, and consider teaching from the perspective of professional inquiry.

Coaching has also been used by Schön (1987) to describe approaches for use in pre-practice settings. In Schön's version, the practicum, or student teaching experience, as the setting for coaching as it approximates the world of practice, allows for greater experimentation and reflection than is possible in actual practice. The coach is a more knowledgeable partner offering guidance in performing, questioning, and interpreting the learning experience—all aspects of professional inquiry. Although Schön's description of coaching is confined to the preservice practicum, it can also be seen to have implications for the mentoring of novice teachers.

Developing a Continuum of Professional Inquiry

Professional inquiry offers teacher educators and supervisors a way to think about learning to teach in terms of a continuum of skills and practices along which teachers develop during the course of their careers. It allows teacher education programs and supervision to function as related efforts engaging teachers in common practices that promote their development as skilled and reflective professionals. A continuum of professional inquiry also reflects shared rather than contradictory assumptions, as follows:

• *Learning to teach is an ongoing process.* Operating on this assumption, teacher educators, supervisors, and university faculty who prepare supervisors would forge links between preservice and inservice programs. Such links would introduce students to ways of thinking about and studying practice that they could expect to be part of inservice supervision. Joint efforts involving teacher educators and school districts should be undertaken to ensure continuity of teachers' learning once they enter practice. Also, programs to prepare teachers and those preparing administrators should collaborate and offer coursework at both undergraduate and graduate levels in such areas as peer coaching, the process of learning to teach, school leadership roles, and action research.

• *Teachers actively participate in determining the direction of their professional growth.* In their work with prospective teachers, preservice faculty would conceive of their role as one that goes beyond the transmission of technical skill to one of providing students with opportunities for engaging in systematic study of and reflection on their developing practice. The emphasis in supervision would be on working *with* teachers, not working *on* them. Supervisors would assist teachers in analyzing and understanding their practice and would help them gain information to better explain and direct their own teaching.

• *Both preservice education and supervision focus on the effects and meanings—intended and unintended—of teachers' practice.* Beginning in teacher education programs and continuing in supervision, teachers would examine practice from empirical, hermeneutic, and critical perspectives that would allow them to develop their own theories of practice. The importance of such personalized, practical knowledge of teaching lies in its potential for preparing professionals who, as Shulman (1986) describes them, can explain and communicate to others the reasons for their teaching decisions and actions.

Responses from the Field

Jane McCarthy, a Preservice Supervisor

Many preservice programs are successful in producing teachers who are skilled and thoughtful practitioners; who look at classroom contexts as constantly changing, dynamic entities; and who work at framing questions in ways that will help them be more effective. These programs also encourage future teachers to think of learning to teach as a lifelong challenge

A number of U.S. programs promote such practices and are organized to prepare teachers to engage in them. Certainly these preservice programs are not yet in the majority, but they do seem to be the wave of the future. What such programs have in common is their emphasis on experiences intended to introduce teachers to the kind of "professional inquiry" called for in this chapter.

One way such programs promote professional inquiry is to provide students with opportunities throughout their preservice work to consider what they are learning in terms of actual practice situations. When teacher education students are introduced to techniques and strategies in isolation from practice, they usually fail to incorporate these techniques into their professional repertoire. It is this lack of exposure to schools and classrooms that causes many beginning teachers to use a very narrow range of teaching behaviors that do not change much over time. It is possible, however, for preservice programs to involve students from the earliest stages of their programs in real schools and to encourage them to work collaboratively among themselves and with practicing teachers. Such experiences prepare teachers for a career in teaching in which they are engaged in continual action research.

Another characteristic of preservice programs that prepare teachers for "professional inquiry" is that they encourage students to make professionally sound decisions that are particular to a specific educational setting and to justify those decisions. A reflective inquiry approach to teacher education provides the experiences in the field and in the classroom that will equip teachers to recognize the unique characteristics of any given classroom.

Preparing preservice teachers to be reflective practitioners is a necessary, but not sufficient, condition for success in the school context. The close collaboration of preservice educators with teachers and administrators in the field is a crucial link in the process. We know that our teacher education students will continue their reflective practices in the field only if such practices are encouraged and rewarded. It is crucial that our colleagues in the field be involved in the preparation process so that the value of reflective practice is shared at all levels.

Marlene Johnson, an Inservice Supervisor

Linking preservice education and inservice supervision through professional inquiry sounds exciting, but as a school district supervisor, I am only too aware of how far away we are from making that concept a reality. In my experience, the best efforts of teachers, supervisors, and administrators to make significant changes in instruction in their schools are undermined by policies that they are powerless to affect—policies such as mandated curriculums, testing, class size, teaching schedules, and teacher evaluation.

In numerous instances, exceptional teachers have shared with me their dilemmas of having to choose between providing the most appropriate instruction for their students or providing the instruction that will lead to higher test scores or better teaching evaluations. Fortunately, these teachers usually choose what is best for students, frequently at their own expense. However, I suspect there are many more teachers who either don't think to question educational policies and practices, or who simply do what is expected of them and remain silent about any alternatives.

A conversation I had recently with a principal demonstrates how difficult it is to move beyond the constraints of mandated policies and traditional practices. This principal was concerned that although the students in her building were performing above average on the state-mandated tests, they could not apply the skills to think critically about reading material on their grade level. The principal believed that although solutions to this problem were possible, such solutions weren't going to happen because she and the teachers were powerless to address the structure of the system that perpetuates the problem. As long as the teachers feel pressured by the district and the state to prepare students for standardized tests, they will be hesitant to alter their teaching practices to accomplish nontested learning objectives.

* * *

This chapter shows how preservice education and inservice supervision can play vital roles in establishing school environments in which professional inquiry leads to real changes in teaching and learning. However, teachers, supervisors and university faculty must do more than engage in professional reflective inquiry among themselves. They must also act to build structures at school, district, state, and national levels to give teachers the flexibility they need to be professionals and reward them for efforts at inquiry.

References

Clift, R., P. Holland, and M. Veal. (1990). "School Context Dimensions That Affect Staff Development." *Journal of Staff Development* 11, 1: 34–38.

Cogan, M. (1973). *Clinical Supervision.* Boston: Houghton Mifflin.

Drebeen, R. (1968). *On What Is Learned in Schools.* Reading, Mass.: Addison-Wesley.

Garman, N. (1981). "The Clinical Approach to Supervision." In *Supervision in Teaching,* edited by T. Sergiovanni. Alexandria, Va.: ASCD.

Garmston, R. (1987). "How Administrators Support Peer Coaching." *Educational Leadership* 44, 5: 18–26.

Goldhammer, R. (1969). *Clinical Supervision: Special Methods for the Supervision of Teachers.* New York: Holt, Rinehart and Winston.

Joyce, B., and B. Showers. (1982). "The Coaching of Teaching." *Educational Leadership* 40, 1: 4–10.

Noffke, S., and K. Zeichner. (April 22, 1987). "Action Research and Teacher Thinking: The First Phase of the Action Research Project at the University of Wisconsin-Madison." Paper presented at the annual meeting of the American Educational Research Association, Washington, D.C.

Palmer, R. (1969). *Hermeneutics.* Evanston, Ill.: Northwestern University Press.

Schön, D. (1983) *The Reflective Practitioner: How Professionals Think in Action.* New York: Basic Books.

Schön, D. (1987). *Educating the Reflective Practitioner: Toward a New Design for Teaching and Learning in the Professions.* San Francisco: Jossey-Bass.

Sergiovanni, T. (1981). "Toward a Theory of Supervisory Practice: Integrating Scientific, Clinical and Artistic Views." In *Supervision of Teaching,* edited by T. Sergiovanni. Alexandria, Va.: ASCD.

Shulman, L. (1986). "Those Who Understand: Knowledge Growth in Teaching." *Educational Researcher* 15, 2: 4–21.

Shulman, L. (1987). "Knowledge and Teaching: Foundations of the New Reform." *Harvard Educational Review* 57, 1: 1–22.

Smyth, J. (1985). "Developing a Critical Practice of Clinical Supervision." *Journal of Curriculum Studies* 17, 1: 1–15.

Soltis, J. (1984). "On the Nature of Educational Research." *Educational Researcher* 13, 10: 5–10.

Walker, D. (1971). "The Process of Curriculum Development: A Naturalistic Model." *School Review* 80, 1: 51–69.

IV

The Reflection

12

The Transformation
of Supervision

Peter P. Grimmett, Olaf P. Rostad, and Blake Ford

ead any text on instructional supervision and you will find that its
R *raison d'etre* is to bring about educational change in teachers'
instructional practices. For example, in a review of the supervision
literature, Pajak (1990) states, "Supervision is considered by many
[writers] to be the primary process by which instructional excellence is
achieved and maintained" (p. 1). Such edifying rhetoric is most laud-
able, but what does it mean for teachers?

For some teachers, the press for change in instructional practice
represents a high-pressure disturbance generating much anxiety, internal seething, and agitation, together with a sense that an overwhelming
muddle is busily at work dismantling the stability of their world. For
others, the press for change rekindles waning enthusiasm; stimulates a
sense of wonder, excitement, and mystery about learning; and absorbs
their interest in a manner that inspires a quiet confidence and serenity.

In this chapter,[1] we emphasize that the way in which supervisors
try to bring about change largely determines how teachers respond to
the challenge. Supervisors can mandate change externally; or they can,
together with teachers, build collaborative cultures that encourage the
seeds of change to take root and grow.

Externally mandated change typically has a cataclysmic effect on
teachers' morale, resulting in a strong sense of dependency. Teachers
often feel overwhelmed by the new expectations when their actions are

[1] The case studies cited in this chapter were funded to Peter Grimmett by the Social Sciences
and Humanities Research Council of Canada (SSHRCC) (Grants 410-85-0339, 410-86-2014, and
410-88-0747). We gratefully acknowledge that this work could not have been carried out without
this funding. The opinions expressed here do not necessarily reflect the policy, position, or
endorsement of SSHRCC. We also acknowledge the conceptual assistance of Pat Crehan at the
University of British Columbia and the contributions of D'Arcy Bader, Cindy Drossos, Louise
Guevremont, Robin Hansby, David Langmuir, Maryl Stewart, Janet Tyler, and Carolyn Varah in
data collection, data analysis, and manuscript preparation.

continually shaped by the directives of others. There is an accompanying sense of helplessness and powerlessness when heightened expectations appear to be beyond reach. The constant bombardment of new tasks and continual interruptions keeps teachers off balance. Such "overload fosters dependency" (Fullan 1989, vi)—and powerlessness. And powerless people have a tendency to become despotic toward their underlings. We all have a neurotic need to control people and situations when we feel anxious, helpless, inferior, or insignificant. When teachers experience these feelings, their students become the innocent recipients of such defensive behavior.

On the other hand, with an emphasis on collaborative cultures, teachers experience a heightened sense of teaching efficacy and professional empowerment. They become purposeful and enterprising in their actions. They take on an authority that demonstrates they can lead students into new knowledge, skills, behaviors, and dispositions. They take risks on behalf of students and make commitments to their learning. Developing instructional practice becomes an important professional choice that motivates such teachers to become visionary about what can happen in teaching and learning. In short, they take charge of their professional lives and engage in perpetual learning about their craft.

How, then, do supervisors foster instructional change in a way that nurtures an empowering form of teacher development? The thesis of this chapter is that *teacher development takes place within a culture of interdependent collegiality when teachers reflectively transform their classroom experience.* In this transformational perspective, supervision becomes a process in which teachers develop profound and fresh appreciations of the learners' perspective, the classroom context, and their own role as an active enabler of student learning.

In exploring this perspective, we first suggest that a shift is needed in the dominant practice of supervision—from deferring unduly to the scientific knowledge base of teaching to valuing and respecting the knowledge that resides in the minds of experienced teachers. Such a shift finds its expression in a culture of collegiality; here, we examine this culture as it relates to instructional change. We explore how teachers develop their craft and show how the process of engaging in reflective inquiry is similar to the important discoveries made by scientists. We then examine how teachers use and make sense of the research-based knowledge so revered by proponents of existing supervisory practices.

Finally, we show how a transformational perspective fosters a culture of interdependent collegiality in which teachers reflectively change their classroom instructional practice for the better. To illustrate this perspective, we discuss the recent experiment in teacher development taking place in the Burnaby School District of British Columbia, Canada.

Shifting the Standard in Supervision

An Emerging Focus on Teacher Development

The dominant model of instructional supervision is marked by a disputable assumption: instructional supervisors have access to a scientific knowledge base and set of analytical skills that are beyond the orbit of the regular classroom teacher. Supervisors sometimes talk about "instructional improvement" as if it were something they do to teachers rather than the outcome of carefully nurtured teacher development. Smyth (1989) and Garman (1990) document how, over the past thirty years, the originally well-conceived collaborative processes of clinical supervision have become a sophisticated mechanism of teaching inspection and instructional surveillance.

Current practice of instructional supervision thus leans toward prescriptive, systematic forms of staff development and school improvement. By contrast, the emerging focus on teacher development places teachers and their development at the heart of educational change (see Fullan and Hargreaves 1991, Hargreaves and Fullan 1991)—and in sharp contrast to legislated mandates for school improvement that proceed, top-down, through the supervisory hierarchy. The shift to teacher development provides a humanistic and critical focus on teachers as key personnel in any educational initiative. The context in which development takes place is absolutely vital. Thus work conditions are both a focus for and a target of development.

A Culture of Collegiality

Ever since Little's (1981) classic study of six schools highlighting positive norms and conditions in the work place, the term *collegiality* has taken on something of a mystique—and is sometimes contrived (Little 1989, Hargreaves 1989, Grimmett and Crehan 1991).[2] Despite

---

[2] For an unraveling of the dark side of this mystique, see Little (1989) who, eight years after her ground-breaking study, was forced to conclude that conditions of individualism, immediacy, and conservatism still persisted, creating "weak" versions of collegial relations that did not confront the fundamental purposes of schools. Hargreaves (1989) suggested that many attempts at collegiality were embedded in bureaucratic structures and therefore essentially contrived. Grimmett and Crehan (1991) found evidence of two broad types of contrived collegiality in schools—that which was administratively imposed and that which was organizationally induced.

this growing mystique, Little (1987) argues that by working closely with colleagues teachers gain instructional range, depth, and flexibility from collegiality. Collaborative group work enables teachers to attempt instructional innovations that they would probably not have tried by themselves. But it is not merely the teamwork that creates the willingness to try new things—it is the joint action that flows from the group as teachers shape the shared task and its outcomes. In short, a culture of professional interdependence emerges.

School culture is important because it represents the values that bind people together. Because schools function more like "organized anarchies" (Cohen, March, and Olson 1972) and the educational program itself is "loosely coupled" (Weick 1982), the culture of the school exerts a powerful influence on how teaching and learning take place. Weick (1982) suggests that the culture is the "glue" that holds loosely coupled systems together. Figure 12.1 shows two examples of the beliefs and values found by Little (1981) to constitute a culture of collegiality.

Figure 12.1
Examples of Beliefs, Values, and Norms Found in a Strong School Culture of Interdependent Collegiality

Example 1: Collegiality

TIGHT
- Belief: Talking about and observing teaching builds up shared referents adequate to the complexity of teaching
- Value: Shared referents are preferred over idiosyncratic perceptions
- Norm: Collegial interdependence

LOOSE — Organizational structure for how collegial conditions occur

Example 2: Experimentation

TIGHT
- Belief: Learning accrues from the active pursuit of the demonstration and risk-taking that teaching provides
- Value: Taking risks is preferred over the stagnation resulting from isolationist, avoidance tendencies
- Norm: Experimentation

LOOSE — Organizational structure for how experimentation takes place

Teachers in the schools studied by Little (1981) shared beliefs and values that constituted professional interdependence as a normative basis for action. They believed that talking about teaching and observing it builds up "shared referents for a shared language of teaching . . . adequate to the complexity of teaching, capable of distinguishing one practice and its virtue from another" (p. 12). Such openness to observing, to being observed, and to discussing classroom practice tends to break down isolationist barriers and promote collegial interdependence. Complementing Little is Weick's (1982) "tight-loose" formulation. When teachers are held accountable by tightly structured beliefs and values, the organizational structure in which collegial conditions develop can be loose. In other words, the administrative hierarchy can invest in teachers the power required to make collegiality happen.

> Highly successful leaders practice the principle of power investment. . . . They understand that teachers need to be empowered to act—to be given the necessary responsibility that releases their potential and makes their actions and decisions count (Sergiovanni 1987, p. 121).

A further belief operative in the schools studied by Little (1981) was that teachers learn from taking risks and demonstrating new ideas. The value here is that taking risks is preferred over the stagnation resulting from the isolationist, avoidance tendencies shown by teachers in typical school cultures. Such openness to learning through the active pursuit of risk-taking promotes the norm of experimentation. (For a detailed discussion of the norms and values of typical school cultures, see Grimmett and Crehan 1991, Bird and Little 1986, and Lieberman and Miller 1984.)

A strong school culture, then, sustains those collaborative practices that lead teachers to raise fundamental questions about the nature of teaching and learning. It represents the intellectual ferment within which ideas for educational change can flourish and expand. Conflict is not subversion but a normal aspect of collaboration when teachers engage in the mutual negotiation of purpose and task. As mentioned previously, the beliefs, values, and norms of such a culture are tightly structured, and the bureaucratic control is loose. When these beliefs, values, and norms take on a professional focus, the prognosis for educational change appears to be good.

Reflective Transformation and Teacher Development

Problem Setting and Solving

How do teachers develop their classroom practice? Schön (1988) has suggested that teachers develop in instructional supervision settings[3] when they engage in the "reflective transformation of experience" (p. 25). Reflective transformation involves some form of experimentation in which practitioners attempt to create meaning out of a problematic teaching situation through "problem setting" and "problem solving":

> In real world practice, problems do not present themselves to the practitioner as givens. They must be constructed from the materials or problematic situations that are puzzling, troubling and uncertain. ... When we set the problem, we select what we will treat as the things of the situation, we set the boundaries of our attention to it, and we impose upon it a coherence which allows us to say what is wrong and in what directions the situation needs to be changed. Problem setting is a process in which, interactively, we *name* the things to which we will attend and *frame* the context in which we will attend to them (Schön 1983, p. 40, emphasis in original).

This reframing of a problem situation enables practitioners to make use of their existing "repertoire of examples, images, understandings, and actions" (Schön 1987, p. 66). In this process, reflection engages teachers in a "conversation" with the problematic situation (Schön 1983). Reflective transformation thus engages teachers

> in a kind of "seeing" and "doing" as—seeing their own situation as a version of the one they had observed, . . . a process of metaphor, carrying a familiar experience over to a new context, transforming in that process both the experience and the new situation (Schön 1988, p. 25).

An Example of Reflective Transformation

Grimmett and Crehan (1990) document two episodes in the case of a teacher, Barry. In both instances, Barry seems to be on the verge of engaging in the reflective transformation of his classroom practice. Yet he achieved it in only one of the two episodes.

The first episode involved Barry's naming of the instructional problem: *engaging a distinct group of uninvolved pupils.* Barry's principal, Margaret, essentially refocused the problem around the theme of

---

[3] Schön (1988) prefers to talk in terms of *coaching* rather than *instructional supervision*, but his conception of coaching differs radically from that of Joyce and Showers (1982, 1983).

teacher proximity to pupils, a theme that had emerged in their previous conferences. In other words, Margaret saw Barry's dilemma in terms of the students' physical location in the classroom, rather than their possible difficulty in grasping the concepts he was presenting. Margaret suggested that Barry change the position of the overhead projector; thus, the principal reframed the instructional context according to her definition of the problem, not Barry's. Although teacher development did not occur in this episode, a culture of collegiality appeared nevertheless to remain in place.

In the second episode, Barry named the problem as *dealing with end-of-lesson activities in an educationally sound manner*. (The last part of the lesson had involved the use of newspaper articles to teach mathematical concepts.) Barry suggested that his difficulties came about because the students had worked hard for too long a period of time. Margaret chose to explore what he typically does when such a breakdown occurs up to ten minutes before the end of the lesson. Barry responded that if it occurred with less than five minutes remaining, he ended the lesson. If more than five minutes remained in the lesson, however, he said he sometimes ran out of ideas; and he asked the principal for advice. Margaret empathized with the predicament Barry had described and began to relate how she always used to read poetry to students when she felt they had reached their saturation point. This provided a change of pace for the students, but still fulfilled the teacher's mandate to be educating them. The principal's story immediately fired Barry's interest; he saw, perhaps for the first time, that such backup activities did not necessarily constitute busywork. Through reflection, Barry expanded his conception of teaching.

Barry then experienced a further enriching instance of reflective transformation. He suddenly realized that he could have read something else out of the newspapers he had used in the third and final segment of the lesson. Thus, he saw his end-of-lesson activity as a version of his principal's. Her reported actions served as a metaphor that prompted him to reframe this own teaching in a highly creative, yet exploratory way. He didn't transfer the principal's reported activity, (poetry reading) to the context of his teaching; rather, he transformed both the activity (from reading poetry to reading the newspaper) and his teaching context (from dead-time or busywork to educationally significant work) in the process.

Four factors seem to account for this double portion of teacher development through reflective transformation:

- The teacher himself named the problem that was explored in the conference.
- The principal did not seem to have an agenda of her own and consequently accepted and explored the problem identified by the teacher.
- The teacher felt secure enough in the supportive atmosphere engendered by the principal to take a professional risk in admitting a shortcoming and asking for assistance.
- The principal's empathic sharing of how she tackled a similar problem enabled the teacher to reconstruct his view of backup activities and reframe the context of the lesson in which he had originally experienced the problem.

This kind of development is similar to the experience of exploration and discovery that scientists all over the world have encountered. Teachers engaging in the reflective transformation of their classroom practice essentially experience the scientist's "exploratory impulsion—an *acute discomfort* at incomprehension . . . the rage to know" (Judson 1980, p. 5, emphasis in original). These teachers share the scientist's moments of self-doubt, anxious searching, and eventual accomplishment. Such accomplishment, when it comes, is usually by chance. Something surprises teachers; and, in exploring the perplexity, they derive insights into their practice. Many significant scientific discoveries have occurred by chance, such as Fleming's discovery of penicillin from a wind-blown mold (Judson 1980, pp. 68–85). What distinguishes scientists from other people is that scientists notice such chance occurrences and pursue them vigorously until they satisfy their "rage to know." In this way, as Medewar pointed out, "scientists are building explanatory structures, *telling stories* which are scrupulously tested to see if they are stories about real life" (Medewar, as cited in Judson, p. 3, emphasis added). Teachers engaging in reflective transformation also tell and test stories:

> Story-telling is the mode of description best suited to transformation in new situations of action. . . . A reflective teacher builds her repertoire of teaching experiences . . . not as methods or principles to be applied like a template to new situations, but as stories that function like metaphors, projective models to be transformed and validated through on-the-spot experiment in the next situation (Schön 1988, p. 26).

The case of Barry demonstrates, then, that when the principal told stories about her practice, the teacher was able to transform both the activity under focus and the context of further teaching. Barry's experience also shows kind of collegial interdependence that is associated with teacher development through the reflective transformation of classroom experience. Generally, however, as Smyth (1988) pointed out, this happens all too rarely in instructional supervision. Two things need to happen to facilitate teacher development in this way: (1) supervisors need to act on an alternative way of understanding the role played by research-based knowledge in teacher development, and (2) supervisors need to devise ways in which they can foster a culture of interdependent collegiality in which teachers working together with other teachers can identify and solve their own problems.

A Framework for Understanding Teachers' Use of Research-Validated Knowledge

Kennedy (1984) and Sergiovanni (1986) described two ways in which scientific knowledge is used in making professional decisions. Grimmett (1990) incorporated these to frame three ways in which teachers use research-validated knowledge: instrumentally, conceptually, and metaphorically.

The Instrumental Approach. This approach has a technological orientation, emphasizing research-derived rules to which practice is expected to *conform.* Zumwalt (1982) describes this orientation as "a definable repertoire of knowledge, skills and attitudes that a teacher brings to bear in an effort to create certain changes in learners" (pp. 223, 224). Grimmett (1989) and Grimmett, MacKinnon, Erickson, and Riecken (1990) argue that such an approach serves to justify supervisory insistence that teachers make their classroom practice conform to what research has found to be effective.

The Conceptual Approach. This approach has a deliberative orientation, emphasizing the discussion of the evidence supporting research findings that are deemed useful in informing practice. In this approach, teaching is a clinical process of aggregating and making sense out of an incredible diversity of information regarding classroom practice. Teachers are provided with ways to think about their complex and contextually influenced classroom experience in light of research (Zumwalt, p. 237). In weighing the evidence for or against research findings, teachers act as professionals who must carefully reject or adapt what research has found. Grimmett (1989) and Grimmett, MacKinnon, Erickson, and Riecken (1990) suggest that this approach carries with it the expectation that teachers will use research findings to *inform* their classroom practice.

The Metaphorical Approach. This approach has a reflective orientation, in which research findings connect with teachers' professional images; and teachers are thus able to transform their classroom practice. Schön's (1983, 1987, 1988) problem "naming," "setting," and "reframing" process discussed earlier can help teachers deal with instructional perplexities and dilemmas. This reflective orientation does not lend itself to the transfer of research-validated knowledge, as in both instrumental and conceptual approaches. Rather, research findings can act as a touchstone to a teacher's "professional image" (Connelly and Clandinin 1988)—that filament of a teacher's own experience, personality, and expression. When this connection occurs, teachers use research-validated knowledge metaphorically to *transform* their classroom practice (Grimmett 1989; Grimmett, MacKinnon, Erickson, and Riecken 1990).

Lakoff and Johnson (1980) suggest that metaphor is pervasive in everyday life—in language, thought, and action. These researchers maintain that our ordinary conceptual system is fundamentally metaphorical in nature. Our concepts essentially are products of all our life experiences, personal biography, and professional socialization. The metaphors that permeate our minds structure how we think and act.

In metaphorical transformation, research findings would be a catalyst for seeing new puzzles in teachers' classroom practice, enabling them to reframe tried-and-true patterns of classroom interaction in ways that permit exploration, experimentation, and subsequent improvement. Such transformation of practice, it seems, would stimulate the kind of exciting intellectual inquiry that energizes classroom teachers for the stringent demands of teaching efficaciously.

Fostering a Culture of Interdependent Collegiality

Supervisors who nurture reflective transformation in teachers do so by fostering a culture of interdependent collegiality, the conditions of which were associated by Little (1987)with teacher development. Despite the claims of earlier writers (e.g., Cogan 1973, Goldhammer 1969) that teachers and principals can work together as colleagues, evidence is mounting that teachers generally learn more readily from interactions with other teachers than they do from interactions with supervisors (see Grimmett and Crehan 1988, Smyth 1989). Indeed, Hargreaves and Dawe (1990) maintain that supervision (including the clinical approach) is incompatible with healthy collegial relations because it consists of "hierarchical relations embedded in bureaucratically-driven systems" (p. 25). In their view, clinical supervision is a form of contrived collegiality and rarely can foster the conditions associated with interdependent collegiality.

How, then, can supervisors work toward instructional excellence and achievement along transformational lines? One way would be to reconstruct instructional supervision in terms of learning support groups among teachers, like self-help groups in other areas of society.[4] Such groups could include supervisory personnel if their presence would not bring attention to their hierarchical position in the formal organization. In these groups, teachers could act as researchers of their own practice (Elliott 1990). Teachers, not supervisors, would initiate the learning process in response to particular practical situations or dilemmas. The supervisor would facilitate the group process through sensitive and supportive questioning, crystallizing, and focusing of the collaborative discussion. The supervisor would ensure that the "wisdom of practice" (Shulman 1987) resident in teachers is valued and respected. Such wisdom is typically built up as teachers collaboratively tackle problems or dilemmas. These dilemmas call for proposed changes that may arouse controversy among the group. The supervisor's role at this point is to enable the group to become comfortable with controversy, thereby releasing in them the power to address the issues without fear or favor.

Further, the supervisor would ensure that the issues are "clarified and resolved in free and open discourse, characterized by mutual respect and tolerance and an absence of hierarchical power constraints" (Elliott 1990, p. 48). Supervisors cannot wear their office on their sleeve, nor can they be "puffed up" about what strengths and abilities they possess. Rather, they keep a low profile, functioning like "well-worn shoes" (not noticed when entering a room, but having a definite sense of purpose)[5] and they allow the strengths and abilities of the group members (including their own) to emerge.

In providing organizational support for learning support groups, the supervisor would organize a schedule for each group (or ensure that someone takes responsibility for drawing up a schedule) and allocate appropriate resources, both fiscal and human.

---

[4] In a very real sense, these self-help groups mirror what happens to teachers when they meet in learning support groups. Teachers are otherwise capable practitioners who are frequently disempowered by administrative attempts to mandate educational change. Many teachers experience cataclysmic feelings of powerlessness, isolation, and dependence. Consequently, many question their efficacy as teachers when instructional improvement is discussed only with administrators. Yet something unexpected and professionally energizing happens when these same teachers get together with one another to talk about dilemmas of practice. The group provides the opportunity for intense professional bonding; and the supportive setting fosters a culture of interdependent collegiality (Lieberman 1989 calls this a "professional culture"), which, in turn, encourages teachers to try new alternatives they have discussed.

[5] We are indebted to Carl Glickman, who first brought this reference about leaders by Nancy Austin to our attention.

Supervisors would also reinforce the beliefs and values of interdependent collegiality through taking risks and making commitments. They would attempt to become a member of as many groups as feasible, taking part in the rigorous discussion of teaching and learning that accompanies the observation of classroom practice. Moreover, from time to time, they would bring up their own dilemmas of practice; and their own practice (even their teaching) would be observed and critiqued in a supportive way. In short, supervisors would attempt to model norms of collegiality and experimentation in their work with teachers' learning support groups. In this way, supervisors might have a much more positive impact on student learning than has apparently been the case to date.

Following the collaborative dialogue of the support group, teachers return to their classrooms with provisional plans of action. They can engage in mutual observation and feedback, or they can work alone and videotape or audio-record their actions. The important point is that they collect data on how the proposed practices fare with students in the context of the original dilemma. Teachers then come back to the learning support group, discuss the results, and obtain collegial feedback.

Toward a Transformational Perspective: The Burnaby Experiment

In 1988, the Burnaby School District of British Columbia, Canada, began to change its approach to the supervision and evaluation of teaching. A committee of teachers and administrators looked at the question of professional growth and evaluation. This committee concluded that summative evaluation of teaching rarely (if ever) contributed positively to teachers' professional growth. The committee agreed with McLaughlin and Pfeifer (1988), who suggested that summative evaluation schemes "create an organizational climate where little learning or accountability can take place" (p. 83).

The committee recommended that summative evaluation be replaced by a process emphasizing professional growth. Such a process, formative in nature, would involve teachers working primarily with other teachers. Accordingly, a new contract was negotiated that replaced the mandatory formal evaluation of all teachers with a collaborative model; and every teacher was expected to come up with a professional growth plan by November 1 of each year. The district provided teachers with resources in the form of research information, release time, and carefully selected workshops that would help foster their professional growth. Teachers, in turn, were encouraged to take full advantage of the opportunity to take a greater responsibility for their professional growth.

The professional growth program in Burnaby has three components: (1) school-based professional growth teams, (2) professional growth plans developed by every teacher (and administrator), and (3) a model of collaboration that incorporates reflective dialogue, classroom visitations, and collegial consultation.

The model of collaboration enables teachers to become involved at different levels, depending on their degree of readiness. It is assumed that each teacher will view *dialogue and reflection* as a professional responsibility and will engage in activities that promote discussion and the sharing of professional experiences. In addition, teachers may choose to begin by working with a colleague in some form of *collaborative planning* and *classroom visitations*. Finally, for those teachers who have developed their skills in observation and conferencing, an opportunity to become involved in a process of *peer observation* and *collegial consultation* (including team teaching) is provided.

At Burnaby, numerous sessions were held with teachers throughout the district to introduce the details of the program. Important as these sessions were to the beginning of the program, they were not critical to its success. The key factor was in a deeply embedded set of beliefs and values about collaboration and teacher professionalism that constituted the normative basis for action among teachers and administrators. The groundwork of establishing this culture had taken place for more than a decade.

One of the early avenues for experimentation was a teacher development project coordinated by Peter Grimmett. Many teachers used this opportunity to engage in collegial consultation, to develop their professional growth plans, and to deal with vital issues and dilemmas emerging in their classrooms. One such teacher was Paul, who worked closely with Diane, a colleague in the same department of a secondary school.

The Case of Paul

Paul was a member of the school's professional growth team. His professional growth plan focused on his need to expand his repertoire of teaching approaches. With Diane (also a member of the school's professional growth team), he participated in collaborative planning, reciprocal classroom observation and collegial consultation, and a good deal of reflection on the research that both teachers had been reading. Both Paul and Diane viewed the consultation process as successful when one or both of them discovered something new and practical about teaching. This case shows a teacher coming to a deep insight as a colleague challenges him to think through his own instructional dilemmas.

Paul had taught a lesson along the lines of inductive inquiry and had invited Diane to observe and give feedback. In the post-conference, Paul stated that one of his instructional goals was to stimulate students to want to become involved in the learning process. Although intrigued by this statement, Diane said it was unspecific and began to probe for clarification. She asked him to compare the class under discussion with a different class (at a higher level) in which Paul maintained that he had greater success in stimulating student involvement. During this discussion, Paul suddenly realized that, in the class under discussion, he was asking questions that were beyond the students' level of ability.

Paul's lesson had included a subgroup activity. This activity had begun immediately after his introduction, which included a set of directions for the activity. Diane had attempted earlier in the conference to talk about this aspect of the lesson, but Paul had not nibbled at the bait. The sudden recognition about the level of his questioning appeared to free Paul to look closely at the way he had set up the activity. He began by acknowledging that he might have spent far too much time on giving directions. He elaborated with specific details. He had repeated the directions three or four times, including writing them on the board. Diane asked him how long it took him to put them on the board.

At this point in the conference, a look of recognition came across Paul's face. He realized that he had written the directions after he had given them verbally in three different ways. He also realized that he should have written them on the board at the same time as talking about them. Like a bolt of lightning, it suddenly struck Paul that because he took so much time on the directions at the beginning of the activity, he felt acute time pressure toward the end of the lesson. He realized that it was this sense of running out of time that had caused him to abandon his attempt at inductive inquiry and revert to a more traditional instructional method.

This episode from the case of Paul shows how teachers reflectively transform their classroom practice through intense—but supportive—interactions with colleagues. It also shows that, when working interactively, teachers tend to use research-validated knowledge conceptually and metaphorically, rather than instrumentally. Both Paul and Diane were familiar with the research findings on questioning, use of time, and clarity of direction giving before an activity. However, they did not make use of these findings in isolation, as if each had prescriptions for desirable action in Paul's classroom practice; rather, they used them as a conceptual frame to understand the essence of Paul's dilemma. In the process, the research on use of instructional time acted as a metaphor that enabled Paul to interpret not only his observed teaching but also his personal biography and professional socialization. He began to see his propensity to escape into didactic instruction as a way of coping with the anxiety produced by time pressure. Such understanding is a first step in undermining the powerful hold that habitual practices exert over teachers in their classroom practice. It releases in them fresh appreciations of what is possible and empowers them to do something about it. In short, it frees them to transform their practice.

Teachers' Appreciation of Collegial Consultation

Not only did teachers like Paul gain pedagogically from the experience, but they also acquired a new-found sense of professional esteem. Paul, for example, was amazed at the ease with which he could subsequently speak frankly with a colleague:

> I remember here thinking, my goodness, I'm not [faking it] at all, I really am being open and honest, and I was amazed because this represents a change even from the first pre-conference where I had a feeling of awkwardness about opening up, and now [three observations later] I'm opening up without any degree of discomfort.

What Paul didn't say, but implied, is that he had been reluctant to open up with a supervisor. Other teachers noted this very phenomenon and commented on how much more beneficial collegial consultation was than their previous experience of supervision. One teacher, Nancy, working with Hannah, was definite:

> I feel very supported and very good about this [collegial consultation] happening. It boosts me up, and that is really valuable. I'm not alone in this world. . . . [My advice to other teachers is] find a compatible partner and do it. The rewards are unexpected and powerful.

Brenda, working with Stephanie, a colleague for whom she had tremendous professional respect, focused on the learning opportunities that collegial consultation afforded:

> I see myself [in this process] as much a learner as a teacher. I am as much a learner from Stephanie as I am a teacher of Stephanie. . . .

I think she knows a lot about teaching her subject, about teaching period, about dealing with young people that is very valuable for me to be able to look in on it.

Stephanie, in turn, also appreciated the professional growth opportunities:

I used to tolerate district inservice days when the outside experts flew into town to tell us how to do it. However, I didn't learn anything from them. I guess they served more of a social need than a professional one. Working with Brenda is such a contrast. We focus on real dilemmas of interest. Brenda knows so much and is so supportive, and together we're finding out lots of new things.

Raymond, working with Jennifer, appreciated collegial consultation for the opportunities it afforded to communicate respect and to "shift the expertise":

I could have told her how to do all this stuff, . . . but I don't think that's the point. The point is that she feels comfortable with what she decides to do. . . . I'm not playing dumb, I'm just shifting the expertise.

This last comment contains considerable wisdom. Teacher development along transformational lines involves shifting the expertise from the observer or supervisor to the teacher. Observers respectfully act on the assumption that teachers hold the key to unraveling their own instructional dilemmas, thus fostering the supportive but challenging conditions that permit teachers to engage in the reflective transformation of their classroom experience.

The preliminary results of the Burnaby teacher development project suggest that such transformation occurs when teachers work collaboratively with other teachers in a context framed by a powerful culture of interdependent collegiality.

* * *

Reflective transformation of practice permits teachers to use research-validated knowledge metaphorically as they creatively (like the best scientists) interpret the various dilemmas of practice that daily arise. It also encourages supervisors to view themselves as practitioners, like teachers, learning their craft in a collegially supportive atmosphere. When teachers reflectively transform their classroom experience in accordance with student learning needs, they are likely to witness an improvement in student achievement and attitudes.

References

Bird, T., and J.W. Little. (1986). "How Schools Organize the Teaching Occupation." *The Elementary School Journal* 86, 4: 493–511.

Cogan, M. (1973). *Clinical Supervision*. Boston: Houghton Mifflin.

Cohen, M.D., J.G. March, and J. Olson. (1972). "A Garbage Can Model of Organizational Choice." *Administrative Science Quarterly* 17, 1: 1–25.

Connelly, F.M., and D.J. Clandinin. (1988). *Teachers as Curriculum Planners: Narratives of Experience*. New York: Teachers College Press.

Elliott, J. (1990). "Teachers as Researchers: Implications for Supervision and Teacher Education." *Teaching and Teacher Education* 6, 1: 1–26.

Fullan, M.G. (1989). *What's Worth Fighting for in the Principalship: Strategies for Taking Charge in the Elementary School Principalship*. Toronto: Ontario Public School Teachers' Federation.

Fullan, M.G., and A. Hargreaves. (1991). *Teacher Development and Educational Change*. Philadelphia: Falmer Press.

Garman, N.B. (1990). "Theories Embedded in the Events of Clinical Supervision: A Hermeneutical Approach." *Journal of Curriculum and Supervision* 5, 3: 201–213.

Goldhammer, R. (1969). *Clinical Supervision: Special Methods for the Supervision of Teachers*. New York: Holt, Rinehart and Winston.

Grimmett, P.P. (1989). "Commentary on Schön's View of Reflection." *Journal of Curriculum and Supervision* 5, 1: 19–28.

Grimmett, P.P. (1990). "Teacher Planning, Collegiality and the Education of Teachers." In *Advances in Teacher Education*, edited by L. Katz and J. Raths. Norwood, N.J.: Ablex.

Grimmett, P.P., and E.P. Crehan. (1988). *A Study of the Effects of Supervisors' Intervention on Teachers' Classroom Management Performance*. Final report to the Social Sciences and Humanities Research Council of Canada (Grants #410-85-0339 and #410-86-2014). Vancouver: The University of British Columbia.

Grimmett, P.P., and E.P. Crehan. (1990). "Barry: A Case Study of Teacher Reflection in Clinical Supervision." *Journal of Curriculum and Supervision* 5, 3: 214–235.

Grimmett, P.P., and E.P. Crehan. (1991). "The Nature of Collegiality in Teacher Development: The Case of Clinical Supervision." In *Teacher Development and Educational Change*, edited by M. Fullan and A. Hargreaves. Philadelphia: Falmer Press.

Grimmett, P.P., A.M. MacKinnon, G.L. Erickson, and T.J. Riecken, (1990). "Reflective Practice in Teacher Education." In *Encouraging Reflective Practice in Education: An Analysis of Issues and Programs*, edited by R.T. Clift, W.R. Houston, and M.C. Pugach. New York: Teachers College Press.

Hargreaves, A. (June 2, 1989). "Contrived Collegiality and the Culture of Teaching." Paper presented at the annual meeting of the Canadian Society for the Study of Education, Quebec City.

Hargreaves, A., and R. Dawe. (1990). "Paths of Professional Development: Contrived Collegiality, Collaborative Cultures and the Case of Peer Coaching." *Teaching and Teacher Education* 4, 3.

Hargreaves, A., and M.G. Fullan. (1991). *Understanding Teacher Development*. London: Cassells.

Joyce, B., and B. Showers. (1982). "The Coaching of Teaching." *Educational Leadership* 40, 1: 4–10.

Joyce, B., and B. Showers. (1983). *Staff Development Through Research in Training*. Alexandria, Va.: ASCD.

Judson, H.F. (1980). *The Search for Solutions*. New York: Holt, Rinehart and Winston.

Kennedy, M.M. (1984). "How Evidence Alters Understanding and Decisions." *Educational Evaluation and Policy Analysis* 6: 207–226.

Lakoff, G., and M. Johnson. (1980). *Metaphors We Live By*. Chicago: University of Chicago Press.

Lieberman, A. (1989). *Building a Professional Culture in Schools*. New York: Teachers College Press.

Lieberman, A., and L. Miller. (1984). *Teachers, Their World, and Their Work*. Alexandria, Va.: ASCD.

Little, J.W. (1981). "The Power of Organizational Setting: School Norms and Staff Development." Paper presented at the Annual Meeting of the American Educational Research Association, Los Angeles.

Little, J.W. (1987). "Teachers As Colleagues." In *Educators' Handbook: A Research Perspective*, edited by V.R. Koehler. New York: Longman.

Little, J.W. (1989). "The Persistence of Privacy: Autonomy and Initiative in Teachers' Professional Relations." Paper presented at the Annual Meeting of the American Educational Research Association, San Francisco.

McLaughlin, M.W., and R.S. Pfeifer. (1988). *Teacher Evaluation: Improvement, Accountability, and Effective Learning*. New York: Teachers College Press.

Pajak, E. (1990). "Identification of Dimensions of Supervisory Practice in Education: Reviewing the Literature." Paper presented at the Annual Meeting of the American Educational Research Association, Boston.

Schön, D.A. (1983). *The Reflective Practitioner: How Professionals Think in Action*. New York: Basic Books.

Schön, D.A. (1987). *Educating the Reflective Practitioner: Toward a New Design for Teaching and Learning in the Professions*. San Francisco: Jossey-Bass.

Schön, D.A. (1988). "Coaching Reflective Teaching." In *Reflection in Teacher Education*, edited by P.P. Grimmett and G.L. Erickson. New York: Teachers College Press.

Sergiovanni, T.J. (1986). "Understanding Reflective Practice." *Journal of Curriculum and Supervision* 1, 4: 353–359.

Sergiovanni, T.J. (1987). "The Theoretical Basis for Cultural Leadership." In *Leadership: Examining the Elusive* edited by L.T. Sheive and M.B. Schoenheit. Alexandria, Va.: ASCD.

Shulman, L.S. (1987). "The Wisdom of Practice: Managing Complexity in Medicine and Teaching." In *Talks to Teachers* edited by D.C. Berliner and B.V. Rosenshine. New York: Random House.

Smyth, J. (1988). "A 'Critical' Perspective for Clinical Supervision." *Journal of Curriculum and Supervision* 3, 2: 136–156.

Smyth, J. (1989). "Problematizing Teaching Through a 'Critical' Perspective on Clinical Supervision." Paper presented at the Annual Meeting of the American Educational Research Association, San Francisco.

Weick, K.E. (1982). "Administering Education in Loosely Coupled Schools." *Phi Delta Kappan* 27, 2: 673–676.

Zumwalt, K.K. (1982). "Research on Teaching: Policy Implications for Teacher Education." In *Policy Making in Education* edited by A. Lieberman and M. McLaughlin. Chicago: National Society for the Study of Education.

13

Moral Authority and the Regeneration of Supervision

Thomas J. Sergiovanni

When Carl Glickman asked me to write the final chapter of this yearbook, he asked that I write from a *personal* perspective. To me, a personal perspective is one that comes from the heart as well as the mind—to write this way about supervision is to share some private thoughts and dreams about the realities and the possibilities of supervision in the hope that readers will be stimulated to think and feel in a new way.

My vision for supervision is a simple one—it is of a day when supervision will no longer be needed. Think about it. No more "inservicing" teachers to get them to measure up to some standard we have set. No more surveillance systems to ensure that they are doing what we want them to do the way we want them to do it. No more hours spent devising, collecting, or monitoring teacher growth plans. No more worrying about such issues as climate and morale to keep their spirits up while we mold them in our images. No more time, money, or effort spent dreaming up arrangements that will get them to work together. Imagine a supervision with no supervision, evaluation, or inservice as we know these practices today. That is exactly my vision, my dream, my hope for supervision as we approach the 21st century.

Why should we change present supervisory practices? In part, because, despite good intentions, supervision can hardly be counted among education's successes. Most teachers consider supervision to be a nonevent—a ritual they participate in according to well-established scripts without much consequence. In reality, what happens behind the closed classroom door and what happens on the stage of supervision are quite different. Besides, when current forms of supervision are forced on teachers, they typically react in ways that are counterproductive in the long run.

We supervise for good reasons. We want schools to be better, teachers to grow, and students to have academically and developmentally sound learning experiences; and we believe that supervision serves these and other worthy ends. But all of the benefits that we seek can be obtained more easily and in enhanced ways in the natural course of events as teachers and students live and learn together in schools. Supervision, in other words, can just as easily come from the inside as the outside.

Authority for Supervision

The issue of authority is fundamental to any discussion of supervision. Authority is the basis for getting things done in schools. Thus, a key question for regenerating supervision is, What should be the source of authority for developing and shaping policy instruments, strategies, and practices in schools? Present supervisory practices emerge from a particular pattern of authority. If we want to change these practices, then we must restructure their authority base.

Supervisory policy and practice can be based on one or a combination of five broad sources of authority:

• *Bureaucratic*—in the form of mandates, rules, regulations, job descriptions, and expectations. When we base supervisory practices on bureaucratic authority, teachers are expected to respond appropriately or face the consequences.

• *Psychological*—in the form of leadership, motivational technology, and human relations skills. When we base supervisory practice on psychological authority, teachers are expected to respond to our personality and the pleasant environment we provide, behaving appropriately for the rewards we make available in exchange.

• *Technical-rational*—in the form of evidence derived from logic and scientific research. When we base supervisory practice on the authority of technical rationality, teachers are expected to respond in light of what is considered to be truth.

• *Professional*—in the form of informed and seasoned craft knowledge and personal expertness. When we base supervisory practice on professional authority, teachers are expected to respond to common socialization, accepted tenets of practice, and internalized expertness.

• *Moral*—in the form of obligations and duties derived from widely shared values, ideas, and ideals. When we base supervisory practice on moral authority, teachers are expected to respond to shared commitments and interdependence (Sergiovanni in press).

These sources of authority, along with the assumptions they derive from, the strategies they require, and their consequences, are elaborated in Figure 13.1 (beginning on page 206). Each of the five is legitimate and should be used in supervision. But it makes a difference which source or combination of sources is primary.

Authority for today's supervision rests in a combination of bureaucratic, psychological, and technical-rational sources. The necessity for this combination stems from the fact that teaching is viewed as individual, rather than collective, practice. As long as teaching is understood as individual practice, these sources of authority will be primary and we will be stuck with the supervisory practices that we have today. If, on the other hand, a vision of teaching as collective practice were to emerge, professional and moral authority would be the driving forces for supervisory practice. Supervision would then emerge from within educators rather than being externally imposed, ending forever supervision as we now know it.

Necessary Conditions for Change

Three things must happen for teaching to be transformed from individual to collective practice:

1. We must take seriously the professionalization of teaching.
2. The metaphor for schooling must change from organization, instructional delivery system, processing plant, clinical setting, market, garden, and so on to community.
3. We must value collegiality as a professional virtue.

In Chapter 1, Linda Darling-Hammond and Eileen Sclan provide compelling reasons why upgrading the profession of teaching makes sense. They also present an overview of the policy initiatives needed for this to happen. Their chapter is must reading because it explains the very practical reasons why professionalizing teaching is an imperative.

Professionalizing Teaching

The current context for teaching practice is too idiosyncratic, nonlinear, and loosely connected to support alternative conceptions of teaching. Teachers, like other professionals, cannot be effective by

Figure 13.1
Sources of Authority for Supervisory Policy and Practice

Source	Assumptions	Supervisory Strategy	Consequences
Bureaucratic Authority Hierarchy Rules and regulations Mandates Role expectation Teachers are expected to comply or face consequences.	Teachers are subordinates in a hierarchically arranged system. Supervisors are trustworthy, but you can't trust subordinates very much. Goals and interests of teachers and supervisors are not the same, so supervisors must be watchful. Hierarchy equals expertise; supervisors know more than teachers do. External accountability works best.	"Expect and inspect" is the overarching rule. Rely on predetermined standards to which teachers must measure up. Identify teachers' needs and "inservice" them. Directly supervise and closely monitor the work of teachers to ensure compliance. Figure out how to motivate teachers and get them to change.	With proper monitoring, teachers respond as technicians executing predetermined scripts. Their performance is narrowed.
Psychological Authority Motivation technology Interpersonal skills Human relations Leadership	The goals and interests of teachers and supervisors are not the same, but can be bartered so that each group gets what it wants.	Develop a school climate characterized by high congeniality among teachers and between teachers and supervisors.	Teachers respond as required when rewards are available, but not otherwise. Their involvement is calculated, and their performance is narrowed.

Teachers will want to comply because of the congenial climate provided and to reap rewards offered in exchange.	Teachers have social and psychological needs; and if many of these needs are met at work, the work gets done. Congenial relationships and harmonious interpersonal climates make teachers content, easier to work with, and more cooperative. Supervisors must be expert at reading needs and must have other "people" skills to successfully barter for compliance and performance increases.	"Expect and reward." "What gets rewarded gets done." Use psychological authority in combination with bureaucratic and technical-rational authority.	

The Authority of Technical Rationality

Evidence defined by logic and scientific research. Teachers are required to comply in light of what is considered to be truth.	Supervision and teaching are applied sciences. Knowledge of research is privileged. Scientific knowledge is superordinate to practice. Teachers are skilled technicians. Values, preferences, and beliefs don't count, but facts and objective evidence do.	Use research to identify best practice. Standardize the work of teaching to reflect best practice. Inservice teachers. Monitor the process to ensure compliance. Figure out how to motivate teachers and get them to change.	With proper monitoring, teachers respond as technicians executing predetermined steps. Performance is narrowed.

continued

Figure 13.1—*continued*
Sources of Authority for Supervisory Policy and Practice

Source	Assumptions	Supervisory Strategy	Consequences
Professional Authority *Informed* craft knowledge and personal expertness. Teachers respond in light of common socialization, professional values, accepted tenets of practice, and internalized expertness.	Situations of practice are idiosyncratic; therefore, no one best way exists. "Scientific knowledge" and "professional knowledge" are different, with professional knowledge created in use as teachers practice. The purpose of "scientific" knowledge is to inform, not to prescribe practice. Authority cannot be external, but must come from the context itself and from within the teacher. Authority from context comes from training and experience. Authority from within comes from socialization and internalized values.	Promote a dialogue among teachers that makes professional values and accepted tenets of practice explicit. Translate the dialogue into professional practice standards. Provide teachers with as much discretion as they want and need. Require that teachers hold each other accountable in meeting practice standards. Make assistance, support, and professional development opportunities available.	Teachers respond to professional norms. Their practice becomes collective; they require little monitoring, and their performance is expansive.

Moral Authority

Felt obligations and duties derived from widely shared community values, ideas, and ideals.	Schools are professional learning communities.	Identify and make explicit the values and beliefs that define the center of the school as community.	Teachers respond to community values for moral reasons. Their practice becomes collective, and their performance is expansive and sustained.
	Communities are defined by their center of shared values, beliefs, and commitments.	Translate these values and beliefs into informal norms that govern behavior.	
Teachers respond to shared commitments and interdependence.	In communities:	Promote collegiality as internally felt and morally driven interdependence.	
	What is considered right and good is as important as what works and what is effective.	Rely on ability of community members to respond to duties and obligations.	
	People are motivated as much by emotion and beliefs as by self-interest.	Rely on the community's informal norm system to enforce professional and community values.	
	Collegiality is a professional virtue.		

following scripts. Instead, they need to *create knowledge in use* as they practice becoming skilled surfers who ride the wave of the pattern of teaching as it unfolds (Sergiovanni 1987). This ability requires a higher level of reflection, understanding, and skill than has traditionally been the case. This level of skill can only come from increased efforts to strengthen teaching as a profession.

The authority of professionalism shares some similarities with the authority of technical rationality. Both, for example, rely on expertness. But the authority of technical rationality presumes that the expertness of the knowledge itself is primary. Further, it presumes that this knowledge exists separately from teachers and context. Thus, the teacher's job is simply to apply the knowledge in practice. The teacher, in other words, is subordinate to the knowledge base of teaching.

Professional authority, on the other hand, presumes that the teacher's expertness counts the most. Knowledge does not exist separately from teachers and context. Thus, teachers are superordinate to the knowledge base, using it metaphorically to inform but not to prescribe practice. Professional authority is a very powerful force for governing what teachers do. But for it to take hold we need to significantly increase our investments in teacher preparation, professional development, school restructuring, and other efforts to upgrade teaching.

There is another dimension to professionalism that takes us beyond specialized knowledge, competence, dedication to service, and autonomous decision making. This dimension implies a standard of behavior that has virtuous qualities and a commitment to excellence that has moral overtones. It is the moral imperative embedded in the ideal of professionalism. Being a professional implies a commitment to the virtues and ideals that make one's responsibilities morally understandable. Professional practice is, therefore, both skilled service and the application of virtue.

In teaching, the application of virtue means a commitment to exemplary practice, which results in the accomplishment of valued ends and, as Alasdair MacIntyre (1981, p. 170) points out, the strengthening, enhancement, and growth of the practice itself. This latter point is key because there is a difference between being concerned with one's teaching practice and being concerned with the practice of teaching. Concern for the practice of teaching is directed to the broad issues of teaching, including knowledge, policy, and practice, and to the more practical problems and issues teachers face every day in their own classrooms and schools. With respect to the latter, it is not enough for one to teach competently in the company of others who may be having difficulty or to have special insights into teaching not shared with others. Like the Three Musketeers slogan goes, it is "All for one and one for all."

Changing the Metaphor for Schooling

The second of the three conditions needed to transform teaching from individual to collective practice is changing the metaphor for schooling. Metaphors help create mindscapes that frame what and how we think, contribute to the development of our practical theories of supervision and teaching, and become the basis for our practice. The language we use, in other words, creates the reality that we are forced to live.

Let's consider, for example, the key management and supervisory issues that emerge when schools are viewed as "instructional delivery systems." Here are some that come to my mind: identifying and developing targets, goals, steps, procedures, timetables, and schedules that compose the best delivery routes; properly training deliverers and then providing them with clear instructions as to what to do and how to do it; developing a monitoring system to ensure proper delivery; providing additional training to correct mistakes and better align what deliverers do with what they are supposed to do; and putting into place an evaluation scheme that measures the extent to which the system is working. Though perhaps known by other names, these are the issues that too often dominate today's supervision.

What happens when we change the metaphor? If, for example, we think about schooling as taking place within a "learning community," the issues that come to mind are likely to resemble these:

• How will this learning community be defined?

• What relationships among parents, students, teachers, and administrators are needed for us to be a community?

• What are the shared values, purposes, and commitments that bond this community together?

• How will we work together to embody these values?

• What obligations do members have to the community?

• How will obligations be enforced?

These images suggest a very different kind of supervision from those that emerge from the instructional delivery system metaphor. What is true changes as we change our metaphor for schooling. The supervisory concepts, rules, and practices that are valid for schools understood as instructional delivery systems are not valid for other schools that are viewed as learning communities, and vice versa. Thus, one way to change supervisory practice is to change the metaphor for schooling.

How can schools be understood as learning communities? Communities are defined by their centers—repositories of values, sentiments, and beliefs that provide the needed cement for bonding people together in a common cause. Centers govern what is of worth to a community and provide a set of norms that guide behavior and give meaning to community life (Shils 1961, p. 119).

As key members of the learning community, teachers have a special obligation to help construct the center of shared values. This center, in turn, spells out certain morally held duties, responsibilities, and obligations for teachers. Among these are a commitment to do one's best to make the community work well. In practical language, this means teachers working diligently, practicing in exemplary ways, keeping abreast of new ideas, helping other members of the learning community succeed, and doing whatever else is necessary for the community to function and flourish. It means, in other words, changing one's practice from individual to collective.

Valuing Collegiality

If we decide to take professionalism seriously and if we change the metaphor for schooling, then our present understanding of collegiality as something interpersonal or organizational will have to change. This brings us to the third condition for changing our current supervisory practices—we must value collegiality as a professional virtue.

There is now widespread agreement in education circles that collegiality among teachers is an important ingredient in promoting better working conditions, improving teaching practice, and getting better results. This agreement is being translated into a variety of efforts to get teachers to work together, to share their experiences, and to help each other. But efforts to date, as pointed out by Peter P. Grimmett, Olaf P. Rostad, and Blake Ford in Chapter 12, have been disappointing. Too often collegiality is confused with congeniality, or it is contrived rather than real.

As Roland Barth (1990) points out, the difference between congeniality and collegiality is important. Congeniality refers to the friendly human relationships that exist in a school, which are characterized by loyalty, trust, and easy conversation among the faculty. When congeniality is pervasive, a strong informal culture aligned with social norms emerges in the school. But the norms may not be aligned with the school's purposes; and when they are not, congeniality can be detrimental. Congeniality is often a byproduct of supervisory strategies and practices that rely too heavily on psychological authority.

Contrived collegiality is certainly better than no collegiality, but it is still not the same as the real thing. According to Grimmett, Rostad, and Ford, teachers engage in the actions associated with collegiality on the basis of radically different beliefs and values. Contrived collegiality, they maintain, is either administratively imposed or organizationally induced. In other words, the basis for teachers' behaving like colleagues rests in bureaucratic authority or psychological authority or some combination of both.

The real thing, by contrast, is connected to the existence of a set of norms and values that defines the faculty as a community of like-minded people who are bonded together in a common commitment. Because of shared work goals and a common work identity, they feel obligated to work together for the common good. The source for such collegiality rests in professional and moral authority. On the one hand, it is expressed in the form of loyalty to the school and the shared values that make it a community. On the other hand, it is expressed as a form of respect for and connectedness to the professional expertness of one's colleagues and the shared commitment to the goals and values of the profession. As professionals, teachers are not only concerned with their teaching practice but with the practice of teaching itself—and their concern requires them to act collegially. In this sense, as Ihara (1988) explains:

> Collegiality is better defined in terms of having the proper professional attitude or orientation. To take this approach to collegiality is to consider it as a kind of professional virtue, a trait or characteristic that is meritorious from a professional point of view (p. 57).

With the three conditions in place, teaching practice changes from individual to collective. The primary source of authority for supervision changes from bureaucratic, psychological, and technical-rational to professional and moral. Under these circumstances, external supervision will no longer be needed. It will be replaced by a supervision that comes from within the individual. This supervision will be concerned with promoting a dialogue that makes professional and community values and beliefs explicit. These will then be translated into professional practice standards and informal community norms. Teachers will have a great deal of discretion concerning what they do and how they do it, and they will hold themselves accountable for meeting these standards and abiding by community norms. A system of assistance and support, shaped by teachers, will be made available for those who choose to use it. First in the minds of everyone will be the moral obligation to practice in exemplary ways on behalf of valued ends and with a concern for the practice of teaching itself.

* * *

Not only would such a dream make a nice reality, it is the only reality that is practical if we want to bring about long-term improvements in schooling. Are teachers capable of making this kind of commitment? If one agrees with Amitai Etzioni (1988) that morality in the form of what we believe, emotions in the form of how we feel, and social bonds in the form of shared norms are the major motivators for determining our personal and collective behavior, then the answer most certainly is yes.

References
Barth, R. (1990). *Improving Schools from Within*. San Francisco: Jossey-Bass.

Etzioni, A. (1988). *The Moral Dimension Toward a New Economics*. New York: The Free Press.

Ihara, C.K. (1988). "Collegiality as a Professional Virtue." In *Professional Ideals*, edited by A. Flores. Belmont, Calif.: Wadsworth.

MacIntyre, A. (1981). *After Virtue*. Notre Dame, Ind.: University of Notre Dame Press.

Sergiovanni, T.J. (1987). "Will We Ever Have a TRUE Profession?" *Educational Leadership* 44, 8: 44–51.

Sergiovanni, T.J. (In press). *The Moral Dimension in Leadership*. San Francisco: Jossey-Bass.

Shils, E.A. (1961). "Centre and Periphery." In *The Logic of Personal Knowledge: Essays Presented to Michael Polanyi* (pp. 117–131). London: Routledge and Kegan Paul.

About the Authors

Carl D. Glickman is the editor of *Supervision in Transition*. He is the Director of the Program for School Improvement in the College of Education at the University of Georgia, Athens.

Frances S. Bolin is Associate Professor of Education at Teachers College, Columbia University, New York.

Peter J. Cistone is Professor of Educational Leadership and Policy Studies at Florida International University, Miami, Florida.

Renee Clift is Associate Professor in the Department of Curriculum and Instruction at the University of Illinois, Urbana-Champaigne.

Amy Bernstein Colton is Staff Development Consultant in the Ann Arbor Public Schools and University Adjunct in the Teacher Education Department at Eastern Michigan University, Ann Arbor.

Linda Darling-Hammond is Professor of Education at Teachers College, Columbia University, New York.

Charles Divita, Jr., is Professor of Adult Education and Human Resource Development at Florida International University, Miami.

Gerald O. Dreyfuss is Assistant Superintendent of the Dade County Public Schools, Miami, Florida.

William Ellis is the Assistant Superintendent of Schools of the Windham Southeast Supervisory Union, Brattleboro, Vermont.

Carol J. Ericson is Superintendent of the Roseville Independent District #623, Roseville, Minnesota.

Pam Francis is Program Specialist for Curriculum and Staff Development at the Central Intermediate Unit #10, West Decatur, Pennsylvania.

Blake Ford is Director of Instruction in Burnaby School District 41, Burnaby, British Columbia, Canada.

Andrew Gitlin is Associate Professor in the College of Education at the University of Utah, Salt Lake City.

Peter P. Grimmett is Associate Professor in the Faculty of Education at Simon Fraser University, Burnaby, British Columbia, Canada.

John E. Grossman is President of the Columbus Education Association, Columbus Public Schools, Columbus, Ohio.

Daniel Heller is English Department Head at Brattleboro Union High School, Brattleboro, Vermont.

Patricia E. Holland is Assistant Professor in the Department of Educational Leadership and Cultural Studies at the University of Houston, Texas.

Susan James is Chapter 1 Coordinator at Windham Southeast Supervisory Union, Brattleboro, Vermont.

Marlene Johnson is a doctoral student at the University of Houston, Texas.

Jean A. King is Director of the Center for Applied Research and Educational Improvement at the University of Minnesota, Minneapolis.

Jane McCarthy is Associate Professor in the Department of Instructional and Curricular Studies at the University of Nevada, Las Vegas.

James Nolan is Assistant Professor in the Department of Curriculum and Instruction at the Pennsylvania State University, University Park.

Edward F. Pajak is a Professor in the Department of Educational Leadership at the University of Georgia, Athens.

Philip Panaritis is a High School Social Studies Teacher in the New York City, New York, Public Schools.

Karen Price is a Special Education Teacher at Lowell Elementary School, Salt Lake City, Utah.

Olaf P. Rostad is Deputy Superintendent in Burnaby School District 41, Burnaby, British Columbia, Canada.

Eileen Sclan is Research Assistant at Teachers College, Columbia University, New York.

Thomas J. Sergiovanni is Radford Professor of Education in the Department of Education at Trinity University, San Antonio, Texas.

Georgea Sparks-Langer is Associate Professor in the Teacher Education Department at Eastern Michigan University, Ann Arbor.

Mary Lou Veal is Associate Professor in the Department of Exercise and Sport Science at the University of North Carolina, Greensboro.

Nancy L. Zimpher is Professor of Educational Policy and Leadership at the College of Education of The Ohio State University, Columbus.

ASCD 1991–92
Board of Directors

Members at Large

Harriet Arnold, San Jose, California

Marguerite Cox, Director of Instruction, Glenbard Township H.S. District 87, Glen Ellyn, Illinois

Mary Francis, Superintendent, Wrangell City School District, Petersburg, Alaska

Esther Fusco, Babylon School District, Stony Brook, New York

Sandra Gray, Director, K–12 Laboratory School, Southwest Missouri State University, Springfield

Phyllis J. Hobson, Director, Parental Involvement Program, District of Columbia Public Schools, Washington, D.C.

David Jones, Jr., Director of Secondary Programs, Metropolitan Public Schools, Nashville, Tennessee

Ina Logue, Director of Curriculum and Instruction, Allegheny Intermediate Unit, Pittsburgh, Pennsylvania

Alex Molnar, Professor, Department of Curriculum and Instruction, University of Wisconsin-Milwaukee, Milwaukee

Yolanda Rey, Director for Staff Development, El Paso Independent School District, El Paso, Texas

Annemarie Romagnoli, Principal, Little Tor Elementary School, New York City, New York

Susan E. Spangler, Director of Elementary Curriculum, Millard Public Schools, Omaha, Nebraska

Judy Stevens, Director of Elementary Instruction, Tomball Independent School District, Houston, Texas

Beverly M. Taylor, Director of Professional Growth, Curriculum Design for Excellence, Oak Brook, Illinois

Elizabeth C. Turpin, Principal, Lansing School District, Lansing, Michigan

Nancy Vance, Associate Director for Professional Development and the Beginning Teacher Assistance Program, Virginia Department of Education, Dinwiddie County, Virginia

Belinda Williams, Paterson Board of Education, Paterson, New Jersey

P.C. Wu, Professor of Educational Leadership and Director, University of West Florida, Pensacola

Hilda Young, New Orleans, Louisiana

Affiliate Presidents

Alabama: Edward Hall, Assistant Superintendent, Talladega County Board of Education, Talladega

Alaska: Mark Hanson, Associate Director, Southeast Regional Resource Center, Juneau

Arizona: Rosalina Baldonado, Assistant Principal, Marcos de Nitza High School, Tempe

Arkansas: Diann Gathright, 1st Vice President, DeQueen-Mena Education Cooperative, Gillham

California: Ruben Ingram, Superintendent, Fountain Valley School District, Fountain Valley

Colorado: Jane Dooley-Stuart, Curriculum Coordinator, Aurora Public Schools, Aurora

Connecticut: Christine Roberts, Professor of Education, University of Connecticut, Storrs

Delaware: Maureen Ladd, Newark

District of Columbia: Saundra McCray, Resource Assistant, Lenox School

Florida: Fran Winfrey, Director of Federal Projects, North Miami Beach

Georgia: Pat Stokes, Assistant Superintendent, Carrollton City Schools, Carrollton

Hawaii: Michael Dabney, St. Louis High School, Honolulu

Idaho: Mary Ann Ranells, Director of Curriculum, Nampa School District #131, Nampa

Illinois: Beverly Taylor, Consultant, Oak Brook

Indiana: Tony Lux, Assistant Superintendent, Merrillville

Iowa: Richard Hanzelka, Director of General Education, Mississippi Bend AEA #9, Bettendorf

Kansas: Donald Hurst, Assistant Superintendent, Hays Public Schools, Hays

Kentucky: Robert Prickett, Coordinator of Educational Administration, Western Kentucky University, Bowling Green

Louisiana: Bill Miller, State Department of Education, Baton Rouge

Maine: Judith Stallworth, Superintendent, M.S.A.D. #51, Cumberland Center

Maryland: Margaret Trader, Director of Curriculum, Washington County Board of Education, Hagerstown

Massachusetts: Lyn Huttunen, Superintendent, Randolph Public Schools, Randolph

Michigan: Olga Moir, Wayne County RESA, Wayne

Minnesota: Pamela Myers, Westonka Schools, Mound

Mississippi: Tommye Henderson, Staff Development Coordinator, Columbus Public Schools, Columbus

Missouri: Kay Wright, Principal, Butler Public Schools, Butler

Montana: Dave DeBoer, Principal, Lockwood Schools, Billings

Nebraska: Patrick Geary, Staff Development Director, E.S.U. #3, Omaha

Nevada: Francine Mayfield, Principal, Whitney Elementary School, Las Vegas

New Hampshire: Ken Didsbury, Humanities Chair, Tilton School, Tilton

New Jersey: Dennis Buss, College Instructor, Rider College, Lawrenceville

New Mexico: Bettye Bobroff, Director of Instruction, Bernalillo Public Schools, Bernalillo

New York: Robert Plaia, Assistant Superintendent, South Huntington Schools, Huntington Station

North Carolina: Sarah Leak, Director, Metrolina Consortium, Charlotte-Mecklenburg Schools, Charlotte

North Dakota: Charles DeRemer, Director, Educational Support Programs, Department of Public Instruction, State Department of Education, Bismarck

Ohio: Jack Conrath, Superintendent, Whitehall City Schools, Whitehall

Oklahoma: Blaine Smith, Assistant Superintendent, Tulsa Public Schools, Tulsa

Oregon: Thomas Zandoli, Principal, Yaquina View Elementary School, Newport

Pennsylvania: James Nolan, Professor, Penn State University, State College

Puerto Rico: Georgina Torres, Director of Graduate Studies, Catholic University of Puerto Rico, Ponce

Rhode Island: F. William Davis, Superintendent, Narragansett Public Schools, Narragansett

South Carolina: William Jenkins, Associate Superintendent, York County School District #3, Rock Hill

South Dakota: Jeri Engelking, Assistant Professor of Education, University of South Dakota, Vermillion

Tennessee: Mark Smith, Associate Vice President for Academic Affairs and Dean of Evening and Summer Programs, Christian Brothers University, Memphis

Texas: Judy Stevens, Executive Director, Elementary Education, Spring Branch ISD, Houston

Utah: Patti Harrington, Principal, Provo

Vermont: Darlene Worth, Director of Curriculum, South Burlington Schools, South Burlington

Virgin Islands: Sandra M. Lindo, Coordinator of Intermediate Grades, Department of Education, St. Thomas

Virginia: Thomas Bentson, Associate Superintendent, Manassas City Schools, Manassas

Washington: Ellen Wolf, Superintendent, Walla-Walla School District, Walla Walla

West Virginia: Patricia Pockl, Supervisor, Ohio County Schools, Wheeling

Wisconsin: Dean Isaacson, Director of Instruction, Platteville School District, Platteville

Wyoming: Leslie Madden, Director, Teacher Center, Douglas

Alberta, Canada: Michael Dzwiniel, Teacher, Harry Hinlay High School, Edmonton

British Columbia, Canada: Owen Corcoran, Superintendent of Schools, Burns Lake

Germany: Heidi Tobin, Aschaffenburg Elementary-Junior High School, DoDDS

Ontario, Canada: Nancy Maynes, Lincoln County Board of Education, St. Catherine's

The Netherlands: Ruud Gorter, Director, Association of Educational Advisory Centers, The Hague

Singapore: Ang Wai Hoong, Director, Curriculum Development Institute, Singapore

St. Maarten: Josianne Fleming-Artsen, Principal, Board of Methodist Agogic Center, Philipsburg

United Kingdom: Carolyn Mikula, Assistant Principal, Woodbridge High School, DoDDS

ASCD Headquarters Staff

Gordon Cawelti, *Executive Director*
Diane Berreth, *Deputy Executive Director*
Frank Betts, *Director, Curriculum/Technology Resource Center*
John Bralove, *Director, Administrative Services*
Ronald S. Brandt, *Executive Editor*
Helené Hodges, *Director, Research and Information*
Susan Nicklas, *Director, Field Services*
Michelle Terry, *Director, Professional Development*

Maria Acosta
Francine Addicott
Dianna Allen
Teddy Atwara
René Bahrenfuss
Vickie Bell
Kimber Bennett
Sandy Berdux
Jennifer Beun
Karla Bingman
Gary Bloom
Joan Brandt
Dorothy Brown
Kathy Browne
Robert Bryan
Colette Burgess
Edward Butler
Angela Caesar
Barbara Carney-Coston
Sally Chapman
John Checkley
RC Chernault
Eddie Chinn
Sandra Claxton
Lisa Manion Cline
Carrie Conti
Adrienne Corley
Cristine Craun
Agnes Crawford
Elaine Cunningham
Marcia D'Arcangelo
Keith Demmons
Becky DeRigge
Gloria Dugan
Shiela Ellison
Gillian Fitzpatrick
Chris Fuscellaro
Sally George

Sonja Gilreath
Regina Gussie
Dorothy Haines
Vicki Hancock
Vonda Harlan
Mary Harrison
Dwayne Hayes
Davene Holland
Julie Houtz
Angela Howard
Debbie Howerton
Harold Hutch
Arddie Hymes
Peter Inchauteguiz
Jo Ann Jones
Mary Jones
Teola Jones
Michelle Kelly
Stephanie Kenworthy
Leslie Kiernan
Shelly Kosloski
Ana Larson
John Mackie
Indu Madan
Lynn Malarz
Larry Mann
Jan McCool
Dawn Meads
Clara Meredith
Susan Merriman
Jackie Miles
Ron Miletta
Ginger Miller
Frances Mindel
Nancy Modrak
Cerylle Moffett
Karen Monaco
Dina Murray

Carlita Nivens
Jonathan Nobles
John O'Neil
Jayne Osgood
Millie Outten
Kelvin Parnell
Jayshree Patel
Margini Patel
Sydney Petty
Carolyn Pool
Jackie Porter
Ruby Powell
Vernon Pretty
Pam Price
Lorraine Primeau
Gena Randall
Melody Ridgeway
Judy Rixey
Jay Robbins
Rita Roberts
Gayle Rockwell
Cordelia Roseboro
Carly Rothman
Margaret Scherer
Beth Schweinefuss
Bob Shannon
Carolyn Shell
Valerie Sprague
Lisa Street
Susan Thran
Cole Tucker
Judi Wagstaff
Judy Walter
Dave Warren
Milton Washington
Pamela Williams
Scott Willis
Carolyn Wojcik

Current ASCD Networks on Supervision

ASCD sponsors numerous networks that help members exchange ideas, share common interests, identify and solve problems, grow professionally, and establish collegial relationships. Two current networks may be of particular interest to readers of this book.

Instructional Supervision

Contact: J. McClain Smith, Coordinator, University Programs, Hilliard City Schools, 5323 Cemetery Road, Hilliard, OH 43026. Telephone: (614) 771-4273. FAX: (614) 777-2424.

Mentoring Leadership and Resources

Contact: Richard Lange, Director of Staff Development, Prospect Heights Public Schools, 834 Inverrary Lane, Deerfield, IL 60015. Telephone: (708) 870-3857. FAX: (708) 870-3896.